KEY CONFLICTS OF CLASSICAL ANTIQUITY

This series is composed of introductory-level texts that provide an essential foundation for the study of important wars and conflicts of classical antiquity. Each volume provides a synopsis of the main events and key characters, the consequences of the conflict, and its reception over time. An important feature is the critical overview of the textual and archaeological sources for the conflict, which is designed to teach both historiography and the methods that historians use to reconstruct events of the past. Each volume includes an assortment of pedagogical devices that students can use to further their knowledge and inquiry of the topics.

ROME'S GOTHIC WARS
FROM THE THIRD CENTURY TO ALARIC

Michael Kulikowski
UNIVERSITY OF TENNESSEE-KNOXVILLE

CAMBRIDGE
UNIVERSITY PRESS

32 Avenue of the Americas, New York NY 10013-2473, USA

Cambridge University Press is part of the University of Cambridge.

It furthers the University's mission by disseminating knowledge in the pursuit of education, learning and research at the highest international levels of excellence.

www.cambridge.org
Information on this title: www.cambridge.org/9780521846332

First published 2007
First paperback edition 2008
Reprinted 2013

A catalogue record for this publication is available from the British Library

Library of Congress Cataloguing in Publication data

Kulikowski, Michael, 1970–
Rome's Gothic Wars from the third century to Alaric / Michael Kulikowski.
  p.   cm. – (Key conflicts of classical antiquity)
Includes bibliographical references and index.
ISBN 0-521-84633-1 (hardcover) – ISBN 0-521-60868-6 (pbk.)
1. Rome – History – Germanic Invasions, 3rd–6th centuries.   2. Rome – History – Empire, 284–476.   3. Goths – History.   I. Title.   II. Series.
DG312.K85   2007
937´.09 – dc22   2006016381

ISBN 978-0-521-84633-2 Hardback
ISBN 978-0-521-60868-8 Paperback

For T. D. Barnes and Walter Goffart

CONTENTS

❀ ❀ ❀

MAPS

ACKNOWLEDGEMENTS

❀ ❀ ❀

TO QUOTE WITH APPROVAL GEOFFREY ELTON AT THE BEGINNING OF the twenty-first century may seem perverse, even lunatic. Yet for all that Elton was (to borrow a phrase from Averil Cameron) a 'dinosaur of English positivism', his *Practice of History* got one thing absolutely right: the historian has a duty to make history intelligible and, however complex the past may have been, there is nothing in it that cannot be explained to any audience if only we choose the right words. This book aims to do no more than that, to make the first two centuries of Romano-Gothic relations comprehensible to everyone – student, scholar, and aficionado alike – and to explain why, for the specialist at least, Gothic history remains a subject of painful controversy. As an aid to readers for whom this material is unfamiliar, I have included glossaries of persons named in the book and of ancient authors used, and while specialists may find that my citations of primary sources are insufficiently abbreviated, I hope it will help those who are just beginning the advanced study of late antiquity to easily locate the texts I have used.

Even in a book so short, one incurs debts of gratitude to family, friends, and colleagues. I have long relied on my father and my wife for first reactions to my work, and both have read this text, parts of it repeatedly. Andrew Gillett read the whole book in draft; Guy Halsall, Andy Merrills, and Philipp von Rummel each read several chapters; all saved me from error and gave me much food for thought. Sebastian Brather, Florin Curta, and Noel Lenski advised on points of detail and Dr. Alexandru Popa provided me with a copy of his invaluable – but in North America inaccessible – work on the stone architecture of the *barbaricum*. Beatrice Rehl offered sympathetic editorial guidance throughout. Final work on the volume took place while I held a Solmsen Fellowship at the Institute for Research in the Humanities at the University of Wisconsin, Madison. The maps were drawn by the Cartographic

Services Laboratory at the University of Tennessee, under the direction of Will Fontanez, and I am grateful to the Department of History for the subvention which allowed them to be produced at short notice.

I owe my interest in this topic to the Gothic and Roman halves of my education. Tim Barnes and Walter Goffart taught me different things about studying late antiquity, but without them I would neither have wanted, nor been able, to write the volume which I now dedicate to them.

BEFORE THE
GATES OF ROME

LATE IN AUGUST 410, A LARGE TROOP OF SOLDIERS BORE DOWN ON the city of Rome. At their head rode the general Alaric, in the full insignia of a *magister militum*. It was the highest command in the Roman army, won after years of politicking and military success. But Alaric was more than a Roman general. He was also a Gothic chieftain, some might have said a king. As far as contemporaries were concerned, the soldiers who followed him were Goths. Sometimes, to be sure, Alaric had put his followers at the service of the Roman emperor. When he did so, they became a unit in the Roman army. But their loyalty was to Alaric, not to the emperor or the empire, and everyone knew it. Alaric might be a Roman general, but no one ever mistook his followers for Roman soldiers. They were the Goths, and Alaric had led them against regular imperial armies more than once. In the early fifth century, the line between Roman regiment and barbarian horde was a fine one, and Alaric straddled it as best he could. But no one was quite taken in by appearances, and Alaric never succeeded in turning himself into the legitimate Roman commander he so desperately wanted to be.

But he had come very close, to within a hair's breadth of achieving everything a barbarian commander could hope for: a place in the empire's military hierarchy for himself, permanent employment for his followers, food and land and security for their wives and children. Yet each time he had been on the verge of grasping everything he wanted, something had gone terribly wrong, negotiations had broken down, someone he had relied on had betrayed him. For fifteen years he had led his men, and for fifteen years most had remained loyal, through the ups and downs of constant negotiation and occasional battle, through the endless marching from the Balkans to Italy, from Italy to the Balkans, and back again. All that was over now. Alaric could contemplate no further delay, no further negotiation. He was in a fury, his patience finally at an end. It was true that he had never been a patient man. As he himself had recognized at least once, his failures were not always someone else's fault: at times his rage had got the better of him, and he had stormed away from the negotiating table too soon, when a little forebearance might have carried the day. This time, though, it had not been his fault. He had bargained in good faith with the emperor and he had gone all the way to Ravenna to do so, instead of insisting on meeting at Rimini, in between Rome and Ravenna, as he had done in the past. He had, in fact, done everything that was asked of him. And it had made no difference. He and his men had been attacked, a surprise assault, with no warning and no quarter.

With that, Alaric decided, the emperor had proven once and for all that he could not be trusted. The emperor's name was Honorius, but he had honoured few of the agreements he made with Alaric. Besides, he was a weakling and an incompetent, rumoured to be a half-wit even by those who wished him well. Holed up in the coastal town of Ravenna, safe behind marshes and causeways and readily supplied by sea, he was unreachable and the workings of his court inscrutable. Indeed, for the past two years, it had been impossible for anyone, least of all Alaric, to be certain which of Honorius' many courtiers really controlled him, which could really deliver on the promises made in his name. It had not always been thus, for while Honorius' father-in-law, the patrician Stilicho, was alive and in charge, Alaric had a negotiating partner he could trust, more or less. But Stilicho had been dead for two years,

MAP 1. *The Italian peninsula.*

murdered, and the cabal of treacherous bureaucrats that replaced him had never spoken with a single voice.

Even so, Alaric had kept trying to make his peace with the court at Ravenna. Simple-minded he may have been, but Honorius was the legitimate emperor, the son of the great Theodosius. Alaric, like anyone born and raised inside the imperial frontiers, shared the Roman reverence for dynasticism, the seal of legitimacy that inherited power conferred. Even when he challenged Honorius, even when he threatened his very hold on the throne, Alaric could still not suppress the residual loyalty he felt to the imperial purple into which Honorius had been born. That was the only reason it had taken so long for his patience to run out. He had it in his power to deliver the killing blow, to seize the city of Rome itself: the eternal city, no longer an imperial residence, no longer the capital of the world, but still the symbolic heart of empire. Enemies had long believed him capable of such an enormity. The greatest Latin poet of the century, an Egyptian named Claudian, accused Alaric of having a malign destiny to pierce the walls of the immortal *Urbs*, 'the city', as Rome was called. Three times he had threatened, three times he had held back. To make good on his threat, after all, would be the end of all his ambitions, all his hopes: an irrevocable move that would make any future negotiation impossible and place Alaric beyond the bounds of civilized politics forever. He did not want that, had never wanted that, and for two long years he had hesitated.

But his options had now run out. Negotiation was fruitless, and as the recent surprise attack had shown, it could even prove life-threatening. However ambivalent he might be, the time to make good on all his threats had probably arrived. It remained a bitter choice, but after two years of failure, it was becoming easier to make. Alaric got back to the outskirts of Rome some time around August 20th. Nothing he saw there can have made him very happy. For two years, since just after the death of Stilicho, his followers had been camped there, spread out along the banks of the Tiber river that fed the city of Rome. Alaric himself had been on the move quite a lot over the preceding two years, riding back and forth across the Appenines and up the coast road to Rimini and Ravenna. Most of his followers had not. Each time he rode out to negotiate with the imperial government, only picked troops had gone with him. Their dependents, and the larger part of the fighting men necessary to defend them, remained behind in the vicinity of Rome. It was more than just a matter of protecting the women and children. They were needed as a reserve, and as a threat, a visible reminder that at any time he wanted, Alaric could seal Rome off from the outside world. His soldiers were, ultimately, the basis of his power, and their value as a threat increased with their proximity to Rome.

The government in Ravenna was afraid of the threat, but that had done Alaric and his followers little enough good. Years had passed since they had fought a proper battle: the massacre of a small imperial force sent from Dalmatia in 409 hardly counted, and Alaric had failed to deliver what all ancient armies, barbarian or Roman, demanded of their leaders: victory, wealth, security. That his men still followed him despite that was perhaps a testament to magnetic leadership. More likely it was because they had no choice, because he was the only link they had with an imperial government that might eventually give them enough to retire in peace and put an end to their endless, fruitless traveling. Now, though, inactivity and boredom were a menace. Alaric had commanded troops in the field for nearly two decades and he knew full well the limits of military discipline. Every time he had stayed stationary for long, bits of his following had melted away. He had always been able to find new followers in the aftermath of later triumphs, but now he'd seen little success for two years. As the hope of negotiation with Ravenna grew more and more distant, he could not afford to lose a single man capable of bearing arms. Worse still was the haunting prospect of mutiny. Better commanders than he had gone down beneath the blows of their own troops. Kept occupied, soldiers had no chance to wonder whether a change of leader might not improve their own prospects. Sitting idle, even loyal troops might get worrying ideas, and recently Alaric's men had been given far too much leisure to contemplate his failings.

The environment was not helping. Rome in August is a sultry and oppressive place, the air a blanket of heat and stench. To this day as many Romans as can manage it leave the city for the month. In antiquity, it was not just uncomfortable but positively unhealthy. The Tiber and its trade sustained the city's life, but its banks bred death in the shape of mosquitoes and the malaria they carried. Malaria is endemic to central Latium and even native Romans suffered. Foreigners suffered worse and the disease could cripple whole armies; until the nineteenth century, the city was a pestilential graveyard for the many northerners who tried to conquer it. Alaric's followers were mostly children of the Balkans and the Danube. Their tolerance for Roman conditions cannot have been very high. Immobility weakened them further, as the waste of men and horses piled up and bred diseases and the spectre of food shortage loomed ever larger.

Alaric's Goths were neither a proper garrison, reliably housed and fed by the state, nor the proprietors of their own farmlands from which they might perhaps extract a living. Halfway between a besieging army and a band of refugees, they would have had a hard time anywhere in Italy, but the suburbs of Rome imposed difficulties uniquely their own. Rome was a huge city, its population numbered in the hundreds of thousands. Its own urban territory could not begin to feed it, and the mass of the city's people were totally dependent on the import of grain from Africa, which arrived at Portus, the city's main harbour, some fifteen kilometres down the Tiber on the Tyrrhenian coast. Some of this grain belonged to the Roman state and was distributed for free, but much of it belonged to the senatorial owners of vast African estates who sold it on the open market. If the grain ships failed to arrive, the city began to starve and the senators, their rich houses and their grain warehouses, suffered first from the anger of the urban mob. Alaric monitored Portus even more closely than he did Rome itself, and twice already he had brought Rome to its knees by cutting off the steady stream of shipping up the Tiber from the sea.

But by 410, even when Alaric let the citizens of Rome eat, there might not be enough food to go around. He and his followers had to feed themselves from the same sources as did the rest of the city. The highest official in Africa was loyal to Ravenna and had held back the grain ships for much of the year, while after two years of Gothic residency near Rome, any stored surplus had been depleted. The suburbs could never produce enough food to feed the city, and now they could no longer feed the Goths either. Even worse, foraging further afield, out into the more distant corners of Latium and north into Etruria, could only make up so much of the difference. The whole region had been blighted by two years of periodic siege and the Gothic occupation. Roman soldiers were proverbially voracious, destructive of the very provincials they were supposed to be defending. But provincial Romans were at least used to such rapacity and viewed the half-random, half-legal, expropriation of their crops in the same way they did the weather, as one of the many miseries that unkind fate showered upon them. The farmers of central Italy – unlike those of frontier provinces that frequently experienced the misery of soldiers and barbarian raiders on the doorstep – had little experience of soldiers and still less of barbarians. The Gothic occupation was a novel blow, and one they sustained with difficulty. For the first time in decades, there was an army at the doorstep likely to eat up the crop without payment, and robbing the farmer of any incentive to grow a surplus for market.

In a similar way, the landlords who might have lined their pockets selling food to the quartermasters of a regular imperial regiment were suspicious of Alaric's Goths. To be sure, Alaric could wave his imperial commission about and claim that he and his followers were entitled to the same supplies as any other unit of the Roman army; yet everyone knew that his relations with the emperor might change at any minute, and with them his status as a legitimately constituted member of the military hierarchy. Who would pay for the food his Goths ate, if the Roman state ceased to take responsibility for them? Far better to hide it or not to grow it at all than to give it away for free. And so those fields that had not been ruined by marching feet, those farms that had not had their seed grain eaten by hungry mouths, lay fallow, their intricate irrigation systems falling into decay. The rich loam of northern Europe might sustain that sort of neglect, but Italian soil was thin and poor, barren if not lovingly tended: even seven years later, a Gallic poet named Rutilius Namatianus, bent as he was on trumpeting the imperial recovery after the dark night of Gothic terror had passed, had to admit that central Italy lay desolate, a wasteland where crops should have sprouted. The modern scholar should have no more illusions than Alaric had at the time: hungry soldiers are angry soldiers, and Alaric's room for manoeuvre was shrinking to almost nothing at all.

His only comfort can have come from the fact that things were very nearly as bad for the Romans inside the city. Rome, as we have seen, was huge and that made it hard to defend. The city was walled, of course, and had been for well over a hundred years, ever since the threat of an earlier barbarian assault during the reign of the emperor Aurelian. The Aurelianic walls snaked for almost nineteen kilometres, enclosing not just the original seven hills of the city, but even the hill of the Janiculum and much of the neighbourhood of Trastevere, on the west side of the Tiber river. Four metres thick, fifteen metres tall in many places, and studded with 381 towers every thirty metres or so, the wall was and remains an impressive construction. Archaeology has uncovered repairs to these walls in many places dating to the first years of the fifth century, presumably a reaction to Alaric's initial invasion of Italy. While such repairs may well have been psychologically important, the city would never have stood up to a genuine assault – it covered too much ground, more than a hundred square kilometres, and its population was overwhelmingly civilian. Even decades earlier, when a unit of elite troops had still been stationed inside the city, Rome had never been put to the test of a real assault. The threatened attack under Aurelian had never materialized, and during the civil wars of the early fourth century, Italian conflicts had been prosecuted in open battle well beyond the city walls, without threat of siege. Had Alaric ever wanted to take the city by storm, it could not have held for long. But thus far he had not wanted to seize Rome, only to strangle it, to force its great men to their knees and induce them to wring from the emperor the concessions he wanted.

That expedient had worked more than once, for no amount of aristocratic resistance could blunt the power of famine. Alaric held Portus, the key to whether Rome ate or went hungry, and he could cut off the food supply more or less whenever he chose to. The plebs might be the first to starve, but they would vent their rage on their senatorial neighbours before they collapsed. It was this threat, more than anything, that had served in the past to reconcile the Roman senate to Alaric. Some senators actually came to prefer Alaric to the emperor in Ravenna, and nearly all feared Alaric on their doorstep far more than they trusted Honorius. It was not just that Honorius was feeble, but that he was the son of Theodosius. The same dynastic legitimacy that conferred on Honorius a certain resilience also earned him the dislike of many Roman aristocrats who had resented the strident Christianity of Theodosius himself. By the later 300s, the cities of the empire were very largely Christian, and the mass of the population in Rome itself was as well. But more so than elsewhere in the empire, the city of Rome was filled with reminders of the pagan past, generations' worth of enormous temples, some of them half a millenium old. An eclectic paganism remained a badge of honour among some of the oldest and most distinguished senatorial families. With them, devotion to the old gods was both a sincerely held belief and a reproof to all the petty aristocrats and jumped-up provincials who ruled the Christian empire and packed the imperial court. Little as they liked Alaric, many senators felt a certain satisfaction in his open defiance of Honorius. Indeed, a few went so far as to place their bets on Alaric rather than Honorius, and for a short while in 409 and 410, a member of the Roman senate had taken up the imperial purple and challenged Honorius' right to the throne with Alaric as his backer. That experiment had gone badly for all concerned, and by August 410, even those Romans who had been most willing to accommodate the Goths had little to hope of their mercy at this point.

Worse still, the threat from outside led to bloodletting within. Roman culture had always viewed a purge as a good way to stabilize the body politic in the face of external threat, and many a Roman vendetta was settled while the Gothic army camped before the walls and people looked for a neighbour whom they could blame. Serena, niece of Theodosius, widow of Stilicho, and thus cousin and mother-in-law of the reigning emperor, was strangled on suspicion of collusion with Alaric, with the open approval of the emperor's sister Galla Placidia. She was not the only victim, and famine and disease soon made matters worse: 'Corpses lay everywhere', we are told, 'and since the bodies could not be buried outside the city with the enemy guarding every exit, the city became their tomb. Even if there had been no shortage of food, the stench from the corpses would have been enough to destroy the bodies of the living'. We can gauge the scale of discontent by a totally unexpected reversion to the old gods. Roman pagans not only blamed the Gothic menace on the Christian empire's neglect of Rome's traditional religion, but were emboldened to say as much in public. They claimed that Alaric had bypassed the town of Narnia in nearby Etruria when the old rites were restored, and argued that pagan sacrifices – banned for twenty years – should be offered on the Capitol, the greatest of Rome's hills on which sat the temple of Jupiter Capitolinus, the foremost god of the Romans. Some Roman Christians, impressed by such arguments, sought the views of the bishop of Rome, who forbade any public sacrifices but gave permission for the rites to be carried out in secret. Such secrecy would have robbed the rites of their efficacy, and the whole project was abandoned. This dramatic story may not be entirely authentic, yet the fact that contemporaries could imagine that the head of the Roman church might consent even to the secret performance of pagan rites – in a city so pious that disputed elections for the city's bishop could end with hundreds of partisans lying dead in church aisles – is the best possible testimony to the fear that Alaric had instilled. However, given that parts of the population had turned to cannibalism to feed themselves, we should perhaps expect any number of extreme measures.

And so, in the scalding heat of August 410, neither Alaric nor the Romans could take much more. On the night of the 23rd, Alaric decided to make the ultimate confession of failure, to countenance the overthrow of all his hopes and dreams. He would let his Goths sack Rome. On the morning of the next day, they did, and for three days the violence continued. The great houses of the city were looted and the treasures seized were on a scale that remains staggering: five years later, when Alaric's successor Athaulf married his new bride, he gave her 'fifty handsome young men dressed in silk, each bearing aloft two very large dishes, one full of gold, the other full of precious – nay, priceless – gems, which the Goths had seized in the sack of Rome'. Supposedly out of reverence for Saint Peter, Alaric left untouched the church on the Vatican that housed his tomb, and in general the Goths made an effort not to violate the churches. But however much some might take comfort in that slight forebearance, the verdict of the world was shock and horror: 'The mother of the world has been murdered'.[1]

***

Alaric's sack of Rome was the climax of a career that had begun fifteen years before in the Balkans, where a very large number of Goths had been settled by Theodosius in 382. Those Goths, in turn, were for the most part veterans of the battle of Adrianople, the worst defeat in the history of the Roman empire, in which a Gothic force annihilated much of the eastern army and killed the emperor Valens. The Gothic history that culminated in Adrianople and the Theodosian settlement of 382 stretches back still further, to the first decades of the third century A.D. Alaric's story, in other words, is just one among many different Gothic histories one can reconstruct from the third and the fourth centuries. But it is in some ways the most important one, and certainly the most symbolic: Romans at the time and later did not remember the sack of Rome by 'some Goths'. For them, Rome had been sacked by Alaric and *the* Goths. We remember the sack of Rome in the same way, and a recent television series on the barbarians devoted almost the whole of its episode on the Goths to the story of Alaric. There is nothing wrong with remembering the past in this way, choosing a profoundly shocking moment to symbolize a much larger series of historical events. Alaric's career was a watershed in both Roman and Gothic history, and no one can dispute that the sack of Rome was its climax. Symbolic dates and events help us remember, but historical reality is always more complicated, always messier.

We will return both to Alaric and to Rome, the stricken 'mother of the world', before we reach the end of this book, but before that we have to deal with a great deal of just such messy historical reality. The book sets out to answer two main questions: first, how did Gothic history develop in such a way that the unprecedented career of Alaric became possible? And second, how do we know what we think we know about the Goths? That last question is very important, and it is not usually asked in an introductory book like this one. Most introductions to a subject try to adopt a tone of omniscience which implies that, even if complex historical events are being simplified, whatever is included can be regarded as certain fact. Unfortunately, however, there are large stretches of history in which even the most basic facts are either unknown or else uncertain because of contradictory evidence. Many times, the way we resolve those contradictions has as much to do with how modern scholarship has developed as it does with the evidence itself. As far as I am concerned, the curious reader is not helped by attempts to disguise the difficulties we face in trying to understand the past. In fact, a false sense of certainty takes much of the excitement out of history. For that reason, I offer no apologies for introducing readers to uncertainty and controversy in the history of the Goths. The road to the past is bumpy, and there is often no single destination at the end of it. Reconstructing the past, and reaching conclusions about it, requires historians to make choices, and in this book I always try to offer explanations for the choices I have made. Throughout the book, we will look not only at Goths and their history, but at the ancient writers who give us our only access to Gothic history and are fascinating and important figures in their own right.

We will also look at modern debates about the Goths. Gothic history is a controversial subject among modern scholars, who support their own positions with an intensity that most people reserve for their favourite football team or rock band. Anyone who writes professionally about the Goths, even if only a little bit, has to take a position in the heated debate about who the Goths were, where they came from, and when their history can really be said to begin – I am no exception. But instead of merely outlining the possible options and explaining which one I choose, I have devoted a part of chapter three to explaining exactly *why* the Gothic past is so controversial – after all, it is not football or music, which, if they are any good, are meant to inspire passionate controversy. By doing this, I hope to give readers a glimpse not just of how historians wrestle with the evidence that past ages have left behind, but how, in doing so, we are deeply affected by many centuries of modern thinking about the past. More so than is the case with many other historical problems, the history of the Goths is still caught up in questions that our ancestors were already asking in the Renaissance. Although such a long heritage of debate might be a cause for frustration, in fact part of the excitement of Gothic history is the way it puts us in touch with the intellectual history of the culture we still live in, as well as the ancient history of barbarians and Romans. All the same, it is those Romans with whom we must begin, because it was the Roman empire that created the Goths as we know them, and Roman writers who tell us most of what we know about them.

THE GOTHS BEFORE CONSTANTINE

CHAPTER ONE

THE GOTHS HAD A MOMENTOUS IMPACT ON ROMAN HISTORY,
appearing as if out of nowhere in the early decades of the third
century. When we first meet them, it is in the company of
other barbarians who, together, made devastating incursions
into the eastern provinces of the Roman empire. The mid third century,
particularly from the 240s till the early 300s, was an era of constant
civil war between Roman armies, civil war that in turn encouraged
barbarian invasions. Contact with the Roman empire, and particularly
with the Roman army, had helped to militarize barbarian society, and
opportunistic raids all along the imperial frontiers exploited Roman
divisions and distraction in the civil wars. When the Goths first appear,
it is in this world of civil war and invasion. Unfortunately for the modern
historian, it is not always easy to distinguish third-century Goths from
other barbarians. The problem stems from the way ancient writers talked
about barbarians in general and the Goths in particular.

'SCYTHIANS' AND GOTHS

To the Greek authors who wrote about them, the Goths were
'Scythians' and that is the name used almost without exception to

describe them. The name 'Scythian' is very ancient, drawn from the histories of Herodotus, which were written in the fifth century B.C. and dealt with the Greek world at the time of the Persian Wars. For Herodotus, the Scythians were outlandish barbarians living north of the Black Sea in what are now Moldova and Ukraine. They lived on their horses, they ate their meat raw, they dressed in funny ways, and they were quintessentially alien not just to the world of the Greeks, but even to other barbarians nearer to the Greek world. Greek historical writing, like much of Greek literary culture, was intensely conservative of old forms, and canonized certain authors as perfect models to which later writers had to conform. Herodotus was one such canonical author and his history was regularly used as a template by later Greek historians. In practice, this meant that authors writing 500 or 1,000 years after Herodotus talked about the world of their own day in exactly the same language, and with exactly the same vocabulary, as he had used all those centuries before.

For Greek writers of the third, fourth and fifth centuries A.D., barbarians who came from the regions in which Herodotus had placed the Scythians were themselves Scythians in a very real sense. It was not just that classicizing language gave a new group of people an old name; the Greeks and Romans of the civilized imperial world really did believe in an eternal barbarian type that stayed essentially the same no matter what particular name happened to be current for a given tribe at any particular time. And so the Goths, when they first appear in our written sources, are Scythians – they lived where the Scythians had once lived, they were the barbarian mirror image of the civilized Greek world as the Scythians had been, and so they were themselves Scythians. Classicizing Greek histories often provide the most complete surviving accounts of third- and fourth-century events, and the timelessness of their vocabulary can interpose a real barrier between the events they describe and our understanding of them.[1] However, the testimony of our classicizing texts sometimes overlaps with that of less conservative writings that employ a more current vocabulary. Because of such overlaps, we can sometimes tell when actions ascribed to Scythians in some sources were undertaken by people whom contemporaries called Goths.

1 Alpes Poeninae
2 Alpes Cottiae
3 Alpes Maritimae
■ Legions

0 _____ 500
Miles

MAP 2. *The Roman Empire at the time of Septimius Severus.*

THE EARLIEST GOTHIC INCURSIONS

Because of this complicated problem of names in the sources, we cannot say with any certainty when the Goths began to impinge upon the life of the Roman empire, let alone precisely why they did so. The first securely attested Gothic raid into the empire took place in 238, when Goths attacked Histria on the Black Sea coast and sacked it; an offer of imperial subsidy encouraged their withdrawal.[2] In 249, two kings called Argaith and Guntheric (or possibly a single king called Argunt) sacked Marcianople, a strategically important city and road junction very near the Black Sea.[3] In 250, a Gothic king called Cniva crossed the Danube at the city of Oescus and sacked several Balkan cities, Philippopolis – modern Plovdiv in Bulgaria – the most significant. Philippopolis lies to the south of the Haemus range, the chain of mountains which runs roughly east-west and separates the Aegean coast and the open plains of Thrace from the Danube valley (all cities are shown on map 4 in chapter four). The fact that Cniva and his army could spend the winter ensconced in the Roman province south of the mountains gives us some sense of his strength, which is confirmed by the events of 251. In that year, Cniva routed the army of the emperor Decius at Abrittus.[4] Decius had persecuted Christians, and Lactantius, a Christian apologist of the early fourth century, recounts with great relish how Decius 'was at once surrounded by barbarians and destroyed with a large part of his army. He could not even be honoured with burial, but – despoiled and abandoned as befitted an enemy of God – he lay there, food for beasts and carrion-birds'.[5]

THE BLACK SEA RAIDS

Gothic raids in Thrace continued in the 250s, and seaborne raids, launched from the northern Black Sea against coastal Asia Minor, began for the first time. What role Goths played in these latter attacks is unclear, as is their precise chronology. The first seaborne incursions, which took place at an uncertain date between 253 and 256, are attributed to Boranoi.[6] This previously unknown Greek word may not refer to an ethnic or political group at all, but may instead mean simply 'people from the north'. Goths did certainly take part in a third year's seaborne raids, the most destructive yet. Whereas the Boranoi had damaged sites like Pityus and Trapezus that were easily accessible from the sea, the attacks of the third year reached deep into the provinces of Pontus and Bithynia, affecting famous centres of Greek culture like Prusa and Apamea, and major administrative sites like Nicomedia.[7] A letter by Gregory Thaumaturgus – the 'Wonderworker' – casts unexpected light on these attacks. Gregory was bishop of Neocaesarea, a large city in the province of Pontus, and his letter sets out to answer the questions church leaders must confront in the face of war's calamities: can the good Christian still pray with a woman who has been kidnapped and raped by barbarians? Should those who use the invasions as cover to loot their neighbours' property be excommunicated? What about those who simply appropriate the belongings of those who have disappeared? Those who seize prisoners who have escaped their barbarian captors and put them to work? Or, worse still, those who 'have been enrolled amongst the barbarians, forgetting that they were men of Pontus and Christians', those, in other words, who have 'become Goths and Boradoi to others' because 'the Boradoi and Goths have committed acts of war upon them'.[8]

Ten years later, these assaults were repeated. Cities around the coast of the Black Sea were assaulted, not just those on the coast of Asia Minor, but Balkan sites like Tomi and Marcianople. With skillful seamanship, a barbarian fleet was able to pass from the Black Sea into the Aegean, carrying out lightning raids on islands as far south as Cyprus and Rhodes. Landings on the Aegean coasts of mainland Greece led to fighting around Thessalonica and in Attica, where Athens was besieged but defended successfully by the historian Dexippus, who would later write an account of these Gothic wars called the *Scythica*.[9] Though only fragments of this work survive, Dexippus was a major source for the fifth- or early sixth-century *New History* of Zosimus, which survives in full and is now our best evidence for the third-century Gothic wars. As Zosimus shows us, several imperial generals and emperors – Gallienus, his general Aureolus, the emperors Claudius and Aurelian – launched counterattacks which eventually brought this phase of Gothic violence to an end. Gothic defeat in 268 ended the northern Greek raids, while Claudius won a smashing and much celebrated victory at Naissus, modern Niš, in 270.[10]

AURELIAN AND A PROBLEMATIC SOURCE

In 271, after another Gothic raid across the Danube had ended in the sack of several Balkan cities, the emperor Aurelian (r. 270–275) launched an assault across the river that probably had considerable success. Aurelian was an extremely capable soldier, and one who spent his five-year reign in continuous motion from one end of the empire to the other, rarely out of the saddle, and rarely pausing between campaigns. A Gothic war is entirely in keeping with the evidence for Aurelian's movements, and a late fourth-century collection of imperial biographies which we call the *Historia Augusta* records that Aurelian defeated and captured a Gothic king named Cannobaudes.[11] Here, however, we run into the sort of problem with the sources that we will encounter more than once in the pages that follow. The *Historia Augusta* is the only Latin source we have for large chunks of third-century history, and even where it refers to events known from Greek historians, it often preserves details that they do not. If it could be trusted, its circumstantial and anecdotal content would be invaluable. Unfortunately, the whole work is heavily fictionalized, its anonymous author sometimes using older – and now lost – texts as a jumping off point for invention, sometimes making things up out of thin air. The biographies of late third-century emperors are the least reliable part of the work, and some of them contain no factual data at all. For that reason, even though he appears in many modern histories of the Goths, we cannot be entirely sure that this Gothic Cannobaudes was a real historical figure.

In this case, however, we are able to confirm at least part of the *Historia Augusta*'s testimony from another type of evidence altogether, because inscriptions make clear that Aurelian did definitely campaign against Goths. From a very early stage in Roman history, whenever a Roman general won a victory over a neighbouring people, he would add the name of that people to his own name, as a victory title. When the Roman Republic gave way to the one-man rule of the empire, the honour of such victory titles was reserved for the emperor, and whether he won a victory personally, or whether a general won it in his name, it was the emperor alone who took the victory title. In this way, a Persian campaign would allow the emperor to add the title *Persicus*, a campaign against the Carpi would make the emperor *Carpicus*, and so on. Since these victory titles became part of the emperor's name, they were included in the many different types of inscriptions, official and unofficial, that referred to the emperor. This provides a wealth of information for the modern historian, because victory titles often attest campaigns that are not mentioned by any other source. Thus in the chapters that follow we will sometimes be able to refer to a particular emperor's Gothic campaign only because an inscription happens to preserve the victory title *Gothicus* – as in the present case, Aurelian's use of the name shows that he did in fact fight against the Goths and felt able to portray that campaign as a success. We can also infer that success from the fact that his Gothic victory was still remembered a hundred years later, and from the rather limited evidence for Gothic raids in the decades immediately following his reign: although we hear of more seaborne raids in the mid-270s that penetrated beyond Pontus deep into Cappadocia and Cilicia, after that Goths disappear from the record until the 290s, by which time major changes had taken place in the empire itself.[12]

EXPLAINING THE THIRD-CENTURY INVASIONS

As the past few pages have demonstrated, the earliest evidence for Gothic invasions of the empire is not well enough attested to allow for much analysis, but that does not mean we should underestimate its impact. The letter of Gregory Thaumaturgus gives us a rare glimpse into just how traumatic the repeated Gothic raids into Asia Minor and other Greek provinces could be. But it does not answer basic questions of causation: what drove these Gothic raids, what made them a repeated phenomenon? The Graeco-Roman sources are content to explain barbarian attacks on the empire with an appeal to the fundamentals of nature itself: to attack civilization is just what barbarians do. That sort of essentialist explanation can hardly be enough for us. Rather, we need to seek explanations in the historical context. Now it happens that the third century was a period of massive change in the Roman empire, which saw the culmination of social and political developments that had been set in motion by the expansion of the Roman empire in the course of the first and second centuries A.D. Against this background, the first appearance of the Goths and the Gothic raids of the third century become comprehensible. Roman expansion had transformed the shape of Europe and the Mediterranean basin. It affected not just the many people who became Romans for the first time, but also the political constitution of the empire and even the many different peoples who lived along the imperial frontiers. One by-product of these changes was a cycle of internal political violence in the third-century empire that produced and then exacerbated the instability of the imperial frontiers.

The Roman empire had been a monarchy since the end of the first century B.C., when Augustus (r. 27 B.C.–A.D. 14), the grand-nephew and adoptive heir of Julius Caesar, put an end to a full generation of civil war that had ripped the Roman Republic apart. Augustus brought peace to the empire, but it came at the expense of the free competition amongst the Roman elite that had created a Roman empire to begin with. In its place, Augustus founded an imperial dynasty that lasted until A.D. 68. By that year, when the regime of the detested emperor Nero collapsed and he himself committed suicide, three generations had passed since the end of the Republic. The imperial constitution was fully entrenched – what mattered most was the relationship of the emperor to the powerful clans of the Roman elite, particularly the senatorial families of Rome itself, who now competed amongst themselves for the emperor's favour and the offices and honours it bestowed. Until 68, emperors had been made at Rome, and loyalty to the dynasty of Augustus had been an essential element in their creation. The civil wars of A.D. 68/69 changed that forever: their eventual victor was Vespasian, a middle-aged commander born of a prosperous but undistinguished Italian family and raised to the imperial title in the eastern provinces of the empire, just as some of his immediate rivals had seized the purple in Spain or Germany. This revealed what Tacitus called the *arcanum imperii*, the 'secret of empire' – that an emperor could be made outside Rome.[13] Italy remained the centre of the empire, but it was no longer the sun around which provincial planets revolved. These provinces increasingly had a life of their own and political influence that could, in time, impose itself on the Italian centre.

To be sure, the provinces might be very different from one another, and they might stand in different relationships to the imperial capital in Rome. Some provinces, like Spain, southern Gaul, or the part of North Africa that is now Tunisia, had been part of Rome's empire for a century or more. Others, like Britain, much of the Balkans, or what is now Morocco were only a generation away from their conquest by Roman armies. Well into the late third century, these different provinces continued to be governed according to many differing *ad hoc* arrangements that had been imposed on them when they were first incorporated into the empire. But all the imperial provinces were more and more integrated into a pattern of Roman life and ways of living, much less conquered territories administered for the benefit of Roman citizens in Italy. Indeed, the extension of Roman citizenship to provincial elites was an essential element in binding the provinces to Rome. As provincial elites became Roman citizens, they could aspire to equestrian or senatorial rank, and with it participation in the governance of the larger empire. Already by A.D. 97, a descendant of Italian immigrants to Spain named Trajan had become emperor. Trajan's successor Hadrian was likewise of Spanish descent, while his own successor and adopted son came from Gallia Narbonensis, the oldest Roman possession in Gaul.

ROMAN CITIZENSHIP AND ROMAN IDENTITY

These provincial emperors are the most impressive evidence for the spread of Roman identity to the provinces, but the continuous assimilation of the provincial elites into the Roman citizenship was ultimately more important in creating the sense of a single empire out of a territorial expanse that stretched from the edge of the Arabian desert to Wales, from Scotland to the Sahara. These imperial elites could communicate with one another, linguistically and conceptually, through a relatively homogeneous artistic and rhetorical culture. This culture was founded on an educational system devoted almost exclusively to the art of public speaking, the rhetorical skills that were necessary for public, political life. Mainly Greek in the old Greek East, frequently Graeco-Roman in the Latin-speaking provinces of the West, this elite culture nurtured an aesthetic taste devoted, in Greek, to the fashions of the Classical and early Hellenistic period and, in Latin, to those of the very late Republic and early empire. It thereby provided a set of cultural referents and social expectations shared by Roman citizens and Graeco-Roman elites from one end of the empire to the other, and allowed them to participate in the common public life of the empire at large, even if they came from wildly divergent regions.

The use of Roman law, which came with the acquisition of Roman citizenship, provided a framework of universal jurisdiction that, for the elites who used it, also overcame regional differences. Because of the growing elite participation in the Roman world and its governance, those lower down the social scale began in time to feel some measure of the same integration, helped along by the hierarchies of patronage that permeated the whole Roman world. The cult of the Roman emperors, and of the personified goddess Roma, was another effective means of spreading the idea of Rome and participation in a Roman empire to the provinces. Greg Woolf has examined in detail how incorporation into an ordered network of provincial government – with the assimilation of local elites into Roman citizenship – could transform an indigenous society.[14] In northern and central Gaul, less than two generations after the organization of the local tribal territories into a Roman province, both old Celtic noble families and the larger Gallic population had learned to express traditional relationships of patronage and clientship, power and display, in Roman terms, eating off Roman tableware, living in Roman houses, and dressing as Romans should. The same process is observable in the Balkans, at a slightly later date but at the same relative remove from the generation of the conquest. In the Greek world, ambivalent about its relationship to a Latin culture that was younger than – and partially derivative of – Hellenic culture, assimilation was more complicated, but even if Latin culture had little visible presence, the sense of belonging to a Roman empire was very strong in the ancient cities of the East.

This convergence on a Roman identity within the empire culminated in a measure taken by the emperor Caracalla in A.D. 212. Caracalla was himself the heir of an emperor from Africa – Septimius Severus, a man who could attest indigenous Punic ancestry in the very recent past. Much given to giganticism and delusions of grandeur, Caracalla undertook all sorts of massive building projects, and it is in this light that we should understand his decision to extend Roman citizenship to every free inhabitant of the empire in 212. The effects of this law, which we call the Antonine Constitution from Caracalla's official name of Antoninus, were varied. It both acknowledged the convergence of local elites on a Roman identity and encouraged its continuation, but it also created the dynamic of political violence which dominated the middle and later third century. Once all inhabitants of the empire were Romans, any of them could actively imagine seizing the imperial throne if they happened to be in an opportune position to do so. This was a radical step away from the earlier empire in which only those of senatorial status could contemplate the throne. The Graeco-Roman reverence for rank and social status was extraordinary, and there was a world of difference between accepting the son of a provincial senator as emperor and accepting a man whose father had not even been a Roman citizen. And yet by the middle of the third century, such recently enfranchised Romans not only seized the throne, but their doing so quickly ceased to occasion surprise and horror among the older senatorial nobility.

WARFARE AND THE RHETORIC OF IMPERIAL VICTORY

If the expansion of citizenship and the broadening definition of what it meant to be Roman permitted such men to imagine themselves as emperor, it was increasing military pressures that made their doing so

practicable. Much earlier, in the era of Augustus when Roman government was for the first time in the hands of one man, the security
of monarchical rule was by no means guaranteed. The authority of
the emperor – or *princeps*, 'first citizen', as Augustus preferred to be
called – rested on a number of constitutional fictions related to the
old public magistracies of the Republic. More pragmatically, however,
the authority of Augustus and his successors rested on a monopoly of
armed force: that is to say, it rested on control of the army. Empire
could not exist without army, and it is hardly an exaggeration to say
that the whole apparatus of imperial government developed and grew
ever more complex in order to redistribute provincial tax revenues from
the interior of the empire to the military establishments on the frontiers. These armies were the ultimate sanction of imperial power, and
they needed not only to be paid but also to be kept active: soldiers
were far less inclined to mutiny or unrest when they were well supplied and occupied in the business they were trained for, rather than
in more peaceable pursuits. This made periodic warfare consistently
desirable.

The regular experience of warfare, in turn, fed into the pre-existent
rhetoric of imperial victory and invincibility which provided part of the
justification for imperial rule: the emperor ruled – and had the right
to rule – because he was invincible and always victorious in defending
Rome from its enemies. Thus even after imperial expansion stopped
early in the second century, the need for Roman armies to win victories
over barbarians was ongoing. The result was a constant stream of border
wars, which allowed emperors to take victory titles and be seen to
fulfill their most important task – defending the Roman empire from
barbarians and from the eastern empire of Parthia, the only state to
which Roman emperors might reluctantly concede a degree of equality.
As we shall see in a moment, the militarization of the northern frontier
had for many years had a profound effect on the barbarian societies
beyond the Rhine and Danube, but at the start of the third century, a
more acute transformation took place on the eastern frontier, again as
a result of Roman military intervention.

From Parthians to Persians
on the Eastern Frontier

Caracalla is the pivotal figure here as well. In 216 he invaded the Parthian empire, the creation of the central Asian dynasty that had displaced the Hellenistic Seleucids as the rulers of Iran and Mesopotamia during the last centuries B.C. Since the defeat of the Republican general Crassus at Carrhae in 53 B.C., Parthia had possessed an iconic quality as the mortal enemy of Rome that was not matched by the actual strength or competence of the Parthian monarchy. A Parthian war might be a significant ideological goal for a Roman emperor – it avenged Crassus, imitated Augustus, and followed in the heroic footsteps of Alexander the Great – but victories in Parthia could actually be quite easy to win. The Parthian empire was fractious, and its kings faced almost continuous revolts in their far-flung eastern provinces. Thus when Caracalla determined to luxuriate in the easy triumph of a Parthian victory, he unwittingly destroyed the Parthian monarchy. It was replaced by a much more dangerous foe, a new Persian dynasty known as the Sassanians. A Persian nobleman, Ardashir (r. c. 224–241), revolted against the overlordship of the crippled Parthian dynasty and by the middle of the 220s had defeated the last Parthian king.

Under Ardashir's son Shapur I (r. 240–272), the Sassanian monarchy not only imposed itself upon the old Parthian nobility and the subject peoples of the Parthian empire, but also undertook repeated assaults on the Roman empire – Greek and Roman authors attributed to him the ambition of restoring the ancient Persian empire of the Achaemenid dynasty, which had been conquered by Alexander the Great 600 years earlier. Caracalla was murdered in 217 while still on his Parthian campaign, but the new Sassanian Persia became the chief focus of his imperial successors. Not only was there the continued lure of a prestigious Persian victory, there were sound strategic reasons for the imperial focus on the East: Persian raids on the eastern provinces – unlike barbarian attacks on other frontiers – threatened the permanent annexation and removal of the provinces from imperial control. Yet the relentless draw of Persia might distract imperial attention from problems on other fronts, and failure against Persia could be fatal to an emperor's hold on his throne – the last Severan emperor, Alexander Severus, was murdered after failures on the Persian front, and innumerable third-century emperors faced usurpations in distant provinces as soon as they had turned their attention to the East. The rise of the Sassanians was therefore one of the catalysts for the third century's cycle of violence. When, as had not been the case a hundred years earlier, a claim on the imperial throne could be contemplated by any powerful Roman and not just the great senatorial generals who had dominated the politics of the second century, then even a minor local crisis – a mutiny, say, or a Persian or barbarian raid – might prompt the local population or the local troops to proclaim a handy leader as emperor to meet the crisis. Having accepted the imperial purple, the new emperor had no choice but to defeat and replace whoever was presently claiming the title. Civil war was inevitable in those circumstances, and the pressures of civil war left pockets of weakness on the frontiers which neighbours could exploit. In consequence, for almost fifty years, a vicious cycle of invasion, usurpation and civil war became entrenched, as even the briefest survey of the mid third century will suggest.

USURPATION, CIVIL WAR AND BARBARIAN INVASIONS

When Alexander Severus was killed in 235, rival candidates sprang up in the Balkans, in North Africa and in Italy, the latter promoted by a Roman senate insistent on its prerogatives. Civil war ensued for much of the next decade, and that in turn inspired the major barbarian invasions at which we have already looked, among them the attack by the Gothic king Cniva that ended in the death of Decius at Abrittus in 251. Decius' successors might win victories over such raiders, but the iron link between invasion and usurpation was impossible to break. This is clearly demonstrated in the reign of Valerian (r. 253–260), who was active mainly in the East, and that of his son and co-emperor Gallienus (r. 253–268) who reigned in the West. Our sources present their reigns as an almost featureless catalogue of disastrous invasions which modern scholars have a very hard time putting in precise chrono-logical order.[15] We need not go into the details here, and instead simply note the way foreign and civil wars fed off each other: when Valerian fought a disastrous Persian campaign that ended in his own capture by the Persian king, many of the eastern provinces fell under the control of a provincial dynasty from Palmyra largely independent of the Italian government of Gallienus. Similarly, every time Gallienus dealt with a threat to the frontiers – raids across the Rhine into Gaul, across the Danube into the Balkans, or Black Sea piracy into Asia Minor and Greece – he was simultaneously confronted by the rebellion of a usurper somewhere else in the empire. Thus Gallienus had to follow up a cam-paign against Marcomanni on the middle Danube by suppressing the usurper Ingenuus, while the successful defence of Raetia against the Iuthungi by the general Postumus allowed him to seize the imperial purple and inaugurate a separate imperial succession which lasted in Gaul for over a decade.[16] Even when Gallienus attempted to imple-ment military reforms to help him counter this cycle of violence, the reforms themselves could work against him: he created a strong mobile cavalry that allowed him to move swiftly between trouble spots, but soon his general Aureolus, who commanded this new force, seized the purple for himself and Gallienus was murdered in 268, in the course of the campaign to supress him. As we have now come to expect, his death inspired immediate assaults on the frontiers, by 'Scythians' in the Balkans and across the Upper Danube into the Alpine provinces as well.

Again, a full list of invaders and usurpers is an arid exercise and one unnecessary here. The successors of Gallienus – Claudius, Aure-lian, Probus, and their many short-lived challengers – faced the same succession of problems as their predecessor had done. Claudius success-fully defeated an invading army of Scythians twice, at Naissus and in the Haemus mountains, and won for himself the victory title *Gothicus* which assures us that those Scythians were Goths.[17] We have already seen that Aurelian won a Gothic campaign, but his energies and atten-tions were constantly distracted by other invasions, some reaching as far as Italy, and by the civil wars in which he suppressed the independent imperial successions in Gaul and the East. Aurelian fell to assassins, and so too did his immediate successor Tacitus, the latter struck down while in hot pursuit of Scythian – perhaps Gothic – raiders deep in the heart of Asia Minor.[18] Though Probus managed to hold the throne for a full six years, he too was killed in a mutiny that broke out in the face of yet another Balkan invasion, and his praetorian prefect Carus was proclaimed emperor by the legions.[19]

THE ACCESSION OF DIOCLETIAN

We get our first indication that authors of the fourth century had come to understand the connection between internal Roman dissension and barbarian invasion with reference to the death of Probus. As the historian Aurelius Victor put it, writing around 360: 'all the barbarians seized the opportunity to invade when they learned of the death of Probus'.[20] In response, the new emperor Carus left his elder son Carinus in charge of the western provinces and led an army against the Quadi and Sarmatians on the middle Danube before launching the invasion of Persia during which he met his end – supposedly struck by lightning, perhaps the victim of assassination.[21] The accession of Diocletian at Nicomedia in 284 prompted the inevitable war against Carinus. The latter had restored the Rhine frontier in 283, but by marching east to face Diocletian he allowed new barbarian raids on the Gallic coast. Carinus was defeated and killed at the battle of the Margus in 285, and in that same year, the victorious Diocletian campaigned against the Sarmatians on the Danube. He also appointed a colleague in the imperial office, a fellow soldier named Maximian, who campaigned on the Rhine.[22]

This was a significant step and one with major repercussions for the longevity of Diocletian's regime. By appointing a co-emperor with whom he was on good terms and who would regard him as his benefactor, Diocletian hoped to give himself the breathing space needed to secure his hold on the throne and prevent rival usurpers appearing in parts of the empire where he could not be himself. The plan worked to a degree, although it took time. Only the appointment in 293 of two caesars, or junior emperors, allowed Diocletian and Maximian to suppress several provincial revolts and secure the frontiers. The evidence of these efforts is visible all along the imperial frontiers, for instance in the so-called Saxon shore forts along the Channel and North Sea coasts of what are now England, France, Belgium and the Netherlands. More important for the history of Roman relations with the Goths is the Diocletianic programme of fortification along the Danube. This consisted both of brand new constructions, as at Iatrus, and also of enlarged and refurbished early imperial fortifications, as at Augustae and Oescus.

DIOCLETIAN AND THE GOTHS

Such improvements were not simply measures of passive self-defence – they were also bases from which imperial campaigns could be supplied and supported. Already in the 280s, Diocletian and Maximian showed a renewed imperial willingness to campaign beyond the frontiers, and Maximian's general Constantius – his caesar after 293 – won several spectacular victories against Franks on the lower Rhine. Meanwhile, Diocletian campaigned on the Danube against Tervingi and Taifali, winning victories in 289 and again in 291. That campaign is significant for us because it marks the first appearance of the Tervingian name in Greek or Latin writing. Our source is a panegyric – a speech in praise of the emperor Maximian, delivered in Gaul in 291 – and it refers to the Tervingi as *pars Gothorum*, which is to say, a section of the Goths.[23] As we shall see in the following chapters, the Tervingi were throughout the fourth century the most important subdivision of the Goths. They were the Gothic group with which the Roman empire had the most regular dealings, and for that reason they are the one about which we know the most. It was the Tervingi with whom the emperor Constantine would conclude a lasting peace in the 330s; descendants of these same Tervingi made up the majority of the Goths who crossed the Danube into the Roman empire in 376, eventually taking part in the Balkan settlements from which Alaric himself would emerge.

For all these reasons, therefore, this first hint of the Tervingi's existence will automatically seem significant to the modern historian of the Goths. We cannot, unfortunately, tell just how important these third-century Tervingi were at the time, particularly as they are mentioned in the same breath as the Taifali, a group of barbarians who often appear together with the Goths in later sources, but always in an inferior position. What is more, this couple of lines in the panegyric of 291 is the last we hear of the Tervingi or any other Goths for more than a decade. By that point, the internal politics of the empire had changed dramatically yet again. As we shall see, the joint reign of Diocletian and Maximian broke the vicious political cycle of the preceding half century. In the process of doing so, they reinvented the governmental system of the Roman empire, strengthening the central government and laying the foundations of a political system that lasted for several hundred years. Just as important, by finally establishing a secure hold on the imperial office, Diocletian and his colleagues were also able to secure more stable relations with barbarian groups along the frontiers. We will return to the government of Diocletian and to the imperial frontiers in chapter four, paying particular attention to the lower Danube. There, by the 320s, the Goths were unquestionably the dominant political force immediately beyond the frontiers, a position they had achieved partly because the emperors wanted them to. In the meantime, however, we must turn to an important interpretative question which is raised by our discussion of third-century invasion and civil war.

If, as we have suggested, the middle of the third century can be defined by this constant cycle of internal and external violence, we are still left to ask why it was that barbarian groups along the northern frontiers could exploit imperial weakness, and particularly imperial rivalry, so successfully and widely. After all, this ability was something quite new, unknown in the early empire, when imperial generals could rampage at will through the land beyond the imperial frontiers. Then, the central European lands beyond the Rhine and Danube were a patchwork of very small political units that could be brought together for coordinated action only for very short periods of time, if at all. That is the situation depicted in the classic account of Tacitus' *Germania*, written in A.D. 98, and corroborated by the political history of the period. The later second and the third centuries stand in very sharp contrast to this early imperial picture. Now, beginning in the 160s and 170s, barbarian groups along the northern frontiers challenged the empire in ways that had always eluded them previously, and did so on a scale never before seen. If we are to understand this exponential growth in the ability of Rome's northern neighbours to pose a threat to the empire, we need to look at the social and political history of barbarian Europe. There, during the first and second centuries, society was transformed in ways that paralleled changes inside the imperial provinces.

THE ROMAN EMPIRE AND BARBARIAN SOCIETY

CHAPTER TWO

JUST AS AN INCREASINGLY COHERENT ROMAN IDENTITY WAS spreading throughout the Roman provinces, so too were major social changes at work in the barbarian societies of northern and central Europe. Soon after the Antonine Constitution made all the inhabitants of the empire Roman citizens for the first time, a new word appears in our sources to describe the world outside the empire: *barbaricum,* the land of the barbarians, and the antithesis of the civilization that was synonymous – and coterminous – with the empire.[1] The catalyst for social change in the *barbaricum* was the simple fact of the empire's existence and with it the growth of Roman provincial life. That fact is hardly surprising, particularly in light of modern studies showing how advanced and relatively complex societies exert unconscious pressures to change on less developed neighbours. The Roman empire was, by the standards of the ancient world, a very complex state. The sophistication of its economic life and its hierarchies of government impinged upon the peoples who lived in its shadow. As provincials became Romans, so they provided instructive models to neighbouring peoples outside the provincial structure, and offered a conduit by which the more portable aspects of Roman provincial life – from luxury goods to a monetized economy – were transmitted to lands that were not, or not yet, provincial.

We can conceive of Roman cultural influence as a series of concentric circles radiating out beyond the Roman frontier. In the band nearest to the frontier, it can sometimes be hard to distinguish the archaeological culture of the natives from their neighbours on the Roman side of the frontier, at least below the level of the social elite; indeed, the fact of imperial government and its regular demands for taxation may have been the only real factor distinguishing a Pannonian peasant on one side of the Danube from a Quadic peasant on the other. Further away from the frontier, differences became starker. Roman export goods, where they could be found at all, were luxury items and Roman coins circulated as bullion not money. Still further out, in Lithuania or Scandinavia, only the most portable of Roman goods are visible – coins, medallions, and the occasional weapon or piece of armour – and from the Roman perspective, these distant people were half-legendary. Even here, however, one finds traces of Roman economic power imposing itself on the indigenous population: on the island of Gotland, for instance, the quantity of Roman coin finds is out of all proportion to the regional norm and seems to suggest a regional distribution centre to other parts of ancient Scandinavia. Such distant regions had products that were valued inside the empire – semi-precious material like amber, but also slaves and raw materials like animal pelts. Such materials leave no trace in the archaeological record available to us, but we can still study the regional distribution of Roman products in central Europe. Such distribution patterns indicate the existence of well-established trade routes from east to west and, especially, from north to south, and it is likely that supplying the economic needs of the Roman empire helped to organize political units far beyond the Roman frontier.[2]

BARBARIANS AND THE ROMAN ARMY

Be that as it may, economic and political interdependence is strikingly visible closer to the imperial frontier, particularly in the context of the Roman army. From the first century onwards, many barbarians served in the Roman army, and the proportion of such barbarians probably increased as the provincialization of the imperial interior made army service less and less attractive to Roman civilians. The benefits of service in the army to a barbarian from beyond the frontier were substantial – not only did service in an auxiliary (non-citizen) unit pay well, it brought with it Roman citizenship after honourable discharge and often a substantial discharge bonus. As we shall see, the Goths were enmeshed in this pattern of service with the Roman army from very early in their history. Even if the famous inscription of a soldier's son named Guththa, who died in Arabia in 208, may or may not refer to a Goth, Gothic troops are definitely attested among the Roman units defeated by the Persian king Shapur and commemorated by him in a famous inscription.[3] Service in the Roman army had profound effects on Rome's neighbours, and not just those who enlisted. Many barbarians who served in the army became entirely acclimatized to a Roman way of life, living out their lives inside the empire and dying there as Roman citizens after long years of service. Others, however, returned to their home communities beyond the frontier, bringing with them Roman habits and tastes, along with Roman money and products of different sorts. Their presence contributed to the demand for more Roman products beyond the frontiers, which helped increase trade between the empire and its neighbours. Roman installations on the frontiers found a ready market for their goods among barbarians close to the frontier, and Roman coins that found their way out into barbarian lands often found their way back through trade.

Depending upon one's political standpoint, this sort of economic influence may seem quite sinister or it might seem benign. Either way, it certainly represents what modern commentators call 'soft power'. Rome's 'hard power' was equally enormous, and could have a painfully severe impact on its neighbours when it was exercised. Even in times of peace, Roman military power was always present as a threat. As we saw in the last chapter, military victories were a vital legitimizing device for imperial power and very few emperors were secure enough on their thrones to pass up the occasional aggressive war. The need for imperial victories translated into periodic assaults upon the neighbours, the imposition of tribute, the taking of hostages, the collection of slaves, the pillaging of villages by Roman soldiers. Roman military pressure was by no means relentless – it could hardly be so after the imperial frontiers ceased to expand – but it was never beyond the realm of possibility. Every generation born along the imperial frontier at some point experienced the attentions of the Roman military. The empire and its army were thus in and of themselves an ongoing spur to social change in the barbarian societies that flanked the imperial provinces: barbarian leaders had every incentive to make themselves more potent militarily.

IMPERIAL POLICY TOWARDS BARBARIAN KINGS

Paradoxically, this drift towards greater military competence amongst the barbarians was only exacerbated by direct Roman interference in barbarian life. Roman dogma held that all barbarians were dangerous and that it was therefore best to keep them at odds with one another as much as possible. In order to keep barbarian leaders in a state of mutual hostility, Roman emperors frequently subsidized some kings directly. This support built up royal prestige and hence governing capacity, while reducing the importance of those leaders who were denied the same support. This type of interference allowed emperors to manage not just relations between barbarians and the empire, but also the relationships among different barbarian groups. Along the barbarian fringe of the empire, access to luxury goods – whether coin or the various items that could be made from the same precious metals as coin – was often as important as the items themselves. The ability to acquire wealth meant the ability to redistribute it, and to be able to give gifts enforced a leader's own social dominance. In other words, conspicuous wealth translated into active power. For these purposes, gold and silver were especially important, and were the dominant medium for storing wealth. Distribution patterns of silver coinage beyond the Roman frontier tend to vary according to the political importance of particular regions at particular times: in Germania, for instance, we find huge concentration of 70,000 silver *denarii* in just a few decades between the reigns of Marcus Aurelius (r. 161–180) and Septimius Severus (r. 193–211), when campaigning along that frontier was regular and intense. What that and other evidence demonstrates is that emperors and their generals regularly manipulated political life in the *barbaricum* through economic subsidy. Yet this strategy, however necessary it might seem within the mental paradigms of Roman government and however effective it might be, was also fraught with dangers.

Raising the status of some leaders above that of their neighbours and natural peers could provide them with both means and motive for military action that they would otherwise have lacked. Leaders buttressed by Roman subsidy were able to attract more warrior clients into their following, thus enlarging the political groups they led. As with Roman soldiers, barbarian warriors were better behaved when kept employed at the tasks for which they were suited. Fighting one's barbarian neighbours was useful in this respect, but nearby Roman provinces – with their accessible wealth and a road system that made it easy for raiding parties to move rapidly about – became a hugely tempting target when imperial attentions were preoccupied elsewhere. The attractions of Roman wealth, combined with the hostility that might be generated by periodic incursions of Roman soldiers, meant that there were strong structural reasons for barbarian attacks on the Roman frontier. These same structural reasons might occasionally inspire a particularly powerful barbarian king to conceive more grandiose plans.

Examples of this phenomenon are apparent even quite early in the history of the empire, as with the famous Dacian king Decebalus. His power was deliberately shorn up by Trajan (r. 98–117) after that emperor's first campaigns beyond the Danube. This support, however, made Decebalus locally predominant, so that he felt able to break his agreements with the emperor and menace the imperial provinces. It took two years of costly warfare to suppress a threat that had only emerged because of imperial subsidy. The Marcomannic wars of the second century obeyed a similar dynamic. They broke out in the mid-160s for reasons that remain disputed, but they precipitated invasions into the Balkans and northern Italy by neighbours of the Marcomanni. The settlement which Marcus Aurelius (r. 161–180) initially imposed on the region failed precisely because it punished some of the chieftains on the middle Danube and rewarded others. Favoured chieftains first threatened and then attacked their less favoured neighbours, driving them into the imperial provinces and making further imperial campaigns necessary. Third-century emperors continued to manage barbarian leaders according to these long-standing habits, but they did so from a position of much greater weakness than had their predecessors. For that reason, the third century witnessed the multiplication of barbarian disturbances all along the frontiers.

New Barbarian Confederacies

Three major barbarian collectivities appear along the imperial frontier in the third century: the Alamanni, the Goths, and the Franks. Though previously unknown to the Roman world, all three groups went on to be permanent features of late imperial politics. Of the three, the Alamanni are in many ways the easiest to understand. In the course of the third century, many smaller groups of barbarians along the Upper Rhine came to be described collectively as Alamanni, and to take occasional collective action. In the fourth century, they appear as a loose confederacy of different kings who could unite for major campaigns against the Romans under one of their number. This sort of coordinated action never lasted for very long, but the Alamanni were nonetheless conscious of sharing a closer comradeship than they did with other barbarians who were not Alamanni. Roughly the same process is detectable in the case of the Franks. Both they and the Alamanni had come together as large but loosely connected polities, whose consciousness of a basic kinship was a response to the simultaneous lure and threat of Rome. It is very likely that the same sort of pressures account for the rise of the Goths.

In the regions where Goths are first attested in the third century – north of the lower Danube and the Black Sea, east of the Carpathians and the Roman province of Dacia – centrally organized and powerful barbarian groupings are unknown until the Goths themselves appear on the scene. Instead, a variety of Sarmatian and other groups formed small communities at the edges of the Roman provinces, and were generally managed in the same way that the empire managed any other barbarians, with periodic subsidy and periodic military punishment. This was how Trajan had dealt with the Roxolani and Costoboci – two of the region's minor barbarian groups – before, during, and after his Dacian wars. Yet it is quite clear that the barbarians of the lower Danube and the Ukrainian steppe were not, in the first and second centuries, perceived as a threat on the same scale as were those of the middle Danube or upper Rhine. Instead, these regions became really important to imperial strategy only in the course of the third century – exactly when we first begin to hear of Goths. Why should the chronology of barbarian history on the lower Danube differ so much from that of other European frontiers? The answer must lie in large part with the relative pace of provincialization in the region.

THE DACIAN FRONTIER AND THE RISE OF THE GOTHS

The Balkan and Danubian provinces were among the last to be added to the Roman empire. Even after Augustus had fixed a line of communication along the Danube to connect eastern and western empires, the mountainous Balkan interior developed only slowly for generations. The series of forts along the frontier was not backed up by the same development of urbanism and road networks as in Gaul, which meant that models of provincial behaviour were not diffused as quickly in the Balkans as they were in frontier provinces further west in the empire. Indeed, it was not until after 107 – when Trajan created the province of Dacia across the Danube in Transylvania and the Carpathians – that the provincialization of the land south of the Danube began in earnest. The existence of the new Dacian province acted on the people of its periphery in the same way that Roman Gaul affected barbarian Germania – it was a spur to the rise of more structured social organization beyond its borders. Archaeological evidence from the lower Danubian regions is not as abundant as it is for the Rhineland and Upper Danube, but we know that the growth of a provincial Roman culture in Dacia followed the same rhythms as those documented with such precision in Gaul. That is to say, by the end of the second century and within two generations of the conquest, a recognizably Roman provincial culture had developed in a long arc across what is now modern Romania. The reigns of Septimius Severus (r. 193–211) and his immediate successors represent the height of Roman material culture in Dacia.[4] It is thus no coincidence that the culture of the steppe lands east of Dacia began to grow more complex in the third century, nor that barbarian confederacies capable of threatening Roman provinces grew up shortly thereafter: this is exactly what had happened in the case of the Franks along the lower Rhine, and with the Alamanni on the upper Rhine and upper Danube. In other words, even though the absolute chronology of change along the lower Danube differs from that further west, it obeys the same relative pace of change: two or three generations after Roman provincial culture began to develop inside the frontier, new and more sophisticated barbarian polities appeared along the periphery, prompted by both the example of Roman provincial life and the threat of the Roman army. The rise of the Goths should be understood within this interpretative framework, as a product of the provincialization of Dacia and the lower Danube provinces.

That, however, leaves open the question of migration. Even readers with a very casual interest in ancient history will have heard of 'the barbarian invasions' or 'the Germanic migrations' and will probably remember that Rome fell because of them. Popular histories are filled with maps that use arrows to plot barbarian migrations from the distant north and east to the doorstep of the Roman empire and beyond. The Goths always feature prominently on such maps and usually come with a very long arrow attached to their migration. Even among scholars, who nowadays tend to downplay the significance of invasions in explaining why Rome fell, the Goths are often taken to be a paradigm of barbarian migration. As we shall see in the next chapter, the evidence for a Gothic migration out of northern Europe to the fringes of the empire is quite weak. It rests mainly on the evidence of a single ancient source, the *Getica* of Jordanes, around which complicated structures of scholarly hypothesis have been built. For centuries, the idea of a deep Gothic antiquity has been essential to many different visions of the European past. All modern discussion of the Goths, including the present book, is a product of this long historiographical tradition. To maintain, as here, that Gothic history effectively begins at the imperial frontier in the third century may be in keeping with all the ancient evidence, but it is also controversial. To understand why an interpretation that closely reflects the ancient evidence should be out of step with much modern hypothesis, we need to examine the role that the Goths have played in the intellectual history of modern Europe. Only by doing so can we see how little our present-day disputes over the Gothic past have to do with third-, fourth-, and fifth-century evidence, and how much they have to do with the political developments of the eighteenth, nineteenth, and earlier twentieth centuries.

THE SEARCH FOR GOTHIC ORIGINS

CHAPTER THREE

OTHIC HISTORY, AS IT APPEARS IN EVERY MODERN AC-
count, is a story of migration. Traditionally, it begins in
Scandinavia, moves to the southern shores of the Baltic
around the mouth of the Vistula river, and then onwards to
the Black Sea. Depending upon what study one reads, one can find
it stated that written sources, archaeology, and linguistic evidence
all demonstrate that just such a migration took place, if not out of
Scandinavia then at least out of Poland. In fact, there is just a single
source for this extended story of Gothic migration, the *Getica* of
Jordanes, written in the middle of the sixth century A.D., hundreds
of years after the events it purports to record. Other sources, literary
and archaeological, have been brought in to corroborate, correct or
supplement Jordanes' narrative, but his story of Gothic migration
underpins nearly every modern treatment of the Goths, consciously
or not. And yet Jordanes, as we shall see, is not merely unreliable, he
is deeply misleading. To understand why his satisfyingly linear, but
ultimately implausible, account is still so pervasive, we have to understand why the idea of Gothic roots stretching back into the deepest
mists of prehistory has played so important a role in conceptualizing the

northern European past. As we shall see, for the past 500 years the Goths have played an indispensable part in imagining a northern European history untouched by the Graeco-Roman world.

THE NORTHERN RENAISSANCE AND THE GERMANIC PAST

In 1425, the Italian humanist Poggio Bracciolini discovered the only known medieval manuscript of Tacitus' *Germania*. That discovery, and still more the first printing of the text at Venice around 1470, were watersheds in the search for a northern, non-Roman, and ultimately Gothic, past. The *Germania* is a short treatise on the peoples and customs of the region that the Romans called Germany – which is to say the whole vast tract of central Europe beyond the Rhine and Danube rivers which was in many ways a mystery to the Romans. Probably written in A.D. 98 and based in part on earlier sources, the *Germania* uses its description of the primitive Germans as a mirror that can reflect the failings of decadent, civilized Rome. Short as it is, the *Germania* provided early modern thinkers and historians with a lot of food for thought. It opens with a section of ethnography in which Tacitus asserts that the Germans were not immigrants to their lands, but rather pure and uncontaminated by intermarriage with others. This is followed by a long description of German customs, and then by a survey of the different tribes of Germania.

For fifteenth- and sixteenth-century scholars – and for many others since then – the modern Germans (or *Deutschen*, as they are called in their own language) were the direct lineal descendants of Tacitus' *Germani*. And so, for humanists in German-speaking countries, Tacitus' *Germania* offered a hitherto undreamed of prospect – a window onto Germanic antiquity for its own sake, rather than as a mere adjunct to the Graeco-Roman past. In the fifteenth century, the Germanic past could only be conceived as a somewhat shady analogue to Roman history, but the discovery of Tacitus – who after all reported that the Germans were a pure race – legitimated the search for separate, unmixed German origins and led back to other texts that could provide insight into a specially German past. German humanists used Tacitus, medieval authors like Jordanes, Gregory of Tours or Einhard, and stray references in the classical sources as the basis for extrapolation and invention, which allowed them to posit a Germanic past that was older than, and therefore could not depend upon, a Roman past.

The Reformation sharpened discussions of the ancient Germans, as the German Protestant reaction against the contemporary Roman Catholic church seeped into discussion of ancient German resistance to the Roman empire. Thereafter, the increasing domestic impact of European colonialism and imperialism also served to change perceptions of northern European antiquity, largely because it encouraged new ideas about the ranking of civilizations into hierarchies. In the sixteenth and seventeenth centuries, Europeans began for the first time to have regular dealings with Asian and (especially) New World cultures which were understood as primitive according to European norms. In the same way that the myth of the 'noble savage' seemed to be validated by the imagined purity of New World primitives, unbesmirched by European decadence, so too were the ancient Germans fitted into a myth of primitive nobility and moral virtue. That Tacitus had used his *Germani* for precisely this purpose was no end of help, and it was easy enough for moralists and polemicists to take the step from the primitive virtues of the *Germani* to the modern virtues of the *Deutschen*. However, it was only with the rise of Romanticism towards the end of the eighteenth century that the study of Germanic antiquity began to ask the questions that still condition scholarly debates today.

ROMANTICISM AND THE RISE OF MODERN HISTORICAL SCHOLARSHIP

In the latter half of the eighteenth century, Romanticism became the reigning intellectual paradigm for German-speaking thinkers and artists. Romantic ideas about the intrinsic qualities of individuals and whole peoples helped to articulate a sense of belonging and identity in German-speaking lands where – unlike France, Spain, or Britain – no modern nation-state had developed. For that reason, Romantic ideology was an inextricable part of German nationalism throughout the eighteenth and nineteenth centuries. In one of history's most fertile accidents, the rigorous and professional study of the past developed in the German-speaking world at precisely this time. The idea that history is a professional scholarly discipline, with a set of analytical methods appropriate to it, goes back to Germany in the early nine-teenth century, and is particularly associated with Leopold von Ranke (1795–1886), who insisted on rooting statements about the past in doc-uments and popularized the radical new approach to teaching through seminars. As this innovative Rankean model of scholarship was adopted throughout Europe, and as history became a professional discipline in universities across the continent, so too did Romantic ideas about the past – ideas that were closely connected to German nationalism – filter into the wider world of nineteenth-century scholarship. In other words, German Romanticism helped to shape basic concepts about how the historical past should be studied during the very years when history was becoming the formal academic discipline it remains to this day.

HERDER, THE *VOLK*, AND PHILOLOGY

The most important figure in this historical Romanticism was Johann Gottfried Herder (1744–1803). For Herder, the *Volk* – the people – was the focal point of all history. The *Volk* was not a constructed or merely political entity, but rather an organic whole with an eternal core identity expressed in language, art, literature and characteristic institutions. All these were expressions of the *Volksgeist*, the unique spirit of the *Volk*. The *Volksgeist* could not be changed by conquest or by borrowings from other cultures, because it was essentially pure and immutable. Herder's emphasis on language as a marker of the identity of the *Volk* had a par-ticular importance for the subject of this book. At the same time that language was taking a leading place among the many attributes of the *Volk*, so too was a new scientific philology – what we would now call historical linguistics – being developed. Of particular importance was the discovery that many living spoken languages were related both to one another and to other languages that had once existed but were now no longer spoken. The idea of language families that could be plotted in a sort of genealogical table fitted in perfectly with the nineteenth-century search for national origins. Close linguistic community – as, for instance, the various members of the Germanic language family – could be invoked as evidence for deeper sorts of political or ideological community. When retrojected into the distant past, evidence for linguistic community could be used as evidence of politically conscious community action in the past.

It was these linguistic arguments that anchored the Goths firmly to the study of a Germanic past. As we saw in the last chapter, our ancient sources never regarded the Goths as Germans, but rather as Scythians. In the nineteenth century, however, philologists discovered that Gothic belonged to the Germanic language family. It was thus a relative not just of medieval and modern German, but of other Germanic languages like Dutch, English, and the different Scandinavian tongues. This meant that the Goths could be annexed to the world of the ancient Germans on philological grounds. Once that was possible, they could take a central role in a history of the German *Volk*. That Romantic ideal of a single German *Volk* helped provide a conceptual framework for the political unification of German-speaking lands that was brought about by Otto von Bismarck in 1871. With the creation of a united Germany, the study of a German national past became even more important. The chieftain Arminius, who had destroyed three Roman legions at the battle of the Teutoburger forest in A.D. 9, emerged as the most potent symbol of an eternal German spirit; in his modern nationalist incarnation as Hermann the German, Arminius became the subject of a beautiful and famous monument, the Hermannsdenkmal, put up near the town of Detmold as a tribute to a free German nation.[1]

PRE-WAR AND POST-WAR SCHOLARSHIP

Given how important the ancient Germanic past was to the national formation of modern Germany, it will come as no surprise that ancient history was also used to justify some of the nastier manifestations of German nationalism. Nazi foreign policy made much of the purity of the German race rooted in the very remote past. The wide distribution of ancient Germans across the European continent could justify the conquest of modern Germany's neighbours as a 'reconquest' of the former lands of the German *Volk*. Proving the 'Germanic' nature of eastern Europe's original population – on the basis of ancient texts or on the basis of archaeology and physical anthropology – had modern political significance. For that reason, historians and archaeological services followed in the wake of the Wehrmacht as it subjugated large tracts of Europe. The story of a Gothic migration from Scandinavia to the Polish Baltic to the Ukraine was, for obvious reasons, a precious testimony to the true extent of German *Lebensraum*. We nowadays recognize that there was no way for a German historian of the 1930s to avoid some association with the Nazi regime, in the same way that fine Soviet historians had to begin their works with an obligatory chapter of Marxist orthodoxy before getting on with their real subject. As a result, alongside quantities of nationalist and racist tripe, some very important monuments of historical scholarship derive from the Nazi era: to take just one example, even today one cannot study the Goths or any other late antique barbarians without reference to the revised second edition of Ludwig Schmidt's *Geschichte der deutschen Stämme* ('History of the German Tribes'), brought out between 1933 and 1942 and in sympathy with the nationalist ideology of that era.

In the post-war period, scholars across Europe consciously repudiated many of the visibly nationalist aspects of pre-war scholarship on the northern European past, analysing barbarian tribes as social constructs, 'imagined communities', rather than timeless and changeless lines of blood kin. As pan-European institutions developed in the second half of the twentieth century – first through a common market, then through the European Union – this sort of approach was increasingly in keeping with a modern political outlook that aims to make it impossible for Europeans to repeat the nationalist conflagrations of the early twentieth century. Yet despite this conscious distancing, many strands of pre-war and wartime scholarship into the Germanic past survived into the discussions of the 1950s and later. Ideas about Germanic lordship, for instance, with its focus on the role of the aristocratic leader in constituting the *Volk*, are prominent in the post-war scholarship of Walter Schlesinger and influence even the most recent debates about barbarian history. Given that, it is very important for us to be clear about a point of intellectual history: to acknowledge scholarly and intellectual continuities with the historical debates of pre-war or wartime nationalism is not to suggest a continuity of political outlook or motive. One cannot stress that point strongly enough, for recent debates about barbarian society and Gothic origins have been poisoned by the mistaken belief that the intellectual continuity of pre- and post-war scholarship must imply political continuity. That is simply not the case. Yet the fact of this intellectual continuity is of fundamental importance, not for political reasons, but because it shows that even the most self-consciously modern work on the barbarians rests on older scholarship rooted in a quest for Germanic origins. The Goths, and particularly Jordanes' Gothic history, have been central to any such quest since the Renaissance, and much of the continued reliance on Jordanes' is rooted in that time-honoured tradition. Unfortunately, as we shall see, Jordanes' history cannot bear the weight that is placed on it.

THE PROBLEM OF JORDANES

Since Jordanes' Gothic history was first printed in 1515 by the humanist Conrad Peutinger – going through seven more editions in the sixteenth century alone – it has remained the core around which those who want to create a single, deep channel of Gothic history must build. No other source suggests that the Goths had a history before the third century, and if Jordanes' *Getica* had not survived, the study of early medieval barbarians would not have evolved in the way it has. In a sense, the *Getica* of Jordanes is nothing more than the earliest manifestation of the impulse to give a non-Roman past to a non-Roman people, the same impulse at work in the many histories that have followed in Jordanes' footsteps.

Of the man and his work we know nothing save what he tells us: Jordanes was the son of Alanoviamuth and the grandson of Paria, a secretary to the barbarian chieftain Candac. Before he was converted to the life of an observant Christian, Jordanes was himself secretary to a barbarian general in imperial service, one Gunthigis also known as Baza. The names of Jordanes' forebears are certainly barbarian, and he may himself claim Gothic descent depending upon how one reads a difficult passage in the *Getica*.[2] Yet nothing in his extant writings suggests that this Gothic descent had any claim on his sympathies, which were entirely Christian and imperial. Jordanes wrote two works that have survived, the *Romana*, or *Roman History*, and the *Getica*, the accepted short title for his *De origine actibusque Getarum*, 'On the Origin and Deeds of the Goths'. He wrote at Constantinople, in Latin as did many of his contemporaries in that capital of the eastern Roman empire. His *Getica* was written sometime after the year 550, the date of the last allusion detectable in the text, but we do not know how long afterwards. When he wrote, it was as the subject of the emperor Justinian (r. 527–565), who had launched bloody wars of (re-)conquest against three barbarian kingdoms that had grown up in the former western Roman empire during the fifth century. When Jordanes was writing, the Vandal kingdom of Africa had been destroyed by imperial troops, and the Gothic kingdom in Italy was on the brink of total annihilation, an annihilation which the *Getica* wholeheartedly endorses. Yet despite the clarity of Jordanes' pro-imperial perspective in the *Getica*, his Gothic descent has long been thought to offer us a privileged window into the Gothic mind and the ancient Gothic past. This unfortunate assumption is perhaps understandable, but it is further complicated by the textual history of the *Getica*.

JORDANES AND CASSIODORUS

Jordanes dedicates his *Getica* to Castalius, who had asked him to abridge a much larger Gothic history now lost to us – the twelve books on the topic written by the Roman nobleman Cassiodorus.[3] Cassiodorus had served as the praetorian prefect of the Ostrogothic kings of Italy, before giving up on the Gothic cause and going into exile at Constantinople in about 540. Sometime before 533, in his capacity as chief *littérateur* at the Gothic court of king Theodoric (r. 489–526) and his successor, Cassiodorus had written his Gothic history. As befitted the work of a loyal courtier, this history placed at its apex Theodoric and his dynasty, the Amals, showing how a continuous line of Gothic kings had reached down to the great Theodoric. Not one word of Cassiodorus' history remains to us in its own right. Jordanes' *Getica* survives, but its relationship to Cassiodorus is a matter of controversy. Jordanes himself tells us that he had three days' access to Cassiodorus' Gothic history when that author's household steward let him read them. When Jordanes composed the *Getica*, he had no copy of Cassiodorus available and needed instead to work from memory. Jordanes says that although he cannot reproduce Cassiodorus' words, he can reproduce his argument and the factual substance of his account. On the other hand, Jordanes also tells us that he added to Cassiodorus an introduction and conclusion, many items from his own learning, and other things drawn from Greek and Latin writers.[4]

So how close does Jordanes stand to Cassiodorus? Many sixth-century authors – for instance the Greek Zosimus who probably wrote not long before Jordanes – did nothing but cut and paste sections from earlier authors into their own narrative. Jordanes claims not to have done this, but perhaps he is not to be trusted on that point. Perhaps his *Getica* is nothing more than a pale shadow of Cassiodorus' lost history. If that is so, and we do indeed have access to Cassiodorus by way of Jordanes, then we are suddenly in the orbit of the greatest barbarian king of the sixth century, and perhaps in touch with the traditions and memories of his family and his court. The relationship between Jordanes and Cassiodorus is thus a matter of real importance – if one wants to believe the stories of Gothic origins and migrations that one finds in Jordanes, then making him little more than a conduit for Cassiodorus is an invaluable device. Jordanes, of course, tells us all sorts of stories about the Goths, placing their origins some 2,030 years before the time of his writing, and linking them to Biblical, Greek, Roman, and Near Eastern history in a bizarre melange of material from different sources. Most of these stories have held little interest for scholars since the Renaissance – no one has tried to prove the historicity of Philip of Macedon's marriage to Medopa, the supposed daughter of a supposed Gothic king named Gudila.[5] On the contrary, there is just one story in Jordanes that scholars have clung to for centuries – the narrative of Gothic migration out of Scandinavia, 'as if out of a womb of nations'.[6]

One of several conflicting origin stories recounted by Jordanes tells us that the Goths left 'Scandza' in three boats and migrated across the Baltic under king Berig; then Filimer, perhaps the fifth king after Berig, led the army of Goths away from the Baltic and into Scythia near to the Black Sea.[7] Having got the Goths to the Black Sea, Jordanes begins to mention historical names known from Greek and Latin sources closer to the events they record, but these notices are intermingled with all sorts of legendary and pseudo-historical material and Jordanes' implied chronology is impossible to chart coherently. The important thing, from the point of view of Jordanes, is to work all of the stories from his many different sources into a single linear narrative of Gothic history, in which Gothic heroism and strength is effectively unbeatable until finally subdued by Justinian. He dates the beginning of the Gothic relationship with the Roman empire to the time of Julius Caesar, and reads the narrative of that relationship in sixth-century legal terms as a series of official treaties between Goths and emperor repeatedly broken by one party or the other and then renegotiated.[8] This continuous Gothic history from Scandinavia to the Black Sea to the Balkans and on to Italy is the part of Jordanes' narrative which modern scholars have striven so hard to sustain. Providing as he does a narrative of Gothic history that pre-dates Greece and Rome, Jordanes' *Getica* was every bit as precious to northern humanists as was Tacitus' *Germania*. For them, as for modern nationalists, both proved the great antiquity of the German identity. Nowadays, scholars have repudiated such explicitly nationalist aims, but their ongoing reluctance to discard Jordanes' origin and migration narratives resides in a similar unwillingness to give up our only evidence for a Gothic past that pre-dates contact with the Roman empire.

'ETHNOGENESIS'

Even today, some eminent scholars maintain that Jordanes' testimony is both a valid historical source and a repository of Gothic ethnic traditions. Such arguments are generally couched within discussions of 'ethnogenesis', a neologism borrowed from American social science, but now used for the coming into being of a barbarian ethnic group and closely associated with the Viennese historian Herwig Wolfram. Wolfram and his followers argue that barbarian ethnicity was not a matter of genuine descent-communities, but rather of *Traditionskerne* ('nuclei of tradition'), small groups of aristocratic warriors who carried ethnic traditions with them from place to place and transmitted ethnic identity from generation to generation; larger ethnic groups coalesced and dissolved around these nuclei of tradition in a process of continuous becoming or ethnic reinvention – ethnogenesis. Because of this, barbarian ethnic identies were evanescent, freely available for adoption by those who might want to participate in them. Parts of this theoretical model are not new: even nationalist historians of the earlier twentieth century knew that the membership of barbarian tribes ebbed and flowed with success or failure, so that the blood kinship which supposedly held them together was partly fictional. The role of noble families in forming the *Traditionskern* is equally a direct echo of pre-war lordship studies. On the other hand, the impact of the Viennese approach has been enormous and its wide acceptance by a non-specialist audience has made it seem more novel than it is. Until quite recently, popular literature and textbooks on the barbarians were dominated by an essentialist approach to barbarian ethnicity: each named ethnic group was a 'tribe' (*Stamm* in German), possessing essential characteristics that made its differences from other tribes self-evident and its history continuous and unique. Proponents of ethnogenesis-theory, whose research has frequently developed in pan-European symposia, often claim it as the only alternative to the sort of racist and nationalist scholarship that blighted past generations. Although that stance is much exaggerated, ethnogenesis-theory has undoubtedly killed off essentialist views of barbarian tribal identity, an excellent result.[9]

Less fortunately, however, ethnogenesis-theory has permitted its proponents to maintain the historicity of Jordanes' migration stories, treating them not as a tribal migration but rather as the ethnic memory of a small noble group, particularly the Amal family of Theodoric. The only recent treatment of Gothic history to dissent from the Vienna school and its focus on aristocratic traditions is that of Peter Heather. But Heather, too, accepts the basic historicity of Jordanes' migration narrative, viewing it as evidence for the large-scale migration of a free Gothic population whose size was such that its 'Gothic-ness' was widely understood by adult male Goths. Thus for both Heather and Wolfram, as for many earlier scholarly generations, the story of the Goths starts in a distant northern land, far from the Roman frontier, whence either migration or 'ethnic processes' bring the Goths or the Gothic identity to the edges of the Roman world. For both, in other words, the controlling narrative is that of Jordanes.

HISTORICAL METHOD AND JORDANES' GOTHIC HISTORY

But how much faith does Jordanes really deserve? Is he any more reliable on events long past than are other sixth-century Byzantine authors? And, if he is, are his northern migration stories any more reliable than the derivation of Goths from the biblical Gog and Magog? That biblical ancestry was commonly accepted by Greek and Latin writers from the fourth century onwards, and Jordanes himself refers to it.[10] Why should Jordanes' migration story be more credible than his story that the Egyptian king Vesosis made war upon the Gothic king Tanausis, who defeated him and chased him all the way back to the Nile?[11] Along with many other changes in our understanding of ancient historical texts, the past two decades have witnessed a realization that we need to take each of them as a whole, reading it in context and in its entirety. We cannot simply pick and choose among the evidence offered by a text on the grounds of its seeming plausible or 'historical'. We must, on the contrary, demonstrate why, in the whole context in which it appears, a particular piece of evidence is authentic.

There is no way to do that with the origin stories in Jordanes. It is possible that Jordanes, via Cassiodorus, had access to genuine stories told by sixth-century Goths about their distant past; it is also possible that such stories entered Jordanes through a mysterious historian named Ablabius whom he mentions, but who is otherwise unknown.[12] That the Goths told such stories is likely *a priori* and probably confirmed by Jordanes' explicit mention of ancient Gothic songs.[13] Yet even if any one of these lines of transmission is real and the migration from the north was genuinely believed by sixth-century Goths, that does not make it true, any more than the famous origin story of Romulus and Remus is true because Romans in the third century B.C. believed it to be. As modern anthropological studies have shown, oral transmission can preserve astonishingly accurate nuggets of historical data, but the context in which it does so is always distorted. Without outside controls, we have no way of telling which, if any, element of an orally transmitted story might be true. Most of the time – as here – that outside control simply does not exist.

Because of all this, we are not justified in taking Jordanes' *Getica* as the narrative foundation for our own Gothic histories. One of the most important differences between the present book and other recent studies of Gothic history is its evaluation of Jordanes on the same terms as any other Byzantine author of the sixth century. If we take him on those terms, we realize that he has very limited information about, and very limited understanding of, fourth- and fifth-century events, particularly those in the western part of the empire. Where we can discover the source for a particular piece of Jordanes' evidence, or where his evidence finds corroboration elsewhere, then we can use it with appropriate caution. That is the case, for instance, with the third-century Gothic chiefs Argaith and Guntheric, whose sack of Marcianople was mentioned early in chapter one: Jordanes' information almost certainly comes from the reliable third-century historian Dexippus, and a corruption of the chieftains' names is attested in a fourth-century text, the *Historia Augusta*, which also drew on Dexippus. In such circumstances, there can be little objection to accepting Jordanes' evidence as fundamentally authentic. Yet where Jordanes is our sole voice, and where we have no evidence for his source or its reliability, we must leave him to one side. That is clearly the path of caution when it comes to Gothic migration stories, which rest solely on Jordanes. No other source makes this long Gothic history probable.[14] Rather than migrants from the distant north, it is more likely that the Goths who entered imperial history in the earlier third century were a product of circumstances on the imperial frontier.

As we saw in the last chapter, powerful barbarian polities tended to arise on the Roman frontiers in response to the existence of the empire, a function of the changes which complex and imperial cultures can work on neighbouring cultures that are less socially stratified and less technologically advanced. These were the social forces that created the coalitions of the Franks and Alamanni along the Rhine and the upper Danube in the third century, and we have suggested that the Goths on the lower Danube should be understood in the same way. Before we can go on to address that question in more detail, we need to think about how the Goths or any other barbarian group differed from other ones. More particularly, we need to consider the ways in which both Greek and Roman writers, and we ourselves, go about 'telling the difference', as Walter Pohl has put it.[15]

BARBARIAN IDENTITY: GRAECO-ROMAN ETHNOGRAPHY

How do we tell a Goth from a Frank or an Alaman from a Sarmatian? How did the Romans do so? In more abstract terms, how does anyone tell themselves and those with whom they identify from other people with whom they do not? The definition of difference was a pressing concern for Greek and Roman writers, for whom ethnography – the literary description of non-Greeks and non-Romans – was so well known a genre that Virgil could parody it in his fourth *Georgic* with a poetic ethnography of bees. Modern scholars, in trying to explain the ancient sources with all their myriad names of peoples, strive both to understand the criteria by which ancient writers told their subjects apart, and to establish criteria by which we can do the same thing. From these two questions there follows a third: how did the different peoples we meet in our sources tell themselves apart from their neighbours? This question is much more difficult, because none of the peoples to the north of the Graeco-Roman world left behind written sources from which we might extract such information. Archaeology, if we can use it for this purpose, might provide an answer, but as we shall see, reading ethnic or group identity in the archaeological evidence is very difficult in most circumstances. Let us, however, take the contents of the ancient literary sources first.

The three words Greek and Roman sources most often use to describe barbarian groups are *gens*, *natio* and *ethnos* (*gentes*, *nationes*, and *ethne* in the plural). The first two words are Latin, the third Greek, and the modern English derivatives of each word are plain to see. Theoretically, in etymological terms, the word *gens* refers primarily to an extended family, the word *natio* to a community of such *gentes*, but in practice the words were interchangeable and their Greek equivalent is *ethnos*. There is no good English word which we can use to translate any of the three terms. 'Tribe' (equivalent to the modern German *Stamm*) is useful because it implies a sense of community and perhaps a blood relationship (real or fictive), but it also connotes the primitive in a way that only the Latin *gentes* conveys (and even then, only in the plural and when used of non-Romans). 'People' might work, but especially in American English it implies a sense of political purpose which is absent from the Greek and Latin. 'Nation' and 'race' are too weighted down with modern baggage to be of any use. Modern scholars have settled on the boring, but deliberately neutral, word 'group' as the safest way of translating *gens*, *natio*, or *ethnos* in the context of late antique barbarians. This is quite sensible, because it prevents us from implying political or cultural characteristics without meaning to do so. On the other hand, it is very important for us to realize that when the Greek and Roman sources on which we must rely use the words *gens*, *natio*, or *ethnos*, they do indeed mean to imply a coherent, interrelated group of non-Greeks and non-Romans that can be identified as different and which share a sense of belonging together because they do in fact belong together. In other words, the Greeks and Romans did not share our conceptual concerns about the existential nature of barbarian groups – they worried about how to tell such groups apart.

A Distorting Mirror: *Interpretatio romana*

All our evidence for the differentiation of barbarian groups is filtered through ancient Graeco-Roman perceptions of alterity, of the non-Greek or non-Roman. This filter is what scholars call the *interpretatio romana*, the 'Roman interpretation', or perhaps Roman distortion, of the barbarian reality it claims to report. The *interpretatio romana* poses real difficulties, in part because a cognitive disjunction lies at the heart of Graeco-Roman ethnographic thinking. On the one hand, at a very real level Greeks and Romans believed all barbarians were fundamentally the same. The very word *barbaros* may be onomatopoeia, coined in order to describe the sound that came out of barbarians' mouths – a noise like that of animals, rather than language which was the special preserve of the Greeks.[16] Barbarians lacked language and so they were all the same. And yet they were not: ethnography, in fact, existed to tell all those others apart. It set out to abstract from the universal 'other' that was the barbarian a set of *gentes* or *ethne* which gave shape and order to the world beyond civilization. Although Roman generals on the frontiers had very practical experience of, and sometimes extremely detailed information about, the neighbours whom they had to fight, the ethnographic tradition was not as concerned with such practical matters as it was with abstracting reality into analytical categories. These categories might pattern the experience of reality as much as they were derived from it. For this purpose, Greek and Roman writers had a series of criteria that they could use to analyse identity and difference among their barbarian neighbours or subjects. Chief among these were habits of dress and clothing; traditional weaponry or fighting styles; sex habits and gender roles; religion; and perhaps most importantly language.

Unfortunately, each of these classificatory criteria posed interpretative problems for ancient ethnographers, because none of them was infallibly diagnostic of ethnic difference. In the case of language, for instance, there were considerably more *gentes* than there were languages. There were, equally, many fewer fighting styles than there were people who deployed them. And couldn't a set of stereotyped 'barbarian' clothing be used to signify any barbarian in artwork? Public victory monuments have a series of iconographic codes which shout out 'barbarian' to the viewer, be they peaked 'Phrygian' caps, trousers for Germans and Persians, or hair worn in a 'Suevic' topknot. Our ancient writers were fully aware that their classificatory categories were problematical. For that reason, even though they believed that such categories could indeed be used to separate *gens* from *gens*, Greek and Roman authors also deployed ethnographic categories as broad existential sets, into which new or newly encountered barbarians could be slotted as necessary, according to whichever classificatory criteria seemed most empirically appropriate at a given time. Categories like German, Celt or Scythian were very broad, their definitions open to discussion. It was, for instance, a very long time before the distinction between Germans and Celts came to be generally accepted among Graeco-Roman authors, and for many years Germans and Celts were regularly taken to be the same. Or again, while in the third century Dexippus could classify Alamanni as Scythians, no fourth-century author could do the same because the Alamanni were clearly fixed as *Germani* by then.[17] What all this means for us is a constant confrontation with the limitations of our Greek and Roman sources for the barbarians. Their belief in an eternal barbarian type explains the constant identification of the Goths with Herodotus' Scythians, and also explains why fourth-century authors can freely combine ancient or poetic barbarians like the Cimmerians or Gelonians with the very real Iuthungi and Franci of their own day.

These conceptual contradictions, or cognitive disjunctures, are pervasive and because they are all we have, they interpose a real barrier between us and the barbarians. We lack nearly any sense of whether or not such Graeco-Roman categories meant anything to the people who were fixed within them. In the case of such meta-categories as German or Scythian the answer, from all we can tell, is no. Nothing in our sources, even filtered through an *interpretatio romana* as they are, suggests that the later empire's *Germani* felt any kinship amongst themselves, or that Goths and Sarmatians, both Scythians in our sources, were aware of any similarities between themselves. We are on much less certain grounds with more specific ethnonyms – Iuthungi, Iazyges, or Tervingi, for example – which seem to designate groups that shared a sense of kinship and engaged in common actions for that reason. Unlike German or Scythian, these names for smaller groups may have been generated by their users themselves, rather than imposed from outside by Greeks and Romans.

Even if that is true, however, it tells us very little about how a sense of identity was constituted within or between barbarian groups. How did the Tervingi tell themselves apart from the Greuthungi, who both appear in our fourth-century sources as political divisions of the Goths? In other words, can we get at barbarians' own criteria of identity and alterity? Language must surely have been important in creating a sense of alterity. Yet despite the deep rooted nineteenth-century conviction that belonging to the same language family produces some sort of shared identity, too many different *gentes* spoke mutually intelligible languages for a common tongue to contribute much to a sense of identity. Religion may have been more significant – some of our ethnonyms, for instance that of the Suevi, may originally have referred not to political or kinship units, but rather to a variety of groups who shared sacred cult sites. Unfortunately, we have virtually no access to authentic traces of barbarian religion, certainly not enough to chart what function, if any, it had in defining the boundaries of identity and alterity. What of dress? Clothing does have, and has always had, a very important function in expressing identity and alterity. Precisely because it is instantly visible, clothing can serve an emblematic function for those in a position to decode what any particular item of dress, or any combination of such items, means. Greeks and Romans were fully aware of the importance of clothing as a signifier of identity: imperial laws from the fourth century restrict the wearing of 'barbarian' costume in certain places, exemplified by a ban on trousers in the city of Rome from A.D. 397.[18] Yet if we try to move from the recognition that clothing could be used to tell the difference to an analysis of *how* it did so, we run up against one of the most vexed and vexing questions of late antique and early medieval studies: what can archaeological evidence tell us about identity, and ethnic identity more specifically?

ARCHAEOLOGY, IDENTITY, ETHNICITY

The material remains of the frontier regions are an extremely valuable source for barbarian social history, as will become clear in the next chapter, but they are much less useful as evidence for ancient ethnic divisions. Although that fact has been demonstrated by a great deal of recent work – both practical and theoretical – it flies in the face of more than a century of scholarship. The correlation of particular types of material evidence with particular barbarian groups named in the literary sources has long been, and remains, normal practice, as does the tracing of migrations on the basis of artefacts. The origins of these approaches lie in the early twentieth century and are particularly associated with the archaeologist Gustav Kossinna, though they underpin the work of other great archaeologists of the European *barbaricum* like Hans Zeiß and Joachim Werner. Kossinna's *Siedlungsarchäologie* ('settlement archaeology') postulated that materially homogeneous archaeological cultures could be matched up with the ethnic groups attested in our literary sources, and also with the language groups defined by philologists. The shifting extensions of material cultures should therefore be interpreted as the movements of peoples. The rigidity of Kossinna's approach has long been repudiated, but its legacy is pervasive. One widespread belief ultimately rooted in that legacy is that artefacts themselves carry ethnicity: that one particular form of brooch is Gothic, another Vandalic, and that wherever we find such brooches we can locate Goths and Vandals. This 'ethnic ascription' – the attaching of ethnic identity to particular material artefacts – is still ubiquitous in archaeological study of the barbarians, as is the designation of complexes of material evidence with ethnic names drawn from our literary evidence. Ethnic ascription is what allows some scholars to maintain that the Gothic migration recorded in Jordanes is also visible in the archaeological evidence.

Unfortunately, it has now been definitively shown that artefacts do not carry ethnicity in such a fashion.[19] Whether in the cemeteries from which most of our artefacts come or in the remains of barbarian settlements, material evidence tells us a great deal about vertical social relationships – those between different status levels within a society – but much less about horizontal relationships between ethnic or linguistic groups with separate identities. Thus while it is comparatively easy to characterize vertical distinctions within a single archaeological assemblage – such as bigger houses, better grave goods – defining assemblages by contrast to others is much more difficult. For one thing, it is a wholly artificial process that involves selecting out several characteristics – for instance the positioning of weapons in burials, or particular brooch forms or building techniques – and holding them to be diagnostic, either singly or in combination, of a particular archaeological culture. The selection of defining characteristics can itself be a problem, as there is always a danger of taking as diagnostic characteristics that are actually very widely diffused. But even if we avoid that danger, we are still making another problematical assumption: that the characteristics we have selected as definitive are the same ones that contemporaries would have recognized as defining their sense of identity or alterity. That assumption can never be possible in purely archaeological terms. Although we can be sure that some items of dress were used as emblems of identity and alterity – of belonging and exclusion – we need the human voice of the past to tell us which items communicated that sense of identity and how they did so. As we have seen, the only human voice that exists for our late antique barbarians is that of an *interpretatio romana* which is as alien to the barbarian perspective as we are ourselves. For that reason, we cannot be confident that our archaeological cultures really do represent something other than our own selection of dead remains – that they do in fact identify some sense of cultural identity that living contemporaries might have recognized. In consequence, we risk investing the material evidence with a historical significance it does not intrinsically possess. That is to say, we risk turning an abstract set of material markers, which we have ourselves selected, into a historically real group of humans to which we then attribute a collective identity or ascribe collective actions. These intrinsic risks are only exacerbated when we draw a connection between an archaeological culture and a historical group named in our sources.

The Goths and the Sântana-de-Mureş/ Černjachov Culture

It is, of course, sometimes possible to draw a legitimate connection between the material evidence and the barbarians named in our Greek and Roman authorities. If a well-dated material culture is widely present in a region in which our sources locate a named ethnic group over a substantial period of time, then we can say with some certainty that the named ethnic group used that material culture. The correspondence is never absolute, however. All of the archaeological culture zones that we know extend over regions in which the literary sources describe more than one ethnic or political grouping. In other words, a material culture is never identical with a particular ethnic grouping we find in the written sources. The single best illustration of this theoretical position is, as it happens, the Goths themselves. We know that Goths first appear in contemporary literary sources in the early decades of the third century and that, in the company of various other named groups, they posed a threat to the peace of the empire from bases in the region to the north and west of the Black Sea. As we shall see in the next chapter, by the earlier fourth century the Goths had unquestionably become the most powerful group in that region. In that same region – roughly between Volhynia in the north, the Carpathians in the west, the Danube and Black Sea to the south and the Donets to the east – a single archaeological culture is visible from the late third until the early fifth century. This archaeological culture is known as the Sântana-de-Mureş/Černjachov culture and is reasonably well dated on archaeological grounds. That is to say, the region in which the Goths were dominant fell within the Sântana-de-Mureş/Černjachov cultural zone. This means that we can use the socio-historical evidence of that material culture to help describe fourth-century Gothic social structures and economic relations – as we will in the next chapter.

GOTHIC MIGRATION IN THE ARCHAEOLOGICAL EVIDENCE

But does the identification allow us to do more than that? For instance, does the identification of the Sântana-de-Mureş/Černjachov culture with fourth-century Goths allow us to find Goths elsewhere? Many archaeologists and historians would answer yes. The argument has been made most explicitly by Volker Bierbrauer: the Sântana-de-Mureş/Černjachov archaeological culture is Gothic; some of its characteristics – particular brooch and ceramic types, a tendency not to place weapons in graves – are similar to those of the Wielbark culture, which was centred on the Vistula river and lasted from the first to the fourth century A.D.; the Wielbark culture must therefore also be Gothic. Also, because the Sântana-de-Mureş/Černjachov culture is Gothic, and because some artefacts associated with it appear inside the frontiers of the Roman empire, these artefacts must represent the movement of Goths from the Danube to Italy, and thence to Gaul and Spain. Bierbrauer's simplistic ethnic ascription model is extreme, but only because it is articulated so clearly.[20] Unfortunately, many other archaeologists and historians working in the field accept its core assumptions without acknowledging the fact. Even Peter Heather, the most subtle modern interpreter of Gothic history, has written about 'working backwards' from the Sântana-de-Mureş/Černjachov culture to earlier stages of 'Gothic' archaeology.[21] Two separate considerations, one practical, one theoretical, make this approach untenable.

For one thing, the Sântana-de-Mureş/Černjachov culture is extremely diverse. As we shall see in the next chapter, the artefacts, construction techniques, and burial practices found within the Sântana-de-Mureş/Černjachov zone have parallels with earlier cultural traditions within the zone itself, with Roman provincial culture, with the Wielbark and Przeworsk cultures to the north and west, and with the steppe cultures of the east. The Wielbark elements in the Sântana-de-Mureş/Černjachov culture are no more numerous than other elements, so there is no archaeological reason to privilege them over others. Even if Wielbark artefacts were dominant in the Sântana-de-Mureş/Černjachov zone, they would not necessarily signify the same thing in both places: artefacts that are emblematic of one thing in one place may change meaning radically if transposed to another. More importantly still, the closeness of the artefactual connections between the two cultures is not as great as is usually asserted. Indeed, their chief point of intersection is not particular artefacts, but the fact that weapon burials are absent from the Wielbark and rare in the Sântana-de-Mureş/Černjachov zones. In purely logical terms, a negative characteristic is less convincing proof of similarity than a positive one, and the fact that weapon burials are commonest where archaeological investigation has been most intensive suggests that our evidentiary base is anything but representative. Given this, why should the Wielbark–Sântana-de-Mureş/Černjachov connection seem so self-evident to so many scholars? One answer is an old methodology that seeks to explain changes in material culture by reference to migration. The other is Jordanes.

MIGRATION V. DIFFUSION THEORIES

The methodological problem is of long standing. In the early years of archaeology's development as a scientific discipline, it was normal to understand cultural changes as the result of one tribe or people conquering or displacing another and replacing the previous material culture with a new one of their own. This interpretative paradigm goes back in part to the nationalist scholarship of the *Volk* at which we have already looked, in part to the preoccupation of our ancient historical sources with invasion, migration and conquest, and in part to Kossinna's ascription of fixed and defined material cultures to ethnopolitical groupings. In the 1970s and 1980s, some archaeological theorists reacted radically against such migration theories. Working from the simple and obvious observation that the material culture of a place can change radically without the population of that place changing much at all, these archaeologists sought to explain change in archaeological cultures by reference to the diffusion of materials and ideas rather than migration. Diffusionist theory became and remains the norm, particularly amongst British archaeologists.

On the other hand, diffusionist theory, like any theory, can be pushed to unrealistic extremes. It is, after all, a simple fact that people move and have always done so, sometimes over long distances – a fine example from our period is the Sarmatian Iazyges, who moved *en masse* from the vicinity of the Dnieper and Dniester rivers, where Strabo places them at the beginning of the first century A.D., to the Alföld between the Danube and Tisza, where Pliny places them in the 70s A.D., having come at the request of the Quadic king Vannius for aid against the Hermunduri. When people move, they often bring large parts of their native culture with them, however transformed it may be when transplanted into a new environment: one need only look at any large immigrant neighbourhood in the U.S. or Britain to see the truth of this fact. What is more, the conquest of one region by people from another can profoundly alter the culture of a conquered region, with or without massive population shifts: the expansion of the Roman empire is history's best illustration of this. Each of these points contradicts the more extreme statements of radical diffusionist theory, but it is unfortunate that this kind of overstatement has given comfort to those who would rather think solely in terms of migration and conquest. The truth of the matter, as so often, lies in the middle ground. Massive cultural changes can take place without much movement of population; by the same token, large-scale movements of population have obviously taken place in the past, which means that some massive cultural changes should indeed be explicable in terms of migration. Neither migration nor diffusion will suit every case, neither can be denied in every case, and we should always have a reason for asserting one explanation over the other in any given instance.

The deep attachment to migration theories in the case of the Goths – and the reading of connections between Wielbark and Sântana-de-Mureş/Černjachov cultures in terms of Gothic migration – can be explained without any deep engagement with archaeological theory. The reading of both Wielbark and Sântana-de-Mureş/Černjachov cultures is what we might call 'text-hindered' and Jordanes is the culprit.[22] His migration story takes the Goths from Scandinavia to the Baltic and then to the Black Sea. Archaeologists have therefore been called upon not to read the material evidence on its own terms, but rather to prove or disprove the authenticity of Jordanes' text. In 1970, Rolf Hachmann disproved the Scandinavian connection on archaeological grounds, thereby making necessary new theories of ethnogenesis such as we have looked at earlier.[23] But the question has remained the same for the Baltic–Black Sea sequence: can one prove or disprove Jordanes? For an archaeologist of the Goths like Michel Kazanski, this is not even a question: the text of Jordanes tells us the Goths were at the Baltic, then in the Ukraine; therefore the material culture of both regions must be Gothic and we should study it as such.[24] That is precisely what we mean when we say the topic is text-hindered: consciously or not, the archaeological question is always structured by Jordanes, hence an insistence on drawing out the material similarities between the Wielbark and the Sântana-de-Mureş/Černjachov cultures.

If we did not have Jordanes, that connection would not seem self-evident. Taken on purely archaeological grounds, without reference to our one piece of textual evidence, there is no reason to interpret the Wielbark and the Sântana-de-Mureş/Černjachov cultures as close cousins. The Sântana-de-Mureş/Černjachov culture represents an intermingling of many different earlier material cultures, some native to its zone, others not. One might argue, as most do, that the Sântana-de-Mureş/Černjachov culture came into being because of a migration out of the Wielbark regions, but one might equally argue that it was an indigenous development of local Pontic, Carpic and Dacian cultures or of the migration of steppe nomads from the east meeting Przeworsk-culture warriors from the west. In purely archaeological terms, each of these interpretations is equally possible, for as we have seen, Wielbark cultural elements are no more numerous in the Sântana-de-Mureş/Černjachov culture than are the many other cultural traditions that make it up. It is only the text of Jordanes that leads scholars to privilege the Wielbark connection. Indeed, if Jordanes did not exist and we were dealing with truly prehistoric cultures, it is highly unlikely that anyone would draw the same connection.

How the Sântana-de-Mureş/Černjachov Culture Became Gothic

What, then, are we to make of all this? How are we to interpret the origins of the Sântana-de-Mureş/Černjachov culture and the Gothic hegemony with which it coincides chronologically? Is there such a thing as Gothic history before the third century? The answer, at least in my view, is that there is no Gothic history before the third century. The Goths are a product of the Roman frontier, just like the Franks and the Alamanni who appear at the same time. That is clearly demonstrated by contemporary literary evidence, and indeed all the evidence of the fourth and fifth centuries – everything except the sixth-century Jordanes. In the third century, the Roman empire was assaulted from the regions north of the Danube and the Black Sea by large numbers of different barbarian groups, among whom Goths appear for the first time. Not long thereafter, the Goths are clearly the most powerful group in the region, while most of the other barbarian groups with whom they appear in the third century either disappear from the record or are clearly subordinated to them. The most plausible explanation of this evidence is to see one group among the many different barbarians north of the Black

Sea establishing its hegemony over the scattered and hitherto disparate population of the region, which was thereafter regularly identified as Gothic by Graeco-Roman observers.

The archaeological evidence of the Sântana-de-Mureş/Černjachov culture makes sense in these terms as well. The rise to prominence of a few strong leaders created a stable political zone in which a single material culture came into being, synthesized from a variety of disparate traditions. None was more important than the others – as the material evidence clearly shows – and there is no need to look for 'original' Goths coming from elsewhere to impose their leadership and their identity on others. There were, of course, immigrants into the region where the Sântana-de-Mureş/Černjachov culture arose, from elsewhere in northern and central Europe and from the steppe lands to the east as well. But none of them need themselves have been Goths, because there is no good evidence that Goths existed before the third century.

WHAT MADE A GOTH A GOTH AND HOW CAN WE TELL?

That leads us back to the sense of collective identity, the problem of telling the difference that we looked at earlier. How was it that these different people knew that they were Goths rather than something else, or did they? How did Greeks and Romans know it? What marked them off as such? In most cases, context alone would have supplied the clues. There may well have been items of emblematic clothing that established insider and outsider status. But that does not mean we can construct a Gothic costume on the basis of grave finds, because in most circumstances, these items were displayed to other Goths and communicated information about status within the community, not about relations to those outside it. Language probably made a difference, and when Gothic was codified as a written religious language in the fourth century, the use of the Gothic bible will surely have identified its user as a Goth as well as a Christian. But languages can be acquired and many of the philologically Germanic languages spoken in central Europe were mutually intelligible. We have no sources to tell us that specifically Gothic idioms or accents could be used to tell a Goth from a Gepid on the Danube frontier – perhaps they could not. What was it, then, that created a sense of community among the Goths of the later third and the fourth centuries? How was it that they knew what their Greek and Roman observers claim to know – that all these people were Goths?

It is possible that precisely the same Roman elite discourse that is accessible to us nowadays helped cultivate a sense of barbarian collective identity along different stretches of the frontier. Just as contact with the Roman empire shaped, and sometimes created, new social and political hierarchies beyond the frontier, so too Roman ideologies and perceptions may have helped single out elements in the culture of the barbarians that came to define those barbarians' own sense of community. In other words, Roman elite discourses about what a Goth was helped to define how people came to identify themselves as Goths, to codify the signs that conveyed Gothicness. This possibility is not as strange as it might seem at first glance, as post-colonial studies of more recent periods have shown. Modern imperialism has had profound effects in shaping the identity of indigenous and subject peoples – it has been shown, for instance, that the codification of a Sikh cultural, as opposed to religious, identity was largely the result of the British need to have a readily identifiable collective group who could be employed in the colonial army.[25] That a parallel process took place along the frontiers of the Roman empire is actually quite plausible: the diverse small groups whom the Romans called Franks or Goths because they lived in a particular place and were recruited into particular units of the Roman army eventually became Franks and Goths because that was how they were described when they had political dealings with the Roman empire, when, for instance, they were recruited into Roman military units or were defeated by an emperor and described in an imperial victory title. As leaders whom Romans identified as Goths grew in strength and their followers grew in numbers, those followers became more like each other, spurred to it by the military intercourse with the empire next door. If one wants to, it is possible to call this transformation 'ethnogenesis' – new Gothic polities clearly came into being at the end of the third and the start of the fourth century. But it needs no appeal to Gothic aristocrats or royal lines, nor to ethnic traditions or processes, to explain what happened, and whether these new polities were very aware of being a *gens* or an *ethnos* is not something that the evidence can tell us.

The *barbaricum* had always been a vast and changing place when viewed from the Graeco-Roman perspective. Probably its changeability was fully evident to those who lived in it as well. People moved about in that changing world, and alliances shifted repeatedly, sometimes at a great distance from the Roman frontier where neither Greeks and Romans nor we can have any inkling of precise circumstances. Sometimes we see tiny faded traces of changing patterns of alliance, changing patterns of trade and interaction, often no more than a shift in the routes along which Roman coins and luxury goods were dispersed. In the third century, in the region northwest of the Black Sea, the warrior stratum of a heterogeneous population came together to take advantage of imperial civil war and to reap a harvest of as much loot as speed and violence would permit. By the end of the third century, a few of these warriors were powerful enough to coordinate political control over stretches of territory north of the Danube and Black Sea. Sometimes they fought the empire, sometimes they fought each other, sometimes they served the empire, sometimes they came together and acted for their common interest. At their centre were leaders who were seen to be Goths by the Romans and who perhaps saw themselves as Goths as well. Certainly, in time, after being told repeatedly that they were in fact Goths and leaders of Gothic *gentes* with whom the empire would fight and make treaties, there was no question in anyone's mind that they were indeed Goths. Likewise the Sântana-de-Mureş/Černjachov culture must surely be the result of a political stability of long enough standing for stable cultural relations to develop. That stability is attested by the growing political sophistication of the Gothic leaders whom we meet in the course of the fourth century and who form the subject of the next chapter.

IMPERIAL POLITICS AND THE RISE OF GOTHIC POWER

CHAPTER FOUR

OUR ATTEMPT AT EXPLAINING GOTHIC ORIGINS HAS TAKEN us a very long way from our narrative, indeed a long way from the ancient world, and into a discussion of modern intellectual history. The detour has been important. It looked at the way modern accounts of Gothic migration, whether they claim to be supported by historical, archaeological or linguistic evidence, are all in one way or another echoes of Jordanes' sixth-century *Getica*. Consciously or not, modern narratives of Gothic migration are rooted in the very old quest for Germanic origins, a quest to give northern Europe a past independent of Roman history. Unfortunately, as we have seen, contemporary evidence supports neither migration stories nor any narrative derived from Jordanes. On the contrary, it suggests that – like the Franks and the Alamanni further west along the frontier – the Goths were a product of the Roman frontier itself. That conclusion not only makes sense of the evidence of the late third century, it also fits in well with the much better understood evidence of the fourth century.

In the first three decades of the fourth century, as we shall see in this and the next chapter, the Goths became the indisputable masters of the lower Danube, from the eastern edge of the Carpathians to the fringes

MAP 3. *The Roman Empire of Diocletian.*

N

DACIA
RIPENSIS

SCYTHIA

MOESIA
I

MOESIA II

DACIA
MEDITERRANEA

DARDANIA

THRACIA   HALMIMONTUS

PAPHLAGONIA

PONTUS
POLEMONIACUS

PRAEVAL-
ITANA

Constantinople

HELENO-
PONTUS

MACEDONIA

RHODOPE

EUROPA

HONORIAS

ARMENIA I

EPIRUS
NOVA

Thessalonica

HELLESPONT

BITHYNIA

GALATIA

GALATIA
SALUTARIS

CAPPADOCIA I

ARMENIA II

MESOPOTAMIA

EPIRUS
VETUS

THESSALIA

PHRYGIA
SALUTARIS

PHRYGIA
PACATIANA

CAPPADOCIA II

OSRHOENE

LYDIA

PISIDIA

LYCAONIA

CILICIA I

EUPHRATENSIS

ACHAEA

ASIA

CARIA

PAMPHYLIA

ISAURIA

CILICIA II

Antioch

SYRIA I

LYCIA

SYRIA
SALUTARIS

CRETA

CYPRUS

PHOENICE
LIBANENSIS

PHOENICE

PALAESTINA
II

ARABIA

PALAESTINA
I

Alexandria

LIBYA
SUPERIOR

AEGYPTUS

AUGUST-
AMNICA

PALAESTINA
SALUTARIS

LIBYA INFERIOR

ARCADIA

THEBAIS

MAP 4. *Asia Minor, the Balkans and the Black Sea region, showing Roman cities and Sântana-de-Mureş/Černjachov sites mentioned in the text.*

of the Caucasian steppelands. Language itself began to acknowledge these facts. Thus, by the 320s, the lower Danube was known as the *ripa Gothica*, the Gothic bank. Soon thereafter, we find the Greek word *Gothia* designating the tract of land beyond the Danube, a word that was imported into the Gothic language as *Gutthiuda*, the Goths' word for their own lands. This tremendous extension of Gothic power was not inevitable. Instead, the Goths were encouraged to become so powerful because it was useful to the political schemes of successive Roman emperors for them to do so. In other words, just as the Goths themselves were created by the political pressures of life in a Roman frontier zone, so Roman emperors made the fourth-century Goths what they were. The revolutionary reign of Diocletian marks the turning point.

DIOCLETIAN'S NEW ROMAN EMPIRE

In the course of the 290s, Diocletian transformed the Roman empire beyond recognition. A governmental revolution grew out of the emergency measures which Diocletian undertook piecemeal in order to keep himself secure on his throne. The cumulative effect of such measures was enormous. It removed many of the systemic causes of disorder that had plagued the third-century empire, and thereby created the powerful Roman state with which the fourth-century Goths had to deal. As we have seen, the first important step that Diocletian took was to appoint Maximian as his fellow augustus, or co-emperor, in 285. The point of this measure was to multiply the imperial ability to deal with many different threats at one time. An emperor who was on the spot and seen to be doing his job was a powerful disincentive to usurpation by a local governor or general. Diocletian took this principle still further, by appointing two junior emperors, called caesars, as a complement to the two senior augusti. Together, these four emperors would form an imperial college in which the actions of each emperor would symbolically be the actions of all four: a law issued by one emperor was issued in the name of all four, and when one emperor won a victory, all four took the victory title associated with it. This college of four emperors is known to scholars as the tetrarchy ('rule of four' in Greek). For as long as it lasted, the new tetrarchy of Diocletian and Maximian, with their caesars Constantius and Galerius, ensured that an emperor was on hand in nearly every trouble spot of the empire, ready to suppress a looming threat and thereby discourage any local response that might challenge the hold of Diocletian and his colleagues on their thrones. The tetrarchic system was also meant to ensure a smooth succession, as a caesar would be waiting to succeed a senior augustus should the need arise.

Diocletian's reform of the imperial office was accompanied by an elaborate religious ideology that assigned to the ruling emperors divine descent from Jupiter and Hercules, those gods that were most ostentatiously Roman in the traditional pantheon. The tetrarchy also insisted on renewed attention to the imperial cult – the worship of past, deified emperors and of the genius, or protecting spirit, of the living emperor. Both measures were designed to ensure that the gods would smile on and protect the empire. The famous Diocletianic persecution of Christians, widely known as 'the Great Persecution', was a consequence of this tetrarchic ideology, because Christians refused to worship any god but their own and by doing so might endanger the health of the state. If religion was one basis on which Diocletian rested his authority, he took other measures as well, reforming the currency, expanding the army, and re-enforcing the elite guard units that traveled with the emperor. Most importantly, he broke up the very large provinces of the early empire into more than a hundred smaller provinces, while also separating the military and civilian hierarchies in the imperial government. The first measure dramatically reduced the scale of any one official's command, while the second meant that the officials who collected taxes and disbursed state salaries to the soldiers were not the same officials who commanded the troops in the field. Together, both measures undermined the ability of either military or civilian officials to claim the imperial throne for themselves. As we have said, the various Diocletianic reforms were *ad hoc* measures, meant to deal with the many different problems that had afflicted the third-century empire. Yet as a group, they were revolutionary: they not only allowed Diocletian to hold his throne for more than two decades, they also produced a system of government that remained effective even after the tetrarchy itself broke down. In other words, the type of imperial goverment originally outlined by Diocletian and the tetrarchy was in essence the same one with which Alaric had to deal a hundred years later. More important for our immediate purposes, however, Diocletian's reforms meant that for the first time in over half a century, a Roman emperor was secure enough on his throne to deal effectively with barbarians beyond the northern frontier – with serious consequences for the Goths.

THE TETRARCHS AND THE NORTHERN FRONTIERS

This new imperial strength meant that the constant stream of frontier wars slackened considerably in the years before 305, when the augusti Diocletian and Maximian abdicated and passed the senior title on to their caesars Constantius and Galerius, who then appointed two new caesars to serve as their junior emperors. Instead of constantly reacting to events beyond their control, the tetrarchs were increasingly able to decide when and where they wanted to fight along their frontiers. They began to co-opt powerful barbarian leaders into imperial circles, and to manage the affairs of their barbarian neighbours in what they perceived as the best interests of Roman power. This policy can be inferred from obscure, but clearly very important, disturbances along the lower Danube in the 290s and early 300s. We saw in chapter one how Diocletian won a victory over one group of Goths, the Tervingi, as the panegyric of 291 attests. We do not know what prompted the campaign that led to that victory, but the decade that followed seems to have witnessed the substantial growth of Tervingian power. Although this Gothic expansion is not attested by positive evidence, it can be inferred from other known events, most importantly the displacement of an older barbarian grouping. Sometime before early 307, Galerius fought a campaign against the Sarmatians, which is to say in the region between the Danube and the Tisza rivers. Then, in the summer of 307, he attacked the Carpi further east, settling a very large number of them in a Roman province south of the Danube as defeated subjects of the empire.[1]

The willingness of the Carpi – virtually all of them, it seems – to be removed from a territory in which they had dwelt for well over a century is significant. It suggests that the military pressure of a neighbouring barbarian power had become too great for them to sustain and that their attempts to find refuge in the empire had provoked a punitive imperial campaign. The Gothic Tervingi are the barbarian group most likely to have affected the Carpi in this way. We seem, in other words, to see an increasingly powerful Tervingian polity near the mouth of the Danube extending its power at the expense of its immediate neighbours, perhaps with the tacit support of the imperial government. That support can probably be inferred from the fact that the tetrarchs fought no campaigns against the Tervingi after 291. On the contrary, Goths may have been recruited into the imperial army and served with Galerius in Persia, though the only evidence comes from Jordanes and is therefore suspect.[2] It is thus quite likely that the tetrarchs were complicit in the build-up of Tervingian power, viewing them as a favoured barbarian group which could help keep in check other barbarians further up the course of the Danube.

There was a real logic to that approach. While the lower Danube was consistently under the firm control of an emperor resident in the Balkans (first Galerius, then Licinius), the provinces of the middle and upper Danube were the usual setting for confrontations between rivals in the years after 305. Because this imperial preoccupation with the upper and middle Danube lasted for a full two decades after 305, imperial support of Tervingian hegemony in this period is quite plausible. It would, moreover, allow us to make sense of two massive ditch-and-rampart wall systems which were built around this time in Bessarabia and Galatz, well beyond the imperial frontiers. Like the long east-west wall system known as the Csörsz-árok, built beyond the Pannonian frontier in modern-day Hungary, these fortifications are of a quality and on a scale that could not have been attained without imperial approval. From the imperial point of view, it would be useful to have a reliable Gothic ally keeping the lower Danube quiescent. By favouring the Tervingi, allowing fortifications to be built in their lands on such a scale, their strength and security could act as an additional layer of imperial defence, allowing emperors to focus on more immediate threats elsewhere. Imperial support along these lines explains why the Tervingi are so much more powerful when we next meet them in our sources, around the year 320.

THE BREAKDOWN OF THE TETRARCHY

In the meantime, however, the tetrarchic experiment had broken down entirely. Diocletian and Maximian abdicated in 305, for reasons that remain extremely controversial. Galerius and Constantius became augusti, but the choice of new caesars caused problems. Rather than the sons of Maximian and Constantius, who had long been groomed for the succession, two of Galerius' close supporters were appointed as caesars. Before long, however, both the imperial children had seized the purple for themselves. After his father died at York in 306, Constantine was acclaimed emperor, supposedly at the instigation of the Alamannic king Crocus, a client of the late Constantius and an early example of a barbarian noble holding a high position in the imperial army.[3] Maxentius, the son of Maximian, was proclaimed emperor at Rome in the same year, with the support of the Roman populace. Constantine's proclamation was soon recognized by the senior augustus Galerius, but Maxentius was never accepted as a legitimate emperor. For half a decade between 307 and 313 the Roman empire was wracked with civil wars that gradually eliminated most of the key claimants to the imperial title. By 313, there were only two emperors left, Constantius' son Constantine (r. 306–337), now a fervent Christian, in the West, and Licinius (r. 308–324), an old comrade of Galerius, in the East. Despite their violence, the civil wars of 307–313 demonstrate the basic solidity of the Diocletianic reforms, because the hallmarks of the third-century crisis are entirely absent from the post-tetrarchic conflicts: no provincial general made an opportunistic bid for the throne, no provinces broke away under their own imperial succession, and no barbarian kings exploited the situation to launch a major invasion across the frontiers.

Indeed, a firm hand was kept on the imperial frontiers despite active civil war. Even before they had done away with other rivals, Constantine and Licinius between them controlled most of the Rhine-Danube frontier. Both undertook traditional imperial campaigns into the *barbaricum*, Constantine leading Frankish kings in triumph at Trier,

Licinius attacking Sarmatians near the Danube bend.[4] As always, we cannot know precisely what prompted the individual campaigns, but the perpetual demand for imperial victories, combined with a need to control barbarian politics while preparing for internal Roman conflict, can explain most of the fighting. A similar calculation probably lies behind the momentous propaganda decision which Constantine took in 310. In the old tetrarchic ideology, Constantius had been the adoptive son of Maximian, and hence took on his adoptive father's putative descent from the god Hercules, along with the name Herculius that represented it. In 310, however, Constantine repudiated the Herculian name which he had inherited from Constantius. He instead began to claim descent from the emperor Claudius Gothicus, a fiction first attested on 25 July 310.[5] It made sense for Constantine to rid himself of the old Herculian connection after his final break with Maximian and Maxentius in 310, but there may have been more to it than that. Claudius, one of the third century's great military heroes, won his Gothic victories in the Balkans. Constantine's claim to a Claudian descent may be the first indication of the Balkan ambitions he was to demonstrate before too long.

CONSTANTINE AND LICINIUS

Between 313 and 316, Constantine and Licinius maintained the cordial neutrality that had allowed them to work together during the last years of the civil wars, but their truce was uneasy and they came to blows in 316. The western Balkans fell to Constantine in this war. He took over Licinius' residence at Sirmium, dividing his time between that city and Serdica, and leaving his son and caesar Crispus in Trier to guard the Rhine frontier and campaign against the Franks and Alamanni.[6] Constantine's eastern ambitions were now clear, as his choice of residence could hardly fail to demonstrate, and he used the old tactic of disciplining the barbarians to provoke a final confrontation with Licinius. In 323, Constantine campaigned against the Sarmatians on the frontiers of Pannonia, winning one battle, over a king called Rausimod, at Campona in the Pannonian province of Valeria, and a second considerably further downstream at the confluence of the Danube and Morava in Moesia Superior.[7] Coins issued at Trier, Arles, Lyons and Sirmium celebrated

the success with the legend *Sarmatia devicta* ('Sarmatia conquered') and
Constantine took the victory title *Sarmaticus*.[8] He may also have insti-
tuted new celebratory gladiatorial games, as an epigraphic reference to
ludi Sarmatici, Sarmatian games, suggests.[9] Regardless, the campaigns
were a provocation of Licinius, into whose territory Constantine had
marched while attacking the Sarmatians. Almost certainly intentional,
this violation of his fellow emperor's sovereignty led to the final break
between Constantine and Licinius – the latter supposedly melting down
Constantinian gold coins celebrating the victory in order to make the
point as publicly as possible.[10]

In the ensuing civil war, both sides made substantial use of barbarian
soldiers. Licinius had won a victory over the Goths before 315 and peace
terms may have included Gothic service in his army.[11] In the war against
Constantine, Goths fought on the side of Licinius, probably under a
general named Alica. Constantine had used Frankish auxiliaries in his
earlier campaigns and by the time of the war with Licinius, the Frankish
general Bonitus had reached a position of rank in Constantine's army.[12]
As we have seen, barbarians had always served in imperial armies, but
there is some reason to think that the build-up to war between Constantine and Licinius represents a new phase in this phenomenon. For
one thing, the early 320s were the first period since the onset of military crisis in the third century during which rival emperors had ample
leisure to recruit troops for themselves. For another, both Constantine
and Licinius were competing for roughly the same pool of manpower, that is to say, barbarians from the middle and lower Danube –
Sarmatians and Goths, generically "Scythians" – and such competition almost always increases both supply and demand. This increasing
reliance on barbarian recruits is partly hypothetical, but is probably
confirmed by the testimony of the *Caesares*, a satire on his predecessors
written by the emperor Julian, which is scathing about Constantine's
recruitment and subsidy of barbarians.[13] Certainly, as the fourth century progressed, emperors made more and more use of barbarians in
filling up the ranks of the army. That being the case, it seems likely
that the precedent set by Constantine and Licinius in the early 320s was
validated by its very success: Constantine routed Licinius.

CONSTANTINE AND THE DANUBE FRONTIER

That victory allowed Constantine a free hand in the Balkans, which he used partly for grandiose construction schemes. The manpower which these projects required is attested by a dramatic increase in the region's supply of bronze coinage in the late 320s. In the valley of the Porecka near the Iron Gates, a major wall system was put up to control threats from across the river. That was eminently practical, but a more spectacular venture was a new bridge over the Danube from Oescus to Sucidava, which in 328 established a real and a symbolic bridgehead onto what one source now calls the *ripa Gothica*.[14] Constantine also continued the tetrarchic program of constructing *quadriburgia* along the Danube. These small forts, enclosing less than one hectare, were a new development of the early fourth century. They were characterized by a tower at each of their four corners (hence their name), and were built both on the right bank of the river in the Roman provinces of Moesia Secunda and Scythia, and also on the barbarian left bank. Primarily useful for keeping the barbarians under observation, *quadriburgia* could also serve as advance posts for Roman military action. Although the whole Danube frontier received this sort of imperial attention, the lower stretch of the river, and hence presumably the Tervingi beyond it, was the main focus. Thus in parallel to the Oescus-Sucidava bridge, Constantine built a new *quadriburgium* at Daphne, on the left bank of the Danube across from Transmarisca. How should we account for this focus on the stretch of the Danube opposite the lands of the Gothic Tervingi? Perhaps the most obvious explanation is the fact that Goths had fought on Licinius' side in the recent civil war. But the support which the tetrarchs and Licinius seem to have given to the rise of Tervingian power in the region probably also worried Constantine.

CONSTANTINE'S GOTHIC WAR

The later 320s witnessed a series of disturbances beyond the Danube frontier which may have justified such worries. As with the displacement of the Carpi twenty years earlier, these events can be understood in terms of Tervingian threats against their neighbours. First, in 330, a number of Taifali invaded the Balkan provinces, perhaps driven there by the Tervingi.[15] A request for imperial aid from some of the Tervingi's Sarmatian neighbours soon followed, and developed into a major Gothic war. The Sarmatians had long been subject to the usual Roman mixture of subsidy and punishment. The remains of the large Sarmatian defensive systems just to the east of the Danube bend – most famously the Csörz-árok mentioned earlier – were undoubtedly built with Roman permission and suggest the sort of alliance that would have justified the Sarmatians' request for assistance. The extent of Gothic power is revealed by the response to this request. Constantine launched a campaign against the Goths, the first stage of which was won 'in the lands of the Sarmatians', thus beyond the Pannonian section of the Danube frontier.[16] That implies a range of Gothic military action far away from the point where the Goths had hitherto appeared in our sources.

One must surmise that, in the aftermath of Constantine's victory over Licinius, and while he himself was distracted by internal political problems, a Tervingian king had seized the opportunity to expand his hegemony at the expense of barbarian neighbours, although without directly threatening a Roman province. Probably he expected events of the previous two decades to repeat themselves: his defeated enemies would be accepted into the Roman empire and settled there, while he would be allowed to continue expanding his control in the trans-Danubian lands. If that was indeed his calculation, he did not foresee the scale of the imperial response. Constantine sent his oldest surviving son and caesar Constantinus to campaign across the Danube. This imperial thrust, so we are told, drove many Goths (the sources speak improbably of 100,000) into the wilderness to die of hunger and cold. Constantinus demanded and received Gothic hostages, amongst them a son of the Gothic king Ariaric.[17] The defeat of the Goths was followed by a successful campaign against the Sarmatians, who had supposedly proved unfaithful to their agreements with the emperor.

THE PEACE OF 332

Constantinus had won a major and lasting victory that remained worthy of note two decades later: in 355, when Constantine's nephew Julian delivered a panegyric to another of Constantine's sons, the emperor

Constantius, the scale of the Gothic victory could still be celebrated.[18] In fact, for more than thirty years after 332 the lower Danube was at peace. Yet despite its evident importance, we know very little about Constantine's Gothic peace. The limitations of our evidence have encouraged modern scholars into much hypothetical reconstruction along two different lines, the first on the continuity of Gothic leadership, the second on the terms of the peace. In both cases, the testimony of Jordanes is a complicating factor. The real problem is the obscurity of the contemporary fourth-century sources, none of which allows us to gauge how important a king Ariaric was, and none of which tell us how, or whether, he was related to Tervingian leaders of the later fourth century. Instead, we have to infer this information from the limited evidence at our disposal.

The first clue to doing this lies in the location of Constantine's first Gothic campaign. Given that it took place in distant Sarmatia, and given the scale of the tribal displacement that preceded it, we can perhaps infer that Ariaric was the ruler of a very substantial polity. Although we cannot be sure that he was the only Gothic king involved in the war of 332, he is the only one attested by name, probably another sign of his importance. We are on less certain ground when it comes to his connection to later Tervingian leaders. It is widely agreed that Ariaric was the grandfather of Athanaric, the powerful Tervingian chieftain against whom the emperor Valens campaigned in the 360s. However, that genealogical connection is based on the hypothetical identification of Ariaric's unnamed hostage son with the equally unnamed father of Athanaric who is said to have had a statue erected to him in Constantinople.[19] The only ancient source that explicitly connects Ariaric with the Tervingian leaders of the later fourth century is Jordanes.[20] But as we have seen, Jordanes was determined to construct a continuous Gothic history. Given that he elsewhere invents demonstrably spurious connections to provide genealogical continuity, the value of his testimony for Ariaric is suspect. In other words, while some connection between Ariaric and later Tervingian kings is plausible, it can only remain speculative.

The same holds true for the terms of the treaty. Fourth-century evidence is limited, while Jordanes imposes on it an anachronistic Byzantine interpretation. He supposes that Ariaric's Goths became *foederati*, a word that by the sixth century had a technical legal content implying specific responsibilities on the part of both empire and federate allies. In 332, however, the formal status of *foederatus* did not exist, and the word for treaty, *foedus*, is not a technical term. Even though many scholars think that the treaty of 332 invented the type of technical *foedus* known in the sixth century, nothing in the fourth-century evidence makes that plausible. The peace of 332 marks a significant stage in both Roman and Gothic history not because of any legal innovations, but because it was so very decisive. It imposed more than thirty years of peace on the lower Danube or, as bishop Eusebius of Caesarea put it in the *Life of Constantine* that he wrote shortly after the emperor's death in 337, 'the Goths finally learned to serve the Romans'.[21] Indeed, some of the defeated Goths would continue to claim a special loyalty to the Constantinian dynasty for many years, decades later supporting a usurper named Procopius on the grounds of his dynastic connections.[22] In the interim, they offered tribute to the emperor, and provided a large supply of military recruits for the Roman army. Such military service was not explicitly required by the terms of 332, as Eusebius' testimony makes clear: he is nowhere able to state that Goths served in the army as a result of the treaty, even though elsewhere in his *Life* he is consistently very enthusiastic, and very specific, about Constantine's recruitment of defeated barbarians.[23] Regardless, the peace brought benefits to both sides.

THE PEACE AND THE GOTHIC ECONOMY

The frontier was opened to trade all along its length, a most unusual measure, given that Roman emperors had for centuries regulated the export of Roman technology outside the empire. Yet the fact that trade surged all along the river is demonstrated by the large number of bronze coins found in the band of territory north of the Danube. Bronze issues of the late 330s to the early 360s dominate the archaeological record, which suggests that the Gothic side of the lower Danube came to be quite thoroughly integrated into the Roman monetary economy in those years. In fact, the distribution of bronze coins in the region immediately beyond the frontier is very nearly as intense as in the Roman province of Scythia itself.[24] That such coins were used for commercial exchange is placed beyond serious doubt by the existence of locally produced imitations of Roman coins which must have been struck to eke out insufficient supplies of genuine Roman coinage in commercial circulation. It must be noted that bronze coin finds are dramatically concentrated right beside the frontier, generally within fifteen or twenty miles of it, but less so in the Gothic regions opposite Scythia and Moesia Secunda than those across the river from Moesia Prima. Although this fact has led some scholars to question the level of monetization of the Gothic economy, the sheer quantity of low-value coinage beyond the frontier make these objections hard to sustain.

That Roman diplomatic connections with the Gothic elite also increased rapidly from the 330s onwards is suggested by the distribution of Roman silver coins. Much less common in the immediate vicinity of the Danube, silver is instead found in large quantity further north and east, in modern-day Moldova and Ukraine. Unlike the bronze, silver coinage is uncommon in stray finds at industrial and residential sites. Instead, silver *siliquae* are concentrated in small hoards, for instance one found at Kholmskoĕ near Lake Kitaj or another at Taraclia in Moldova. The Kholmskoĕ hoard is especially significant: its ninety-three silver coins of Constantius II were all of the same value and type, struck between 351 and 355, bearing the legend VOTIS.XXX – MULTIS.XXXX, and virtually unused. This fact raises some doubts about whether they circulated as money or as bullion. It is possible that our extant finds of silver coinage are not evidence for trade across the frontier – especially since silver *siliquae* are very rare in the Roman province of Scythia itself – but rather for gift-subsidies to Gothic chieftains whom the empire had an interest in cultivating. All the same, there can be no question that the economy of Gothia was both fairly sophisticated and closely linked to the Roman world. Indeed, archaeological evidence from modern-day Romania, Moldova and Ukraine gives us precious insight into the social and economic world of the fourth-century Goths.

GOTHIC SOCIETY AND ARCHAEOLOGICAL EVIDENCE

As we saw in chapter three, it is very rarely possible to assign a particular material culture to a specific barbarian group known from the written sources. Fortunately for us, one of the few places where we can do precisely that is in the area occupied by the so-called Sântana-de-Mureş/Černjachov culture between the late third and the late fourth centuries. This archaeological culture gets its unwieldy name from two cemeteries, one in modern Romania, one in modern Ukraine, each coincidentally at the edge of the culture's extension, which lies between the Donets river in the east and the Carpathians and Transylvania in the west. The Sântana-de-Mureş/Černjachov culture is dated, partly on independent archaeological grounds, to the same period in which the literary sources show the Goths as the dominant political force along the lower Danube and northwest of the Black Sea. Many barbarian groups other than Goths lived within the Sântana-de-Mureş/Černjachov zone and the culture itself is diverse and derived from several different cultural traditions. However, because it is a new development of the later third century – exactly the period in which the written sources attest the growth of Gothic hegemony – it is likely that Gothic leaders inadvertently created a stable political zone at the edge of the Roman empire in which a new material culture could develop out of numerous different antecedents. Because this new Sântana-de-Mureş/Černjachov culture was the material context in which Gothic history was embedded, it can help us understand the world of the Goths we meet in our written sources.

The geography of the Sântana-de-Mureş/Černjachov region shaped the social diversity of its archaeological culture. The culture extended across three major geographic zones. At its northernmost reaches, it occupied the so-called forest steppe, a broad transition zone between the heavily wooded regions of northern Europe and the open plains immediately north of the Black Sea. This northwestern Black Sea region is actually the westernmost end of the great Eurasian plain, which is at its widest breadth in Central Asia and gradually shrinks to a narrow band along the Black Sea coast to the east of the Carpathian mountains. Unlike the forest steppe to its north, this Black Sea steppe was not heavily wooded, and its drier expanses were better suited to the sort of pastoralist exploitation common to the Eurasian steppe than they were to agricultural cultivation. Several important rivers flow through this region into the Black Sea, among them the Dnieper, Bug, and Dniester, as well as the Sireul (Sereth) and Prut, which join the Danube just before it turns east and enters the Black Sea itself. Along these rivers and their many smaller tributaries there is rich land suitable for the intensive cultivation of food crops, particularly grains. Because of these environmental contrasts, the region has always supported two parallel ways of life, settled agricultural populations in the river valleys coexisting alongside semi-nomadic pastoralists in the steppes. These pastoralists have often had strong cultural, and sometimes political, connections to other nomadic groups further to the east, where the Eurasian steppe becomes broader north of the Sea of Azov and the Caucasus. This coexistence of pastoralists beside sedentary farming populations seems to have characterized the region since prehistoric times and certainly continued to do so deep into the middle ages. In the third and fourth centuries, the nomadic population of the Sântana-de-Mureş/Černjachov zone was in regular contact with the settled population: at a site like Kholmskoě, for example, the remains of a nomad camp are present very close to an agricultural village. Although it was commonplace until recently to read such contrasts between pastoralism and agriculture in ethnic terms (for example, Alan and Sarmatian nomads versus sedentary Goths and Taifali), they are better understood by comparison with Arabia in the same period, where the pastoralist bedouin of the deserts lived alongside the settled populations of the oases and desert fringes, politically but not ethnically diverse.

AGRICULTURAL LIFE

Despite the presence of pastoralists, the Sântana-de-Mureş/Černjachov culture was fundamentally agricultural and the majority of its population were farmers. Settlements were concentrated along the great river valleys and along their tributaries. Even from the quite limited survey data, it is clear that population was dense, with villages scattered every few kilometres along the rivers. Villages could be quite large, sustaining twelve or fifteen families, along with their livestock – mostly cattle, with sheep/goats (almost indistinguishable archaeologically) or pigs as secondary animals, depending on which was better suited to the local topography. Horses were rare in the agricultural settlements, and presumably confined to the use of elites. For the most part, settlements were well organized, with houses in rows. The houses themselves were built in a fashion known from all over central Europe, which scholars always refer to by their German name of *Grubenhäuser* ('sunken houses'). Such *Grubenhäuser* were half-dug into the ground, with varying amounts of the house – sometimes as little as the roof – projecting above the surface. The houses were generally of wood, and sometimes of wattle and daub, but in regions near to the Black Sea stone floors were common. Regardless, the sunken construction maximized insulation in both winter and summer, very useful in a continental climate with considerable variations in temperatures. Another type of house common throughout the *barbaricum* was found alongside the *Grubenhäuser* at many Sântana-de-Mureş/Černjachov settlements. Called *Wohnstallhäuser*, these houses were built of timber and entirely above ground, combining within a single structure a dwelling area for the human residents with stalls for the livestock.

As with the types of houses one finds in the Sântana-de-Mureş/Černjachov zone, there is nothing strikingly unusual about the region's economy, which conformed to the patterns found in all the agricultural cultures of the *barbaricum*. The economy of most Sântana-de-Mureş/Černjachov villages was self-contained. Wheat, millet and barley were the staple grains, and most of what was eaten seems to have been ground at home by hand. Agricultural and woodworking implements made of iron were common, though forge-sites are barely known and we cannot tell whether every village had a blacksmith or whether there were more centralized distribution spots for metal tools. For cooking, hand-made pots were used alongside wheel-turned pottery of considerably higher quality, and many ceramic forms found in the region have long-standing local precedents. Much of this pottery must have been made in the villages where it went on to be used, but there is also evidence for commercial workshops of different types – for instance a well-known glass factory at Komarovo – and for trade in fine wares with the Roman province of Scythia.[25] The bronze and occasionally silver ornaments that are quite common in the grave goods of the region were presumably made in regional workshops and distributed by means of trade. Similarly, workshops for bone combs have been discovered, with production on a scale much too large for purely local consumption.

Long-distance Trade

Trade with the Roman empire and with other more distant regions of the *barbaricum* is also attested. Although some have argued for substantial imports of basic foodstuffs into Sântana-de-Mureş/Černjachov regions from the Roman empire, the evidence is debateable. Mediterranean amphorae have been found at Sântana-de-Mureş/Černjachov sites, presumably a sign of some trade in the grain, oil, and wine that were transported in amphorae. On the other hand, amphorae remains are not extensive and we do not know how widely the Mediterranean preference for olive oil spread beyond the lower Danube – certainly animal fats were preferred to olive oil in most of central Europe. It is similarly hard to imagine an extensive grain trade: various grains, including some not grown inside the empire, were widely cultivated throughout the region, which had historically been able to serve as an important granary for the Greek world of the Mediterranean.[26] Wine, by contrast, might well have been a fairly substantial export into the Sântana-de-Mureş/Černjachov regions, but it will take more detailed study of the amphora evidence for us to be sure.

Wine, as a relatively high-value item not readily available from local sources, probably served the needs of Sântana-de-Mureş/Černjachov elites, as presumably did Roman glass and fine ceramics. It is, however, higher-value goods that most clearly demonstrate the existence of this sort of interaction with the empire. We have seen that Roman bronze coins were common close to the frontier and represent the monetization of the local economy. More striking are the large gold coins – multiples of the *solidus* – worn as medallions inside the *barbaricum*. In the Sântana-de-Mureş/Černjachov zone, such *multipla* are known from between the early third and the early fifth century, but fully eighty percent of the finds cluster in the middle of the fourth century, under Constantius II, Valentinian, and Valens. These *multipla* are distributed in a zone between the lower Danube and Black Sea on the one hand, and the Vistula and Oder rivers on the other, which suggests that they passed from the empire to the Sântana-de-Mureş/Černjachov elites and then onwards through a network of treaty relations into east-central Europe. The absence of such medallions from the Upper Danube and the Rhineland suggests that they are a phenomenon specific to the relations between the empire and the Goths, and in turn between Gothic elites and neighbours further to the north. Examples of portable art more representative of Danish, Scandinavian and northwestern German regions, found at Sântana-de-Mureş/Černjachov sites like the large cemetery at Dančeny, suggest traffic of the same sort in the opposite direction.[27]

The Elite Population

In all likelihood, then, trade and diplomatic activity between the empire and the Sântana-de-Mureş/Černjachov elites brought Roman luxury goods into the *barbaricum*, while gift exchange distributed some of those same goods from the immediate vicinity of the frontier into remoter parts of central and northern Europe. Unfortunately, we know somewhat less about Sântana-de-Mureş/Černjachov elites than we do about other barbarian elites further to the west. Archaeologists have not, for instance, uncovered anything like the same number of fortified sites as were raised by Alamannic chieftains along the upper Rhine. On the other hand, sites like Bašmačka, Aleksandrovka and Gorodok are all distinctly larger than the more usual small villages and all display considerably higher levels of imported Roman amphorae. They were thus probably royal or aristocratic strongholds rather than just farming villages. Traces of fortification confirm that impression. Aleksandrovka, for instance, sited at the confluence of the Ingulec and the Dnieper, was surrounded by a ditch and an earth rampart, and the foundations of the site's walls were of stone with evidence of three towers, the whole design very reminiscent of the late Greek architecture of the Black Sea coast. Palanca, near the Dniester, Gorodok, on the lower Bug, and Bašmačka, near the Dnieper rapids, also had stone walls.[28] All three sites controlled important east-west routes across the region northwest of the Black Sea.

A considerably more intriguing site than any of these can also be interpreted in the context of the Sântana-de-Mureş/Černjachov elite.

The fourth-century village at Sobari, in the modern republic of Moldova between the upper Prut and Dniester rivers, was first discovered in 1950 and has been excavated intermittently ever since then, uncovering remains of eight houses and a ceramic workshop. The village lay near the Dniester river and was walled – three sides of the wall have been found – with large cut-granite stones and smaller rubble fill. What makes the site so impressive is the lavishness of one of the standing structures. Although it may have consisted of only two rooms, one roughly 5.5 × 7.5 metres, the other 7.5 × 10 metres, the building itself is unparalleled in the *barbaricum* for its use of a colonnade, of which sixteen column-bases survive. The building was roofed in the standard Roman fashion, with terra cotta tiles, and more than 14,000 pieces of roof tile have been found. Still more strikingly, at least some of the windows were of glass. We cannot be sure whether this structure was a public building like a church or a temple or whether it was a residence, but it certainly is an anomaly in a village where ceramic finds are otherwise typical of the Sântana-de-Mureş/Černjachov region as a whole. Sobari is nearly 300 kilometres from the Roman frontier, yet whoever built this house did so knowing what an elite Roman settlement ought to have, namely a central structure with columns, a tiled roof and glazed windows. It is not at all far-fetched to see in Sobari the residence of a Gothic lord who had spent some time in the service of the empire, possibly converted to one of its religions, and developed a taste for its aesthetic habits.[29] Much the same interpretation may explain the large farming village of Kamenka-Ančekrak near the Black Sea, where the central structure and its several outbuildings were built of stone and revealed a much higher incidence of imported ceramics than did ordinary houses in the surrounding village.[30]

Nobles like those whose residences we can see at Sobari and Kamenka-Ančekrak were presumably the owners of the few horses known from Sântana-de-Mureş/Černjachov villages, and it may well have been they who were responsible for the relatively small number of wild animal bones found at such sites – hunting was throughout the ancient world an aristocratic pursuit. This same elite can probably account for the treasures discovered in the Sântana-de-Mureş/Černjachov region. Indeed,

the distribution of such treasures may help us to map royal and aristocratic strongholds, if we interpret treasure finds as collection points for
tribute and for the exercise of such governmental functions as existed.
The conspicuous redistribution of portable wealth was a major part of
all barbarian leaders' relationship with their followers and we have considerable, if somewhat later, evidence for the importance of inherited
treasures to the continuity of a barbarian royal line. Unfortunately, in
the Sântana-de-Mureş/Černjachov zone we lack the same sorts of evidence that we have from regions further west along the Danube. There,
from sites like Strásza, Ostrovany, Rebrin, and Szilágysolmlyó we have
a variety of golden fibulae and imperial symbols that must almost certainly represent the direct diplomatic support of the Roman state. The
famous gold hoard of Pietroasele, though found within the Sântana-
de-Mureş/Černjachov region, belongs to a somewhat later period, and
most of the culture's prestige items were of silver rather than gold, for
instance the hoard of silver items of ca. A.D. 380 from Valea Strîmbă.[31]
Regardless of the specific provenances of any particular find, the ability
to display and dispose of valuable treasures was clearly an important
index of social distinction among Sântana-de-Mureş/Černjachov elites.
This social display is particularly evident in the many grave finds from
the region.

The World of the Dead

As is so usual in studies of late antique barbarians, cemetery sites are considerably better known than are settlements, a fact that raises all sorts of
problems because what people take to their graves does not always reveal
what they did or thought in life. All the same, the whole Sântana-de-
Mureş/Černjachov region stands out from the rest of the *barbaricum* for
the striking variety of its funerary customs. Some cemetery sites contain
both cremation burials, whether in an urn or straight into a hole in the
ground, and inhumations, some of them in wooden chambers, some in
more or less elaborate graves with or without stone coverings. In general,
we can observe a trend throughout the Sântana-de-Mureş/Černjachov
region away from cremation and towards inhumation, but cemetery
chronology is too uncertain for us to press that point. Grave goods

vary just as much as do burial typologies. With very few exceptions, the sort of enormously rich 'princely' burials – loaded with gold and silver and known throughout western and north-central Europe – are absent from the Sântana-de-Mureş/Černjachov zone.[32] Most Sântana-de-Mureş/Černjachov graves were unfurnished, some were furnished with pottery alone, some with fibulae (brooches – either one or two). Many bodies were belted, since belt buckles appear in large quantities, and some belts were decorated with hanging ornaments known as pendentives. Weapon burials are even rarer than they are in the Rhineland and upper Danube but by no means unknown. Grave goods might be positioned in different ways in different types of inhumation, while in cremations grave goods were sometimes burned along with the body, sometimes deposited intact with the ashes. In a few inhumations, the body was arranged on a raised platform within the grave, and a very few bodies show signs of deliberate cranial deformation in the skulls of the deceased. Both these latter habits are characteristic of steppe-nomad customs known from earlier and later periods, and quite common further to the east.[33]

These variations in burial type are perhaps the best sign of the diverse cultural traditions that made up the Sântana-de-Mureş/Černjachov culture. Everyday artefacts also show a mixture of nomadic, Roman, northern European, and local traditions, but the diversity of burial ritual in the Sântana-de-Mureş/Černjachov is truly extraordinary. That raises questions on many different levels. Unsurprisingly, differences in burial customs have generally been interpreted in ethnic terms, some rituals and artefacts ascribed to one ethnic group, some to another. But that is problematical. The material culture of the living population was relatively uniform across the Sântana-de-Mureş/Černjachov zone, however many different cultural traditions lay behind it. By contrast, the material culture of the dead was highly differentiated both within and between cemetery sites. In other words, cultural differences are not uniformly distributed across every social context in Sântana-de-Mureş/Černjachov culture, but are confined to the specific context of burial ritual. What is more, no one has been able to demonstrate that the particular ornaments singled out for burial with a dead person were widely used while he or she was still alive. For that reason, although the differences in burial ritual may well reflect different beliefs about the afterlife, there is no evidence that funerary customs and objects differentiated people except at the brief moment during which the body was displayed before its cremation or interment. That fact helps us to interpret Sântana-de-Mureş/Černjachov burials in a more nuanced fashion than a strictly ethnic reading requires.

FUNERARY RITUAL AND WHAT IT TELLS US

The ways in which burial ritual communicates clues about identity has been rigorously examined in the Frankish world, and some of that research can be applied to the Sântana-de-Mureş/Černjachov zone as well.[34] Burial ritual is, at least originally, a reflection of beliefs about the afterlife, but it is also a social ritual for those who remain alive to bury the dead person. Although the materials deposited in tombs are all that we have left to study, they were not meant for us. Rather, they are the surviving traces of a ritual that was viewed and experienced for only a short time by the people who took part in it. This burial ritual not only commemorated the deceased and prepared his or her way into the afterlife, it also helped delineate the social relationships among the people who came together to bury the dead. In other words, contemporary observers both inside and outside the dead person's family would read and interpret burial ritual for the social signals it conveyed. Thus, people buried with more and better goods may have occupied a higher social station than those with less – or at least their living relations will have been asserting the higher status of the deceased, and therefore their own higher status, as the heirs or family of the dead. In the Sântana-de-Mureş/Černjachov zone, there seems to be a correlation between richer grave goods and the alignment of bodies with the head to the north, and this too may have had a status link now lost to us.

However, the sheer heterogeneity of the Sântana-de-Mureş/Černjachov burials is such that purely status-based explanations seem inadequate. Beliefs about the afterlife must also come into the picture, beliefs that differed widely between neighbours. Whether one was burnt or buried, with a sword or without, raised on a wooden platform or deposited straight into the earth would seem self-evidently to reveal different expectations about what was going to happen in death. The question that has most exercised scholars, of course, is whether these differing beliefs reflect ethnic difference, whether we can tell Goths from Gothic subjects on the basis of how they were buried. The answer is complicated by the fact that there are really two separate questions. At some point, the wildly divergent burial customs we meet in the Sântana-de-Mureş/Černjachov zone must have derived from populations with different beliefs about the afterlife. This impression is re-enforced by the parallels that exist between burial rituals in the Sântana-de-Mureş/Černjachov zone and those elsewhere in Europe and central Asia. But the fact of differing derivation – even differing ethnic derivation – does not mean that burial ritual continued to have an ethnic meaning within the Sântana-de-Mureş/Černjachov culture. This is especially true because, thanks to patterns of material preservation, we have no evidence that the population of the zone marked such differences in any context other than that of burial ritual.

That fact suggests that rituals representing different beliefs about the afterlife, which had at one time corresponded to ethnic origins, had no ethnic content within the Sântana-de-Mureş/Černjachov culture. This suggestion may well seem implausible to those who believe that burial ritual is a primordial depository of ethnic beliefs. But it is in fact not at all far-fetched. We know for a fact that groups of people within the same society can have incompatible beliefs about what happens after death without thereby ceasing to share social and ethnic common ground. The best ancient example is the Roman empire itself. There, elite Romans of the second through fourth centuries shared a single material, literary and aesthetic culture, as well as the legal status of Roman citizens, but their religious and philosophical views differed enormously and came from the most various provincial and ethnic traditions. The differences in burial ritual within the Sântana-de-Mureş/Černjachov culture should be interpreted as a parallel to this contemporary Roman reality.

WHY THE SÂNTANA-DE-MUREŞ/ČERNJACHOV CULTURE IS GOTHIC

The Sântana-de-Mureş/Černjachov zone was, in this view, a complex cultural world in which many different historical strands had mingled. It may have been much smaller in scale and less socially varied than its imperial Roman neighbour, but it was not fundamentally different in kind. The wealthy military elite whose status display remains so visible to us led a society that was recognizably Gothic for Graeco-Roman observers. When Romans of the fourth century looked beyond the lower Danube, they saw Goths, divided into different groups like the Tervingi, but Goths all the same. They did not see what they saw at the Danube bend, in the 'land of the Sarmatians', where an ethnically distinct subject population could be distinguished from the Sarmatians. Nor did they see what they saw in the Sântana-de-Mureş/Černjachov cultural zone at a later date, in the fifth century, when distinctly Hunnic masters ruled over many different subject populations, Goths included.

It is, in other words, fundamentally wrong to follow the many modern historians who call the Gothic realm of the fourth century 'polyethnic'. It was polyethnic only in the sense that no culture is totally autonomous and free from the admixture of disparate cultural strands. The Sântana-de-Mureş/Černjachov culture emerged within two generations of the Goths first appearing in contemporary written sources. Its origins are nearly contemporary with the decade in which, according to the literary sources, Goths come to dominate the lower Danube and the northwestern Black Sea region. As we saw in the last chapter, nothing in the material evidence suggests that 'the Goths' came from somewhere else and imposed themselves on a polyethnic coalition; nothing contemporary tells us that Goths 'came' from anywhere at all. Instead, in the crucible of Roman frontier politics, people of very different backgrounds came together under leaders who were defined as Goths in their constant interaction with the Roman empire. The relative clarity of that relationship with the empire led to a stable political system just beyond the frontier in which the material culture we call Sântana-de-Mureş/Černjachov developed. That culture, its agricultural base and its nomadic hinterland, were the foundations on which different Gothic polities grew up and solidified in the course of the fourth century. Some of those polities are deeply obscure, glimpsed only as shadows in our sources. Others, closer to the frontier, were more heavily implicated in the life of Rome's provinces and are therefore quite well known to us. The history of these Gothic groups, and the Tervingi in particular, will occupy us in the next chapter.

GOTHS AND ROMANS, 332–376

CHAPTER FIVE

A S THE LAST CHAPTER SUGGESTED, THE SÂNTANA-DE-MUREŞ/
Černjachov culture was the material expression of Gothic
hegemony in the lower Danube region. That is to say, it was
the product of a relative political stability that the imperial
support for Gothic hegemony ensured. But the same stability held
inherent dangers for the Roman empire. Constantine's defeat of king
Ariaric in 332, and the subsequent thirty years of peace between the
empire and the Tervingi, did nothing to retard the growth of Tervingian military power. Thus when a Roman emperor next came to fight
a major Gothic war, as Valens did in the later 360s, he confronted an
opponent whose power would have surprised Constantine. More shocking still was the Gothic victory at Adrianople which, in 378, wiped
out the larger part of the eastern Roman army. For us, it would be
very satisfying to know just how Gothic power grew so great in this
period. Unfortunately, we know remarkably little about the history
of the Tervingian region in the three decades of peace that followed
Constantine's victory – not even whether we should talk about a Tervingian kingdom or kingdoms – and still less about more distant Gothic
groups.

As we have already seen, it is impossible to be sure whether Ariaric was the only Tervingian king involved in the campaigns of 332, and how or whether he was related to later Tervingian rulers. The evidence for the mid fourth century is just as uncertain. In the year 364/365, we hear of more than one Gothic king sending troops to support an unsuccessful claimant to the imperial throne.[1] But in the later 360s and early 370s, our main narrative sources regard one particular Goth, Athanaric, as the sole leader of the Tervingi, even though they refer to him as *iudex*, 'judge', rather than as king. Other sources, however, demonstrate quite clearly that Athanaric was not the only Tervingian leader: we meet royal figures – a queen Gaatha, and others unnamed – who act in opposition to the *iudex* Athanaric, who is also called *iudex regum*, 'judge of kings', in one, admittedly highly rhetorical, source.[2] Thus, although a judge was clearly superior to a king, the substantive distinctions between them are altogether unclear, despite reams of scholarly speculation. Our Graeco-Roman sources were translating a genuine distinction between the Gothic word for king, *reiks*, a cognate of the Latin *rex*, and the Gothic word for judge, *thiudans*. The fact that *thiudans* was used to translate the Greek *basileús*, 'emperor', in a Gothic martyrial calendar is a significant clue to the importance of the rank, but how much authority a Tervingian judge wielded over a Tervingian *reiks*, and how permanent it was, will always elude us.[3]

CONSTANTINE'S DEATH AND ITS AFTERMATH

Regardless, the short-term consequence of Constantine's Gothic victory was merely to shift the focus of confrontation to a new set of barbarian enemies. In 334, Constantine campaigned against the Sarmatians, probably those who had asked for his help against the Goths in the first place. We are told that the servile population of the Sarmatian lands rebelled against their masters, and that many Sarmatians – 30,000 according to one source – fled into Roman service. Once inside Roman territory, they were divided among the Balkan and Italian provinces.[4] Whatever the shadowy events that had preceded the Gothic war, it is clear that the whole structure of the Danubian *barbaricum* had been deeply disturbed, as old hierarchies of power were overturned. After the

334 campaign, Constantine took the victory title *Sarmaticus Maximus*
to accompany his multiple acclamations as *Gothicus Maximus*. He also
took the title *Dacicus Maximus*, which probably represents a claim to
have restored Trajan's province of Dacia. The Carpathian lands of the old
province were certainly not reannexed and subjected to Roman administration, but new garrisons in trans-Danubian *quadriburgia* and other
small forts probably justified the claims. Nevertheless, Constantine was
a familiar and frightening force beyond the *limes*, as is illustrated by the
large number of barbarian ambassadors present in 335 at the celebra-
tion of his *tricennalia*, his thirtieth anniversary on the throne, which is
described to us by Eusebius, an eyewitness.[5]

The extent of Constantine's prestige is illustrated by the immediate
aftermath of his death in 337: for almost two years, we have no record of
any campaigns against northern barbarians, an unheard of stability given
that barbarian neighbours almost inevitably seized the opportunity provided by imperial successions to raid the Roman provinces. In the year
of his death, Constantine had been preparing for a massive invasion
of Persia, perhaps meant as the culmination of his world-conquering
career. His death bequeathed a legacy of instability on the Persian frontier to his successors, and their own competition made matters worse.
Constantine was succeeded by three sons and two nephews, the latter of
whom died in a massacre of nearly all Constantine's male relatives which
was organized in order to ensure his sons a firm hold on the throne. But
those sons – Constantinus, Constantius II, and Constans – soon came
to blows themselves. The eldest son, Constantinus, was displeased with
his share in the division of the empire. He attacked his younger brother
Constans in 340, but died in the war that followed. Thereafter, Constantius and Constans cohabited more or less peaceably for a decade,
having probably campaigned together against the Sarmatians shortly
before their elder brother's death.[6] When Constans was overthrown by
an army coup in 350, Constantius waged a bitter war against the usurper
Magnentius. In the midst of this civil strife, the inhabitants of the frontier provinces were the greatest losers. Just as it had in the third century,
the defence of the frontiers took second place to the prosecution of
internal disputes, and thus the outbursts of civil war during the 340s

and 350s encouraged barbarian incursions. Along the lower Danube, the peace of 332 continued to hold, the Tervingi honouring its terms and providing soldiers for the military ventures of the emperor Constantius. The Rhine frontier, by contrast, posed almost continuous difficulties. It was there that Constans had faced the revolt of Magnentius, and thence that Magnentius had drained troops in order to prosecute his war against Constantius. The connection between usurpation and barbarian invasion is made explicit in a speech attributed to the emperor Constantius, just before he appointed his cousin Julian as caesar and gave him the unwelcome task of restoring the Rhineland.[7]

OUR MOST IMPORTANT SOURCE: AMMIANUS MARCELLINUS

The source for this speech is Ammianus Marcellinus, one of the greatest historians of all antiquity and our main source for later fourth-century history, including the relationship between the Goths and the empire: without Ammianus, this and the next chapter could hardly be written. Given his importance to our understanding of the Goths, we must take a few moments to look at Ammianus himself before moving on. Ammianus was a Greek from one of the great cities of Syria, probably Antioch. He came from a good family which had been excused from its obligation to serve in the local town council and was instead closely linked to the larger imperial administration. As a young man, Ammianus served as *protector domesticus*, part of an elite group of soldiers who carried out a variety of special functions and often operated in the close vicinity of the emperor himself. *Protectores* frequently went on to command units of active-service troops in later life: the institution can be seen as a sort of officer training academy and more than one *protector* went on to become emperor. Ammianus found himself personally involved in a number of high-profile missions, and ultimately joined the invasion of Persia launched in 363 by the pagan emperor Julian, cousin and heir of Constantius. Unlike his Christian cousins and his uncle Constantine, Julian (r. 361–363) had repudiated Christianity, probably in reaction to the Christian piety of Constantine and his sons, who had murdered all but one of Julian's close relations. Julian's reign saw a determined attempt to undo Constantine's Christianization of the empire, an attempt that fizzled out immediately upon Julian's premature death on campaign. Julian, however, was Ammianus' hero, and Ammianus may even have been an apostate from Christianity just as Julian was. Certainly his promising career came to a sudden halt with Julian's death in 363 and it may be that Julian's more committed pagan followers found their prospects stymied in the Christian reaction against the dead emperor.

Ammianus, his career prospects finished, devoted himself to research and, eventually, to writing the history of the Roman empire. We know that he travelled widely, and that he had moved from his native Greek East to Rome by 384. He wrote much of his history in Rome, perhaps under the patronage of one of the great senatorial families who dominated that city. His work liberally intermixes a political history of the empire with scholarly asides and Ammianus' personal reminiscences. It was probably finished within a year or so of 390 and Ammianus may have died soon afterwards, for we know nothing more of him thereafter. The title he gave his history was *Res Gestae*, literally 'deeds done', and it indicates that the political history of the period it covers – from the reign of the emperor Nerva (r. 96–97) to that of Valens (r. 364–378) – was its primary concern. The surviving version of the text, unfortunately, begins with the start of book 14 and relates the events of summer 353 onwards, before ending, with book 31, just after the death of Valens at the battle of Adrianople in August 378. The structure of the history is complex and we cannot be sure of how it was originally organized, or indeed whether the numbering of the books as we have them is correct – it is possible that the original text consisted of thirty-six books, five of which are now lost and the rest misnumbered.[8] Almost all of Ammianus' Gothic material is contained in the extant book 31, which is structurally and thematically very different from all those that precede it and may perhaps have been initially composed as a separate treatise. Regardless, the pessimism that pervades the *Res Gestae* is shaped by and focused on the catastrophic defeat of Valens by the Goths at Adrianople. The whole narrative is therefore filtered through the understanding of the terrible disaster that was to come, a disaster that Ammianus blames on a failure to honour Rome's ancient traditions. This penetrating gloom must inform our own reading of Ammianus whenever we try to mine his text for information on the events of this period – we must always ask why he says what he says in the way he says it, for he is a master of innuendo and misdirection. On the other hand, he was a keen observer of Roman decline, and understood how Roman failures could lead directly to barbarian successes. Indeed, he alone demonstrates that at least some contemporaries understood and could articulate why the intersection of Roman internecine strife and barbarian invasion was so lethal: the barbarians 'were like wild beasts who have acquired the habit of stealing their prey through the negligence of the shepherds'.[9]

CONSTANTIUS ON THE DANUBE

The greatest barbarian danger, as the narrative of Ammianus shows, lay along the Rhine and the upper Danube, where neglect and the civil war that followed the death of Constans had weakened the frontiers. Both Alamanni and Franks were restive and the latter even succeeded in sacking so important a town as the imperial residence of Trier. Constantius, the last surviving heir of Constantine, was a deeply suspicious man, mistrustful of everyone, not least his own family. But he could not govern alone, certainly not with simultaneous disturbances on Rhine, Danube and eastern front, and even a suspect cousin was preferable to another usurper like Magnentius. Constantius turned to his only surviving male relatives, but the caesar Gallus, Julian's elder brother, proved a disaster and soon met his end at the hands of the executioner. In 356, Julian alone remained and was duly appointed caesar. For half a decade, he campaigned more or less continuously along and beyond the Rhine. Constantius, meanwhile, devoted himself to the Sarmatians and Quadi of the middle Danube in year after year of campaigning. In 358 and 359, Constantius conducted massive punitive raids against Sarmatians and Quadi, and then against the Sarmatians' former subjects the Limigantes. Deliberately sowing terror, Constantius sat in judgement on the many petty kings of the region, allocating territories to different groups.[10] As a result of these campaigns, the Sarmatians were eliminated as a serious power in the *barbaricum*. What is more, the suppression of the Limigantes created a sort of no-man's land opposite the Danube bend between the powerful Quadic chieftains to the northwest and the Tervingian ones to the south and east. Both Quadi and Tervingi were to benefit.

Gothic power was presumably rendered all the more stable by these campaigns. Certainly neither Constantius, nor later Julian, ever felt the need to campaign along the *ripa Gothica* of the lower Danube, which was entirely peaceful between the 330s and the 360s. That peace allowed for the trade relations advertised in the name of a little fort called *Commercium* – 'the marketplace' – and for the recruitment of Gothic soldiers into the garrisons on the imperial side of the river.[11] Such garrison troops are probably responsible for the fairly widespread distribution of Sântana-de-Mureş/Černjachov decorative styles in places like Iatrus south of the frontier, and we know that Constantius was able to recruit many Goths for his Persian campaigns of the later 350s. The price of Constantius' Danubian peace only became clear in the long term. His eventual successors, the imperial brothers Valentinian (r. 364–375) and Valens (r. 364–378), were spared any serious fighting between the Danube and the Tisza rivers where Constantius had suppressed the Sarmatians and Limigantes. But the absence of those troublesome neighbours only strengthened the power of Quadic and Tervingian rulers in their own territories and Valentinian and Valens each died on campaign, against the Quadi and the Goths respectively. Ammianus recounts how, in 361, the emperor Julian declared himself content to leave the Goths to the slave traders, so little did they merit military attention.[12] No doubt Ammianus wrote with the omniscience of hindsight, and wanted to bring home to us the tragic decline in Julian's good judgement that would end in his death on a Persian battlefield. But if Julian really did speak those words or others like them, it was a stunning underestimate of Tervingian power. That power, in no small measure a product of imperial policy, would be revealed in three years of bitter warfare between the Tervingian *iudex* Athanaric and the emperor Valens. Before that, however, another element of imperial policy had begun to impinge heavily on Gothic society, in the shape of Christian missions.

ULFILA AND GOTHIC CHRISTIANITY

In the long years of stability after 332, Constantine's ambition to evangelize the Goths was partly fulfilled. Constantine, as we have seen, had become a devoted Christian, certainly by the year 312 if not before. By the time he won his Gothic victory in 332, he had been implementing pro-Christian policies throughout the empire for several decades, particularly in the Greek East, which he had conquered from Licinius as the liberator of eastern Christians from persecution. He saw himself as a bishop to those outside the empire, and clearly regarded himself as called to evangelize the *gentes* beyond the frontier. The war against Persia which Constantine was preparing at the time of his death was prompted at least in part by his sense of Christian mission. Whether Constantine had explicitly planned for the evangelization of the Goths by 337 is controversial. It is sometimes argued that Constantine deliberately imposed Christianity on those Goths with whom he made peace in 332, but the evidence for that is not good.[13] On the contrary, it may simply have been a matter of chance that an opportunity to bring Christian teaching to the Goths arrived in the person of the Bishop Ulfila, sometimes known as Wulfila or Ulfilas.

Our information on the life of Ulfila is derived from just two sources, a letter written by one of his disciples, Auxentius, and a heavily abbreviated version of Philostorgius' fifth-century *Ecclesiastical History*. Ulfila was descended from Cappadocians taken captive in the Gothic raids of Gallienus' reign, but he himself bore a Gothic name. The date of his consecration as bishop and the start of his mission is debated. He came from Gothia on an embassy to the emperor – perhaps Constantine, perhaps Constantius II – and was consecrated in either c. 336 or c. 341 by Eusebius of Nicomedia and other bishops. Eusebius was an adherent of a variety of Christianity associated with the Egyptian priest Arius who had argued that God the Son was subordinate to God the Father in the holy trinity. Arianism had been condemned as false doctrine – heresy – at the council of Nicaea, convened by Constantine in 325 immediately after his conquest of the eastern empire. In rejecting Arianism, the bishops at Nicaea decided that the Father and Son were identical, of the same substance (*homoousion* in Greek). Despite this, modified forms of Arius' homoean theology – so-called from the Greek word for 'likeness', because it argued that the Father and Son were of like but not identical substance – continued to have considerable appeal, not least to Constantine, who was ultimately baptised by Eusebius of Nicomedia himself. Modern readers – including most professed Christians – are unused to and almost entirely indifferent to theology, and so find it very hard to understand why christological or trinitarian definitions aroused such passions in the early church. They did so because the consequence of getting the definition wrong – of believing the wrong thing about the persons of the trinity – was to compromise salvation. Because, after Constantine, the Roman state took on the task of guaranteeing Christian orthodoxy, the political cost of having one's theological views condemned as heresy was very high. To understand the history of the fourth century, we need to take seriously both the political and the religious significance of theological disputes.

The fact that the Nicene position was not universally accepted by several fourth-century emperors was a particular complication. Constantius II, for one, was a convinced supporter of homoean belief and attempted to enforce it as orthodoxy, even though he was defied by many bishops in the empire who supported the Nicene definition of the trinity. Ulfila was a member of the homoean party, and as a consequence of that fact, the earliest evangelism among the Goths brought Christianity in its homoean form. The homoean tendencies of Gothic Christianity were heavily re-enforced by later events under Valens, a fervent homoean who diligently persecuted his Nicene opponents. When he agreed to let many Tervingi into the empire in 376, he may have made some form of conversion a prerequisite for admission, and he had certainly sponsored missions among them before 376.[14] Valens, however, was the last emperor to support homoean doctrine and, upon his death, an overwhelming Nicene reaction meant that any doctrine with Arian tendencies would thereafter remain a reviled heresy. Over the years, however, Gothic Christians remained committed to their homoean doctrine and its homoean liturgy. When, a hundred years after Ulfila's first mission, a powerful Gothic kingdom existed inside the Roman empire, Arianism functioned both as a defining symbol of Gothic identity, and as a major obstacle to peaceful coexistence between Gothic kings and the Nicene Romans over whom they ruled.

All the same, when his mission began, by 341 at the latest, Ulfila was simply adhering to the form of Christian doctrine endorsed as official orthodoxy by the emperor and those bishops whom he favoured. Ulfila was meant to serve as bishop for all the Christians already in the land of the Goths, but we have no idea how many such Christians there might have been, nor how many of them were descendants of former captives from the Roman empire and how many were converts won beyond the frontier. Within a decade of Ulfila's arrival in Gothic territory, however, the number of Christians must have grown large enough to worry Gothic leaders, who associated the new religion with imperial power and therefore found the loyalty of Gothic Christians somewhat suspect. We do not know what sparked it, or indeed which Gothic leaders were involved, but eight years after Ulfila's arrival in Gothia a persecution of Gothic Christians began. An offhand remark by bishop Cyril of Jerusalem seems to imply that this persecution produced martyrs, though none are known by name.[15] Ulfila and his followers were driven out of Gothic territory and into the empire, where they were granted lands in the province of Moesia Secunda, possibly around the city of Nicopolis.[16] Constantius addressed Ulfila as a new Moses, for leading his people out of servitude in their trans-Danubian Egypt.[17] Inside the empire, Ulfila became heavily involved in the ecclesiastical politics of Constantius' reign and by the time of his death in 383 had been an influential theologian for many years.

THE GOTHIC BIBLE
Ulfila and his followers in Moesia may have maintained close connections with co-religionists beyond the Danube, but we cannot be sure because the evidence comes from the fifth-century church historian Sozomen, who often misunderstands or oversimplifies fourth-century events. It would make good sense if Ulfila continued to be involved in diplomacy between emperors and Goths, yet in the 370s, the bishop of

Tomi on the Black Sea, and not Ulfila, probably had responsibility for all the Christians of Scythia – both the Roman province of that name and the broader Gothic region beyond the frontier.[18] Regardless of that, Ulfila's greatest impact on Gothic history came through his invention of an alphabet in which the Gothic language could be written. He based this alphabet on the Greek, but included new letters which could represent sounds not found in Greek.[19] Ulfila had only one purpose in creating this alphabet – to translate into Gothic the text of the Bible, so as to aid the work of evangelization. He translated into Gothic the whole text of the Bible apart, we are told, from the books of Kings, 'because these books contain the history of wars, while the Gothic people, being lovers of war, were in need of something to restrain their passion for fighting rather than to incite them to it'.[20] This work of translation may well have involved not just Ulfila, but his followers as well, and was probably a product of their time in Moesia, rather than the eight short years they had been able to spend in Gothia. Yet the work they did endured. In the Gothic kingdoms of the fifth and sixth centuries, this Gothic Bible was the basic text for the homoean liturgy, and fragments of the Gothic Bible have been transmitted to us from many different sources. Almost all of these remains come from the New Testament, while only small fragments of Old Testament texts still survive. These biblical texts, however, are the earliest substantial evidence we possess for the morphology and vocabulary of a Germanic language, and are thus of priceless value to modern philologists.

Whether or not Ulfila's mission was a direct product of Constantine's own missionary ambitions, it was clearly a result of the Constantinian peace with the Tervingi. We have no way to correlate the growth of Christianity in Gothia with the meagre scraps of Tervingian history that are known to us during the reigns of Constantius and Julian. But we can be sure that Christianity was indeed spreading throughout the region, as retrospective evidence makes clear. As we shall soon see, the aftermath of Valens' Gothic wars in the 360s brought on a second, much heavier, persecution of Christians in Gothic territory, one that is much better documented in ecclesiastical and liturgical sources. Most of the known victims of this second persecution seem to have been Nicene

Goths, rather than homoeans. That would seem to imply that there were in fact two separate strands of missionary work beyond the lower Danube frontier in this period, however obscure their details may be to us.

TERVINGI, GREUTHUNGI AND OTHER GOTHS

Still more obscure than the rise of Tervingian Christianity is the Gothic world beyond the Tervingi. There is no contemporary evidence, and almost everything we know about the larger Gothic world of the middle fourth century – apart from the archaeological evidence for its social structures, which we looked at in the last chapter – comes from retrospective accounts written after the disaster of Adrianople. Jordanes has much to say about this period, but it is almost all fiction that draws genuine figures from contemporary sources and inserts them into a spurious dynastic history of the sixth-century Ostrogothic king Theodoric the Great. The one thing we can be quite sure of is that beyond the fourth-century territory of the Tervingi there lay another Gothic realm, whose inhabitants were called Greuthungi. The Tervingi and Greuthungi have been interpreted as the linear ancestors of the later fifth-century Visigoths and Ostrogoths, and the long-standing division of the Goths into two sections under separate royal dynasties is a fixture of older literature (and still maintained by supporters of ethnogenesis-theory, with their insistence that royal dynasties transmit ethnic identity). In fact, the division between Visigoths and Ostrogoths is a product of fifth-century politics within the Roman and Hunnic empires, and the names are retrojection from the sixth-century text of Jordanes: they bear no demonstrable relationship to fourth-century divisions. The Gothic groups that emerged in the fourth century, after Adrianople, and in the fifth century, after the collapse of the Hunnic empire, were of thoroughly mixed origin, with connections to several different Gothic polities of the fourth century. Of these, the Tervingian polity is moderately well attested, but our knowledge of the Greuthungi comes almost entirely from a few pages of Ammianus Marcellinus. He, in turn, only mentions the Greuthungi when he describes the destruction of their kingdom by the Huns and the death of their king Ermanaric.

Ammianus actually knew very little about the Greuthungian king-dom. He tells us that Ermanaric ruled 'lands rich and wide' and was a 'most warlike king and, on account of his many and various deeds, feared by the neighbouring peoples'.[21] That, in full, is the only contem-porary evidence for Ermanaric's kingdom that exists. Jordanes, however, expands that account into an elaborate list of peoples over whom Erma-naric held sway, drawing on traditions of classical ethnography and extending this fictional empire as far as northern Russia. Utter non-sense, Jordanes' 'empire of Ermanaric' warrants none of the attention given it by otherwise serious scholars desperate for any scrap of infor-mation on the early Goths. Apart from the single line of Ammianus, the extent of Ermanaric's power must remain a mystery to us. After his kingdom collapsed in the face of a Hunnic attack, we learn of several different groups of Greuthungi whom we cannot positively identify as having once been Ermanaric's followers. That fact suggests that, just as different factions are known amongst the Tervingi in the face of Valens' invasions of the 360s, so amongst the Greuthungi, Ermanaric was not the single source of power. The archaeological evidence we have looked at offers no help, and there is no material difference between the Sântana-de-Mureş/Černjachov territories in which the Tervingi were dominant and those in which Ermanaric's Greuthungi lived. We must, in other words, content ourselves with only a very imperfect sense of Gothic history between the victory of Constantine in 332 and that of Valens in 369, to which we can now turn.

VALENTINIAN AND VALENS

As with so much of the history of the Roman frontier, Valens' Gothic wars are tied up in the internal conflicts of the empire, and particularly the legacy left to him by his predecessors Constantius II and Julian. Julian, when we last saw him, had been appointed caesar by Constan-tius, in the hope that he would restore the Rhine frontier which had been so badly weakened by the usurpation of Magnentius. In 359, after many successes against Franks and Alamanni in the Rhineland, Julian was declared augustus by his troops. Both he and Constantius prepared for civil war, the latter bringing his Persian campaigns to an abrupt end in order to deal with his upstart cousin. A full-blown conflict was only averted by Constantius' timely death, of natural causes, in 361. Julian immediately launched into a hugely ambitious program of reform, aimed both at reversing the Christianization of the Constantinian empire, and at fulfilling the dreams of his uncle and cousin and conquering Persia. After initial successes that brought the army to the walls of the Persian capital at Ctesiphon, Julian's campaign ended in shambles; he himself died of a wound received in a sudden ambush. The army elected an ineffectual officer named Jovian (r. 363–364) to get them out of Persia, which he did at the cost of a humiliating peace-treaty that ceded several important Mesopotamian towns to the Persians. Jovian, a heavy drinker, soon died of self-indulgence, and the army high command elected Valentinian (r. 364–375) as emperor. Valentinian, a *protector* like the historian Ammianus, in turn appointed his younger brother Valens (r. 364–378) as his co-emperor.

The brothers were Pannonian, from the region of Lake Balaton in modern Hungary, and therefore from a region proverbially backward, the punchline in many a late Roman joke. This cultural stereotype deeply affects their treatment in our narrative sources, which invariably depict them as loathsome and cruel, a judgement mitigated only by Valentinian's undeniable prowess as a general. Ammianus, the cultured Greek from Syria, found them unspeakable: Valens was *subrusticum hominem*, a half-witted man, who would have been murdered by his soldiers, had fate not spared him to suffer greater disaster.[22] Everything we know of Valens, in both Ammianus and the rich Greek historical tradition, is uniformly hostile. Our own interpretations of his reign, like those of his contemporaries, remain coloured not just by such slanders, but by his ultimate fate: killed by the Goths, along with most of the eastern Roman army, on the field of Adrianople. It has recently been argued that Valens was by no means a disastrous emperor, and certainly not the incompetent he is so often made out to have been. He was, on the contrary, a more or less average late Roman commander who faced an impossible concatenation of circumstances that ultimately brought him down.[23] Though that assessment may be a trifle generous, there can be no question that both Valens and Valentinian faced formidable challenges upon their accession to the throne.

The prospect of civil war between Julian and Constantius, and the fact that Julian launched his Persian war immediately upon the death of Constantius, led to the customary upheavals along the frontiers. As in the 340s and 350s, these disturbances were worst along the Rhine, though the Quadi, relieved of the pressure of their Sarmatian neighbours, required repeated campaigning by Valentinian to control. This demonstrates the structural dangers inherent in the standard imperial policy towards the barbarians. Constantius' settlement of affairs between the Danube and Tisza had bred resentment amongst the Quadi, who had suffered demeaning punitive raids at the same time as the Sarmatians were suppressed, but it had also so strengthened them that as soon as the opportunity presented itself – as it did with Julian's departure and death – they were able to launch devastating attacks on the provinces of Noricum and Valeria. So confident had the Quadi become in the security of their position that some of their envoys dared to address Valentinian as an equal during the campaigning season of 375. His outrage at this effrontery triggered the stroke which killed him, leaving the western provinces to his sons, one an untested youth named Gratian, the other, Gratian's half-brother Valentinian II, still only a toddler. Since 365, when they had divided the empire and its field army between them, the elder Valentinian and Valens had declined to interfere in one another's affairs. Valens made no effort to intervene in the West upon his brother's premature death, just as Valentinian had left Valens to his fate in the long series of disturbances that had faced him in the decade after 365. The earliest of these was the usurpation of Procopius, and it was from that venture that Valens' Gothic campaigns ultimately stemmed.

THE USURPATION OF PROCOPIUS AND THE BREAKDOWN OF THE GOTHIC PEACE

Procopius could claim kinship with the Constantinian dynasty whose main line had died with Julian. He launched his usurpation at Constantinople in 365, suborning some troops who were *en route* to the Danube frontier, and almost succeeded in bringing down Valens' new and insecure regime. Only the opportune treachery of some old associates of Constantius II saved Valens, and Procopius was captured and executed in 366. Several Gothic kings had lent support to Procopius, supposedly sending 3,000 soldiers, but they excused themselves on the grounds of their treaty with the house of Constantine, whose legitimate heir they had taken Procopius to be.[24] We cannot tell if they believed their own excuses, but we do know their services were well rewarded: the largest hoard of silver coins in Gothic territory, from Caracal on the river Olt in modern Romania, contained nearly 3,000 silver coins, including thirty of Procopius.

Valens, as one can well imagine, had no intention of accepting this sort of excuse. He was in desperate need of a victory to shore up his prestige, badly damaged by a usurpation that had nearly unseated him. The Goths made an easier and more attractive target than did the intractable Persian frontier, and he could portray a Gothic war as well-merited punishment for lending support to a usurper. He seized the Goths who had come to support Procopius and deported them to Asia Minor. Then, in the three summer campaigning seasons from 367 to 369, Valens assaulted the Goths across the Danube. The campaigns were well prepared, as attested by a flurry of laws issued to the praetorian prefect Auxonius, responsible for organizing logistical support. What is more, the importance of the campaigns was widely anticipated in the eastern empire, for Valens received the dedication of a strange treatise, now anonymous, called *De rebus bellicis*, 'On military matters', which recommends both sensible measures well suited to Thracian conditions, and bizarre new war machines that no general could have deployed in reality. The orator Themistius, a great celebrity in Constantinople and a mouthpiece for imperial propaganda since the reign of Constantius, prepared public opinion for the successes that would soon be forthcoming. Sadly for Valens, Themistius' enthusiasm went unvindicated by events.

VALENS' THREE GOTHIC CAMPAIGNS

In the first campaign, launched in summer 367, Valens crossed the river at Daphne on a bridge of boats, which suggests that the Constantinian bridge from Oescus to Sucidava was no longer useable for large-scale military operations. The emperor laid waste the territory beyond the river, but failed to bring any large number of Goths to battle, because they fled into the Carpathians or the Transylvanian Alps in the face of his advance. He was, however, inspired to set a bounty on the heads of any Goth his men could capture, and this allowed him to at least salvage some claims to victory from the campaign.[25] In 368, rains and heavy flooding hampered the army's movements, and Valens spent much if not all of the season encamped beside the Danube to no great military effect. He did, however, undertake a considerable construction campaign, restoring old and building new *quadriburgia* and smaller *burgi*, some of them named after himself or members of his family (for example Valentia, Valentiniana, Gratiana).[26] These building efforts are attested by bronze coins showing a *burgus* on their reverse, and by a fragmentary inscription from Cius that is dated to 368.[27] The third year of the war was more satisfying. After crossing the river at Noviodunum in the Dobrudja, Valens marched a long way into Gothic territory, sowing fear and destruction wherever he went. The Tervingian leader Athanaric gave battle and was defeated, as barbarian armies usually were when a Roman field army could pin them down in a set-piece battle. However, rather than pursue Athanaric in his retreat Valens returned to imperial territory, possibly because of the lateness of the season.[28]

THE TERMS OF THE PEACE

Ammianus Marcellinus, who is our chief source for these campaigns, had reason to underplay their significance, knowing as he did that Adrianople was soon to come. But Valens' three years of warfare had brought real successes. The new Danube forts strengthened Roman defences and the ability to project imperial power against the Goths. In fact, Valens shut down the frontier so effectively that Gothic access to Roman trade goods was systematically denied them. We saw in the last chapter how prominent a role trade with the Danube provinces played in the Sântana-de-Mureş/Černjachov regions, and Valens' measures must have caused real hardship. More even than the battlefield defeat of 369, the shortages of Roman goods throughout Gothic territory forced

Athanaric to sue for peace.[29] The terms of the peace were arranged in late summer 369 by two of Valens' trusted generals, Victor and Arinthaeus. Valens and Athanaric met to solemnize a treaty near Noviodunum, but they did so on boats, midstream, Valens respecting the Gothic king's oath not to set foot on Roman soil.[30] Hostages were given on the Gothic side, the emperor stopped paying subsidies to the Goths, and trade was opened up again, though restricted to just two (unnamed) cities.[31] Yet the separation of the Goths from the empire was not quite as complete as these measures were meant to suggest, for translators from Greek to Gothic continued to receive their imperial stipend, suggesting that the lines of communication were to be kept open.[32]

In the aftermath of this treaty, both sides could claim some sort of victory. The obliging Themistius, addressing the senate of Constantinople in early 370, preserves for us the official line: Valens' philanthropy has inclined him to mercy. Why, after all, should a conquered and subjugated foe be wholly destroyed when he might be preserved and put to use on the battlefield? Valens, for his part, used the cessation of hostilities, and the concomitant propaganda triumph, to deal with growing trouble on the eastern frontier, taking up residence at Antioch in Syria for nearly half a decade. Athanaric, by extracting from the emperor a dignified peace on equal terms, was free to reassert his authority among the Tervingi. He chose to do this in part by launching a persecution of Gothic Christians, which may have led him into war against other Gothic chieftains and provoked further Roman intervention. Certainly, the opposition he experienced gives us some hint as to how low his prestige had fallen in three years of inconclusive warfare against Valens. As usual, the available sources leave much open to debate, and it is not at all clear that Gothic Christians had played any active role in helping Valens or opposing Athanaric before he began to persecute them. But, as had been the case with Diocletian decades earlier, suspicion might be grounds enough for persecution. Not only could Christians appear to poison the health of the state by refusing to honour its protecting deities, they were, from Athanaric's point of view, potentially spies for the emperor. If, as seems quite possible, Ulfila's Gothic community in Moesia maintained ties with co-religionists across the Danube, then

Athanaric's suspicions are thoroughly explicable. In times of peace, this sort of contact might be unproblematic, not much different than the to and fro of trade that so characterized the lower Danube of the mid fourth century. But once the Romans went to war against the Goths, and when Valens' activities cut trade down to a tiny trickle, perspectives were necessarily altered. Gothic Christians might come to look less like fellow subjects of the Gothic kings and more like prospective sympathisers with Valens. If, as the fifth-century church historian Socrates tells us, Valens began to send missionaries into Gothia in 369, the case against Gothic Christians was that much clearer.[33] Persecution followed, its effects well documented in the extant sources.

THE STORY OF SABA

The most extensive of these sources is the *Passion of St. Saba*, written shortly after 373, within a year or two of the death of its protagonist Saba. The *Passion* was sent to Basil, bishop of Caesarea in Cappadocia, perhaps the single most influential Greek bishop of his day.[34] Basil corresponded with the Cappadocian native Junius Soranus, who had been appointed to a military command in Roman Scythia – as *dux Scythiae* – in 373. This sort of letter exchange was a normal part of life for provincial elites, and the accession of a fellow provincial to an imperial office in a distant province usually meant an extension of patronage towards natives of the home region. Maintaining one's network of correspondents was therefore an essential prerequisite of being able to serve one's clients, and Basil's letter collection is one of many that survive to show us how sedulously useful contacts were cultivated. The *Passion of Saba* is still available to us because of just this sort of letter exchange: a Balkan cleric (either Ascholius of Thessalonica or perhaps more likely a simple priest of the same name) seized the opportunity of Soranus' appointment and his known connections to Basil to inform the great bishop of church affairs in the Danubian provinces and beyond. Basil, in gracious reply, flatters the author as a 'trainer of Gothic martyrs', though we have no way of evaluating the truth of that epithet. Regardless, the *dux* Soranus was enchanted by the legend of the holy Saba, sending men across the Danube to collect the saint's relics and ultimately sending them to

Cappadocia, where they would thenceforth rest. The accidental connection of Gothic Christianity and Cappadocia, whence Ulfila's ancestors had been taken more than a century earlier, was thereby perpetuated.

The story of Saba, as portrayed in his *Passion*, must detain us a little longer, for its incidental details offer the only glimpse of Gothic social history we possess apart from the archaeological remains of the Sântana-de-Mureş/Černjachov culture. Saba, we are told, was a villager somewhere in Gothia, perhaps in the region just to the southeast of the Carpathians. He was a Nicene rather than a homoean Christian, and may have been a cantor or lector in the local church (it is not altogether clear whether the reference to his "singing God's praises in the church" should be given such a technical meaning). The *Passion* distinguishes several phases of persecution by the Gothic *megistanes*—'lords' or 'chiefs', perhaps a direct reference to the Gothic king Rothesteus mentioned later in the text, perhaps to his more important followers. In both phases, these *megistanes* tested the loyalty of the villagers by forcing them to eat sacrificial meat. The first time this happened, the pagans in Saba's village decided to trick the supervising officials by substituting meat that had not been sacrificed to the pagan gods for meat that had been. For us, this demonstrates the integration of Gothic Christians into village life and the willingness of their fellow villagers to unite against authority from outside the village, however legitimate it was.

For Greek contemporaries reading the *Passion*, however, it was Saba's actions that proved his sanctity: refusing to go along with the deception, he made a conspicuous show of rejecting the meat altogether, and thus provoked his fellow villagers into exiling him from the village. He was allowed back before long, but promptly stirred up further trouble for himself and the other Christians of the village. When a Gothic noble came to the village for a second time to supervise the consumption of the sacrificial meat, the pagan villagers were going to swear, while eating it, that there were no Christians in the village. Once again, Saba revealed himself and refused to play along. But when the villagers swore that Saba was a man of no account, possessing 'nothing but the clothes he wears', the Gothic lord did no more than order his expulsion from the gathering, on the grounds that a man with no property could neither help nor harm. That response is strong evidence for the essentially political nature of the persecution in Gothic territory: powerful Gothic converts might be a threat, potentially in league with the emperor; a man like Saba was at worst a conspicuous nuisance.

Yet in the final phase of the persecution, Saba's obstinacy reached a pitch that provoked the martyrdom he so clearly craved. Saba was *en route* to another village to celebrate Easter with a priest named Gouththikas, when a miraculous fall of snow prevented his going forward and turned him back to celebrate the feast in his own village with his fellow Christian, the priest Sansalas. Three days after Easter, Atharidus, the son of the Gothic king Rothesteus, arrived in the village with an entourage, specifically to arrest Sansalas. Saba, found in his company, was likewise arrested, but while Sansalas was held captive to face a higher authority, Saba was tortured on the spot. First driven through thorny thickets, then lashed to the axles of a wagon and flogged through the night, he defied his tormentors in the approved manner of one born to martyrdom. A friendly village servant freed him and fed him, but the tortures continued on the following day, when Sansalas and Saba were ordered by Atharidus' men to consume meat that had been sacrificed. Saba naturally refused and was finally condemned to die, on 12 April 372. The soldiers chosen to drown him in the river Musaios, perhaps the Buzaǔ, seriously considered him setting him free: they thought him simple-minded for rejoicing at his coming martyrdom and reasoned that Atharidus would never find out if they just let him go. But Saba, insisting that he could see an army of saints waiting beyond the river to welcome him into heaven, urged them to their duty. So 'they took him down to the water, threw him in and, pressing a beam against his neck, pushed him to the bottom and held him there'. It may have been Sansalas who set down in writing the account of Saba's martyrdom.[35]

OTHER GOTHIC MARTYRS AND THE MOTIVES FOR PERSECUTION

Saba was not the only martyr in this persecution. As St. Jerome put it in his chronicle entry for 369, 'Aithanaric king of the Goths persecuted

Christians, killed many and drove them from their own lands to the lands of the empire'.[36] Quite a few of these martyrs are recorded by name, in several different sources. Of particular significance is the list of martyrs remembered at Cyzicus in Asia Minor, where relics were deposited by Dulcilla, the daughter of an otherwise unknown Gothic queen named Gaatha. Among these martyrs we find the priests Bathouses and Wereka, their unnamed children, the monk Arpulas, eleven named Gothic men, and seven named Gothic women, all killed at the command of the Gothic leader Wiguric.[37] Other names are known from less reliable sources, but the drift of the evidence is clear: while some Gothic leaders favoured Christianity and tried to preserve the memory of their local martyrs, many also supported Athanaric's persecution.

We have already seen why Athanaric might rationally have regarded Gothic Christianity as a threat that needed to be stamped out. Yet in the face of this essentially political explanation, it is worth pointing out that some of his followers will have supported him out of genuine conviction. The story of Saba makes that clear: in the first of his several confrontations with Gothic authorities, Saba was exhorted to eat the sacrificial meat in order to save his soul. Unless this is merely a Christian gloss put on the confrontation by an ecclesiastical author, it would seem that some Goths regarded Christianity not just as a threat to the Gothic state, but also to the spiritual health of converts. All the same, it would be hard to deny that political fears were the foremost motive for persecution. The enthusiasm of leaders like Rothesteus and Wiguric shows that well below the level of the *iudex* Athanaric, it was feared that Christians might form a fifth column more sympathetic to the empire than to pagan Gothic leaders.

That some members of the Gothic aristocracy had converted only made matters worse, for they were in a position to treat with the Roman empire where a man like Saba was not. Emperors were only too keen to encourage dissension among barbarian neighbours, and Athanaric's defeat had damaged his authority, however much face he saved by the peaceful compromise that ended the war. As we have seen, the church historian Socrates reports that Valens used the peace to evangelize the Goths. Socrates also reports that the Tervingian chief Fritigern was one of those converted, that his Christianity caused him to go to war with Athanaric, and that some Roman soldiers were sent to aid Fritigern before the two Gothic leaders made peace. The conversion story is corroborated by Fritigern's probable commemoration in a later Gothic liturgical calendar, though the Gothic civil war is known only from Socrates.[38] Yet it too is plausible. The next time we meet Fritigern – in Ammianus, a more reliable source than Socrates – he is the leader of Tervingi opposed to Athanaric. We cannot know whether Fritigern opposed Athanaric because he was a Christian, or whether he became a Christian because he opposed Athanaric. But it seems quite clear that Athanaric was absolutely right to see the extension of Christianity among Gothic elites as a substantial threat to the political status quo in Gothia. How matters might have turned out in the long run is a moot point. Within four years of Saba's martyrdom the stability of the whole Gothic world had been shattered by obscure but traumatic events that brought many Tervingi to the banks of the Danube, begging for admission to the empire, in the spring of 376.

THE BATTLE OF
ADRIANOPLE

CHAPTER SIX

THE BATTLE OF ADRIANOPLE WIPED OUT TWO-THIRDS OF THE whole field army of the Roman East. It was the worst military disaster of the Roman imperial era, and one of the worst in Roman history. That it was inflicted by barbarians made it instantly controversial, as contemporaries struggled to understand the reasons for the loss. For them, little save divine displeasure could explain such a calamity, so debate centred on which god was angry and why. But from the perspective of the modern historian, the trail of events that led to Adrianople is dotted with human error at every step. The Goths who defeated the emperor Valens at Adrianople in 378 were not a horde of unstoppable invaders. They were, for the most part, the same Goths who had crossed the Danube just two years earlier, in 376, having done so with the full approval of the imperial government. The reception of barbarians into the empire was no unprecedented novelty, but a well-known procedure with centuries of success behind it. Of course, accidents can happen whenever large numbers of people move from one place to another. But the path to Adrianople was no accident. The orderly reception of the Goths broke down through mismanagement and thereafter the imperial government repeatedly exacerbated the problem in a toxic combination of venality and incompetence. And so the crisis marched inexorably onwards to the fatal 9th of August 378.

A modern narrative history is entirely at the mercy of the ancient sources that happen to survive, which condition both its depth and its detail. For the two years before Adrianople, our access to one particular stream of Gothic history grows tremendously larger. The Goths who entered the empire in 376 are better known to us than are any of their predecessors, or indeed any of their contemporaries who remained outside the empire. The pace and scale of our narrative can therefore change with the present chapter. Up till now, we have been able to look at Gothic history in only two ways: first, in a sort of static, analytical overview, based on the archaeological evidence; and second, in brief flashes of narrative when the Goths impinged heavily enough upon Roman imperial politics for our Graeco-Roman sources to leave a record of events. But beginning in 376, for the first time, we learn enough about both Roman and Gothic activity to write a detailed narrative history, one that permits some insight not just into what happened, but also into why and how it did so.

HUNS, ALANS AND GOTHS

The sources do not reach this level of precision until the Goths arrive at the banks of the Danube in 376, and the train of events that brought them there is known in nothing like the same detail as are the two years that followed it. The basic source is Ammianus Marcellinus, supplemented only very rarely by the fragments of Eunapius or the later sources, like Zosimus, that drew on him. Ammianus gives us a satisfyingly linear account: the Huns, a mysterious and lethal new people, appear as if from nowhere, smash the only somewhat less savage Alans, and drive through the Greuthungian kingdom of Ermanaric, pressing a horde of Gothic refugees forward to the Danube where they clamour for entry into the empire. No one can deny the force of Ammianus' account, but it has won rather more credence than it deserves from modern scholars. Ammianus always needs careful handling, but here even more so than elsewhere, because the events he describes took place so far from regions in which accurate knowlege was possible. His account is highly schematic and telescopes what was a long, complicated, and dimly understood upheaval into an implausibly straightforward story of cause and effect.

The Huns of Ammianus appeared from the distant East. For him, they are *bipedes bestias*, 'two-legged beasts': they live on horseback and cannot walk normally as other men do, they scar their children's faces and drink only mare's milk, they never cook their food, but rather place raw meat between their thighs and the backs of their horses in order to warm it up.[1] Eunapius once reported something similar, for Zosimus tells us that Huns could not fight on foot because they even slept on horseback.[2] Whereas scholars once took this evidence very seriously, it is now generally agreed that almost every element in Ammianus' description can be traced to older ethnographic traditions, often stretching back as far as Herodotus, 800 years earlier. Ammianus, we may be fairly certain, had never seen a Hun and nor had most of his readers, who would instead envisage the Huns as the historian intended them to – a patchwork of ethnic stereotypes stitched together to make a composite, but suitably barbarous, whole.

For all that we must distrust it, Ammianus' account may simply be retailing the sort of rumours that were all most Romans ever heard of events beyond the frontier.[3] His own lack of certain knowledge must explain why his narrative of the Hunnic onslaught lacks any chronological markers. The Huns appear suddenly, at some unspecified time, and overcome the Alans who dwell between the Don and the Caspian. Unlike the Huns, these Alans had long been known to Graeco-Roman ethnography. They made periodic incursions into Roman territory, but were for the most part a greater threat to Persia than to Rome. As early as the second century, Arrian (c. 86–160), the Hadrianic governor of Cappadocia and famous historian of Alexander, had written a tactical manual, the *Order of Battle against the Alans*, explaining how a Roman army should be disposed in order to repel the charge of Alanic cavalry. Arrian was a keen observer, but even in his own time, they had been confounded with ethnographic stereotypes in existence since the time of Herodotus, and his sketch of their tactics is not very informative. By the fourth century, Ammianus' sketch of the Alans does little more than a nod towards the conventional Graeco-Roman image of the horse-nomad. Starting from these Huns and Alans, Ammianus narrates a simple chain reaction, one group of barbarians pushing against the next until eventually the massed Tervingi appear on the banks of the Danube.

THE DEFEATS OF ERMANARIC AND ATHANARIC

The Alans, so we are told, joined forces with the Huns after being defeated by them. In the company of their new Hunnic masters, they went on to assault the borders of the Gothic Greuthungi. These Greuthungi were led by the 'most warlike' king Ermanaric, whom we met briefly in the last chapter. Ermanaric determined to make a stand against his enemies, but to no avail. In the end, he committed suicide rather than face the coming horrors. A new Greuthungian king, Vithimir, succeeded him, and like his predecessor determined to make a stand on the battlefield. Unlike his predecessor, he lost his life in battle. Thereafter, his little son Videric was made king, but two *duces* – a generic term which Ammianus uses for subordinate commanders – acted as the new king's guardians and seem to have taken Greuthungian affairs into their own hands. These *duces*, named Alatheus and Saphrax, led the Greuthungi of Videric westwards to the Dniester river. There, according to Ammianus, their plight came to the notice of the Tervingi and their *iudex* Athanaric.[4]

Athanaric, Valens' old enemy, advanced with an army to the banks of the Dniester, where he encamped at a safe distance from the Greuthungi. Sending an advance guard to observe and perhaps intercept the Huns, he waited at the Dniester, but was surprised by the Huns' strategic skill. A party of Huns crossed the Dniester in the night, marched down it to Athanaric's camp and forced him to withdraw into some unnamed mountains, perhaps the foothills of the Carpathians where he had previously sought refuge from Valens. What appears in Ammianus as a tactical retreat was in fact a massive withdrawal, for nearly 200 kilometres separate the Dniester from the line which Athanaric next determined to hold. This ran from north to south above the Danube, just beside the Carpathian foothills, and probably reconstituted the old Roman *limes transalutanus*, parallel to the river Olt and the frontier of the high imperial province of Dacia. Despite the efforts he put into throwing up earthworks and other defences, Athanaric's new measures came too late. Though he repulsed a Hunnic attack somewhere in the region, many of his followers had already deserted him. The *populi pars maior*, 'the larger part of his people', left their stubborn leader to fight his own battles, themselves seeking refuge in the empire. The Greuthungi under Alatheus and Saphrax, for their part, disappear from view until 377, several months after many Tervingi were allowed to cross the Danube into the empire.[5]

THE CHRONOLOGY OF GOTHIC DEFEATS

The foregoing narrative raises more questions than it answers, in large part because it derives exclusively from the last book of Ammianus' history. His account is heavily telescoped: its stages may be well defined, but its actual chronology is almost totally invisible. Even if Ammianus' account is substantially correct – and the very linear trajectory he suggests must be suspect – the series of conflicts among Huns, Alans and Goths will have taken much longer than the headlong rush implied by Ammianus. What is more, it is not easy to sustain his simple 'domino-effect' theory of causation, with the Huns toppling the Alans onto the Greuthungi onto the Tervingi onto the Romans. To be sure, the emergence of the Huns somewhere between the Caspian and the Black Sea probably did spark far-reaching changes in eastern and central Europe. But it is harder to make the case that the Huns were the proximate cause of Gothic collapse, rather than its catalyst. No named Hun appears on the frontiers of the empire until the very end of the 390s, two full decades after the disaster at Adrianople. Even then, it is another three decades before there is evidence for a Hunnic state, or even far-reaching Hunnic hegemony, in the barbarian lands near the empire where the Greuthungi and Tervingi had once held sway.

These facts suggest that, however much Ammianus may have envisaged Hunnic wolves snapping at the heels of the fleeing Goths, the process was altogether more gradual, not to mention more complex. The time frame of these events is unclear from Ammianus, and wholly beyond reconstruction from other sources, despite the best efforts of scholars. A reasonable guess might place the early confrontations between the Huns and Alans, and then between the Huns, Alans and Greuthungi, as far back as the 350s, but that can be no more than speculation. The only certainty is that the disruptions along the Don river and north of the Sea of Azov had not yet been felt along the lower Danube when Valens made his treaty with Athanaric in 369. As we have seen, the persecution in which Saba was martyred was a response to the campaigns of Valens and Saba's *Passion* gives no hint at all of traumatic upheavals to the east. Even though that may be no more than a reflection of the hagiographic genre and its constraints, nothing else in the evidence for Valens' campaigns shows the slightest awareness of trouble beyond Athanaric's realm. Thus when all is said and done, our only firm chronological indicator is the arrival of a large number of Tervingi on the banks of the Danube in spring 376.

Tervingian Petition and Imperial Response

Early in the year, before the start of the campaigning season, masses of Tervingi occupied the northern bank of the river, begging for admission into the empire.[6] They offered to abide peacefully inside the imperial frontiers and to furnish auxiliaries for the Roman army if required to do so.[7] These Tervingi were divided into many different groups, without any overall leadership. The one leader who might have claimed some sort of supremacy, Athanaric himself, was certainly not among them, fearing that the breach between him and Valens was too great for him ever to be admitted to the empire. We hear of two Tervingian chieftains, Alavivus and Fritigern, in the context of the Danube crossing, and it is clear from later events that they led not all the Tervingi, but rather the most significant of several independent bands. Although Alavivus led the negotiations with the empire, Fritigern was perhaps the more powerful of the two chieftains. He was probably better known to the empire, if Socrates' story of his conversion to Christianity in the earlier 370s is correct, and he was certainly the more competent general, for by 377 he was in overall command of the Goths' military operations.[8] As to Alavivus, we can reject outright speculation that he was the father of the later general Alaric, a theory based on nothing more than the alliteration of their names.

Negotiations over terms of entry must have taken quite some time, certainly several months, given that messengers and ambassadors had to travel more than a thousand kilometres to Antioch in Syria before returning to Thrace with the imperial decision. Even if the senior negotiators moved very fast indeed, as a letter of Basil of Caesarea implies, agreements could not have been reached before high summer.[9] How order was maintained in the interim, we do not know, nor how the massed Tervingi were kept supplied with the necessities of life. But since we have no evidence for any disturbances during the ongoing negotiations, we must postulate a firm hand among the Goths, and an assumption on both sides that everyone involved was negotiating in good faith. In other words, the Tervingian leaders must have felt it likely that their petition would meet with success – success which was, to a degree, dependent upon their good behaviour.

From Valens' point of view, the Tervingian offer was both opportune and welcome – every source tells us as much, and there is no reason to disbelieve that evidence or maintain that the Gothic entry to the empire was permitted only because it could not be repelled. The emperor was in the midst of preparing a substantial war against Persia, made necessary by complicated manoeuvres over who should control the kingdoms of Armenia and Iberia. Persian wars were always costly and sufficient manpower could be hard to come by. If the Gothic petitioners were indeed allowed into the empire, that would fulfill the promises that the Valens' orator Themistius had made in 369 at the end of the last Gothic war.[10] In that speech, as we saw in the last chapter, Themistius had been forced to put a good face on a clearly compromised peace, arguing for public consumption that the empire benefited more from sparing its enemies and keeping them alive as potential soldiers than it did from their destruction. What was at the time an argument of necessity, and a weak one at that, could now be made into happy reality for all concerned. The Tervingi could be admitted as humble suppliants, and then formed up into units to be dispersed to the eastern frontier. Given that, it is no wonder that Valens seized the chance which fate had offered him, giving orders that the Tervingi should be allowed to cross the river, fed for a time, and thereafter offered lands to farm; the Goths, for their part, probably gave hostages to the imperial government to guarantee an orderly crossing and settlement.

THE CROSSING OF THE DANUBE

It took several days and nights to transport all the Goths across the river, and Ammianus gives the impression of people coming over in their thousands.[11] Where exactly the transfer took place is unclear, though Durostorum, on a straight road line south to Marcianople, seems the likeliest point. Numbers are likewise not to be had. Eunapius speaks of 200,000 Goths, but few have taken seriously a figure that high. Although it has recently been defended as plausible in light of the constant losses which the Goths suffered in the course of the next six years – to have lost so many, there must have been masses of them to start with – that position gives too little weight to significant re-enforcements which the band received in those same years. Questions of manpower in the ancient world never have clear answers, and the best we can say here is that the scale of later fighting implies that the Goths admitted to the empire numbered at least in the tens of thousands, and perhaps considerably more than that.

If Alavivus and Fritigern were the first to be received, there were other Gothic commanders as well. They came voluntarily, not in response to military defeat by the emperor, which may explain their relative strength. Certainly, few of them were disarmed. Standard imperial practice was to disarm barbarians before they were admitted to the empire, and only then to re-arm them out of imperial arsenals at times and places where they could not pose a threat. In this case, however, whether through corruption, neglect, or the sheer scale of the enterprise, many of the Goths retained the weapons they normally carried, despite the clear intention of the emperor that they be disarmed in the usual fashion.[12] When this oversight was combined with appalling abuse, the situation became volatile indeed. The officials put in charge of the crossing were Lupicinus and Maximus, the first a *comes rei militaris*, the second the *dux* of either Moesia or Scythia. For Ammianus they were *homines maculosi*, 'men of tarnished repute', but that seems like the judgement of hindsight, perhaps even the verdict of a later imperial inquiry into what had gone wrong in the lead-up to Adrianople.[13] Imperial officials were expected to profit from the offices they held, and we should not assume that the exploitation of the Goths by Lupicinus and his officials was in excess of the late Roman norm. Nor should we discount the possibility that limiting the Goths' food supply was a deliberate way of controlling what was, after all, a large and potentially dangerous body of barbarians on imperial soil. By modern standards, however, the abuse was shocking. The food that ought to have been allocated to the Goths was diverted by the generals for sales that would line their own pockets. In its stead, the Goths were offered dogmeat at the price of one dog for one Gothic child enslaved. According to Ammianus, even the children of Gothic nobles could be rounded up and sold on to slavers.[14]

ALATHEUS AND SAPHRAX

While this trouble was brewing, the Greuthungi of Alatheus and Saphrax – those Gothic *duces* who had taken custody of the child-king Videric – also arrived at the Danube, seeking entry into the empire. As Alavivus had done some months before, these two generals now sent envoys to Valens offering terms and asking for succour. Somewhere in the same vicinity, old Athanaric too had arrived, though it is not clear what finally drove him to seek refuge in the empire. We do not know why, but the request of Alatheus and Saphrax was refused. Some have argued that the emperor began to fear the consequences of letting in too many Goths at once, or that the Tervingi already inside the empire had become so restive that additional newcomers would impose too heavy a burden on an already overwhelmed officialdom. Perhaps, though, the treatment of the Greuthungi was simply a very public demonstration of the imperial power over barbarians: after all, the gesture proclaimed that the decision of whether or not to admit different Gothic groups was entirely in the hands of the emperor, who could pick and choose with total inscrutability. That, at least, was the lesson Athanaric learned: seeing the Greuthungian request rejected, he gave up on any prospect of accommodation and retreated to 'Caucalanda', perhaps the

Transylvanian Alps, where he was to remain with his followers for half a decade. But if the deliberate arbitrariness of the imperial position was meant to intimidate the Greuthungi and cool their ardour, it did not do so. Instead, Alatheus and Saphrax bided their time.[15]

The Tervingi, for their part, were understandably dissatisfied, and Lupicinus began to fear unrest. He decided that the time had come to move them, and the coming of spring 377 made possible their dispersal out of winter quarters near the Danube. As Lupicinus and his officials began to organize the relocation of their charges, river patrols were neglected and the Greuthungi of Alatheus and Saphrax saw an opportunity to take for themselves what imperial orders had denied them. They crossed the river in makeshift boats and pitched camp at a great distance from where the Tervingi of Fritigern were being formed up for relocation at Marcianople (now Devnja in Bulgaria).[16] That substantial city, founded by Trajan during the Dacian wars, lay nearly 100 kilometres south of the Danube and was located at the junction of the east-west road to Nicopolis-ad-Istrum with the north-south road that led around the eastern edge of the Haemus mountains and down into open and populous Thrace. It was the ideal place from which to organize a major venture of this sort, and thus served as the headquarters of Lupicinus. At Marcianople, however, the disastrous train of events already underway became unstoppable.

A Treacherous Banquet

Lupicinus invited Fritigern and Alavivus to be entertained as his guests at Marcianople.[17] This was a perfectly normal gesture, for local commanders customarily invited officers in transit through their region to dine with them. If, as we must assume, Fritigern and Alavivus were being treated as the de facto commanders of Gothic units destined for inscription into the Roman army, then their reception and entertainment by Lupicinus makes perfect sense. At the same time, however, banquets were one of the usual venues for treachery in the Roman world. It was at banquets that usurpations were plotted and often set in motion, and it was at banquets that prominent barbarian hostages might be seized and spirited off to captivity.[18] Themselves quite innocent of treachery, Fritigern and Alavivus walked into a trap at Marcianople.

The Gothic leaders took up temporary residence within the city together with a small group of attendants, but Lupicinus kept their main following at a good distance from the town, interposing Roman troops between the Goths and the city walls. Before too long, confused brawling broke out between these two groups, prompted by the Romans' steadfast refusal to allow Goths into the city to purchase supplies, and perhaps by the continued attentions of slave traders. In the riot, a number of Roman soldiers were killed and robbed by the frustrated Goths. News of this reached Lupicinus while he and his guests were taking their leisure and deep in their cups. Clearing his head and seeking to forestall a full-blown revolt, Lupicinus ordered the resident bodyguard of Alavivus and Fritigern to be executed. Though the order was carried out in secret, rumour of it spread rapidly, and the Goths outside the city prepared to storm the walls. Fritigern, conscious of his own danger, convinced Lupicinus that the only way to avert catastrophe was to demonstrate to his followers that he, at least, was still alive. Lupicinus immediately grasped the wisdom of this counsel. Fritigern and those of his attendants who were still living went out to their followers and were greeted rapturously; Alavivus, by contrast, is never heard from again, perhaps killed or retained as a hostage, perhaps even betrayed by Fritigern as a dangerous rival.

THE GOTHIC REBELLION

Then, however, rather than attempt to retrieve the situation and carry on with his reception into the empire as planned, Fritigern made a momentous decision. In the face of constant harassment and sudden betrayal, he would reject the terms under which he had been received into the empire, lead his followers away from Marcianople and into open revolt. He and his Tervingi therefore marched out into the province of Scythia, and as news of Lupicinus' treachery spread, all of the Goths who had crossed the Danube the year before joined Fritigern. Why did things go so very badly wrong at Marcianople? Modern scholars, influenced by the black colours in which Ammianus paints Lupicinus, tend to assume that he plotted treachery from the beginning. That seems unlikely given the normal habits of Roman officialdom. Exploiting the perquisites of office to get rich was one thing, deliberately provoking a rebellion another thing altogether. If Fritigern's Goths were already destined for a secure place in the Roman army, as other Goths in Thrace certainly were at precisely this time, then Lupicinus had nothing to gain from eliminating Gothic commanders who had up to that point kept their following obedient and quiescent. Again, the banqueting at Marcianople, and indeed the separation of commanders and attendants from the main body of troops, was perfectly normal – it is exactly paralleled twenty years before, when the caesar Julian entertained his high commanders at Paris while their units were encamped well away from the city itself. Although Lupicinus must have seen that he had a chance of entrapping the Gothic leaders at Marcianople, it seems most unlikely that he actually planned to do so from the beginning. On the contrary, when riotous skirmishing flared up between Gothic and Roman troop, Lupicinus panicked. That panic, in turn, convinced Fritigern that his only safety lay in rebellion.

Retreating from Marcianople, Fritigern and his followers were pursued by Lupicinus and the army stationed there. Fourteen kilometres from the city, the two forces clashed and Lupicinus' army went down to bloody defeat. The whole of its junior officer corps died on the field, the unit standards were lost, and Lupicinus himself only survived by escaping into Marcianople and shutting up the city behind him. Fritigern's Goths equipped themselves with the weapons and armour of their fallen enemies and went on the offensive, raiding nearby regions, and then ranging further afield, as far south as Adrianople, about 320 kilometres to the south. We can be fairly certain that the rebellion would have been halted in its tracks had Lupicinus been victorious. Success, however, breeds confidence and Fritigern and his followers, tormented by Roman exploitation for long enough, were now in no mood to see reason. To their standards flocked not just the other Goths who had been admitted into the empire, but also the dissatisfied and oppressed of the provinces – slaves, some of whom were Gothic, miners, and prisoners of all stripes. These, in turn, made rebellion easier, for they knew their way around the provinces, knew the roads and imperial establishments, and thus made the task of supplying the rebels far less complicated than it would otherwise have been.[19]

THE REBELLION SPREADS

Gothic units in the Thracian army soon joined Fritigern as well. Two commanders named Sueridus and Colias, in winter quarters at Adrianople with their units, had observed with total unconcern the travails of the Tervingi admitted in 376. Nor did the revolt of Fritigern at Marcianople interest them. The fact that Sueridus and Colias demonstrably lacked any special feeling for fellow Goths is a salutary reminder that only extraordinary pressure of circumstances could turn different groups of Goths into 'the Goths'. In this case, that pressure came from the managerial incompetence of local officials at Adrianople. Early in 377, Sueridus and Colias received their marching orders, detailing them to the eastern front where they were needed for Valens' Persian campaign. When they asked the local authorities in Adrianople for money to equip their units with food for the journey, they were refused by the head of the local city council, the *curia*. Ammianus tells us that the councillor was angry with the followers of Sueridus and Colias for the damage they had done to his suburban property. Now it is true that the quartering of a Roman army – any Roman army, regardless of who composed it – was a severe burden on townsfolk, but the magistrate was not acting solely out of anger. While cities were obliged to house and feed Roman units quartered on them, the legal obligation of the *curia* to give troops supplies for a march was by no means clear. Indeed, on most readings of late Roman practice, imperial officials should have taken charge of equipping Sueridus and Colias' troops for their journey, without involving the *curia* of Adrianople at all.

The *curia* armed and brought out the staff of the local imperial arms factory – the *fabricenses* – and with that force at their back ordered Sueridus and Colias to be on their way at once. Even if the legal right was on their side, for the *curia* to have refused the generals' request with such brusqueness was political stupidity of the highest order. Sueridus and Colias were genuinely shocked by the unexpectedly heavy-handed treatment and made no move to go. At that point, no doubt egged on by their magistrates, the townsfolk and *fabricenses* began to harass the soldiers, pelting them with makeshift missiles and attempting to drive them off by force. Thus provoked, the soldiers of Sueridus and Colias fought back and, as usually happened when imperial troops were turned loose on civilians, massacred whomever they got their hands on. That done, and presumably well armed with the stores from the imperial *fabrica*, they marched their followers off to join Fritigern.[20]

As this one example shows, the Gothic rebellion in Thrace was not a single, planned affair, still less a barbarian migration. It was, on the contrary, a series of local revolts that in time converged into a mass uprising which threatened not just those regions in which the rebels were active, but the security of the Danubian provinces as a whole. There is no point in tracing in detail every skirmish mentioned in our sources.[21] They are too similar and we know too little about how they were connected to one another. However, one vital point is abundantly clear: the Goths under the overall command of Fritigern transformed themselves into a potent fighting force in a very short space of time. Equipped with Roman arms and armour, they also constructed a substantial supply train which allowed them to carry with them foodstuffs and other necessities gathered from the well-stocked regions through which they passed. This large force was made up of Goths from many different backgrounds, as well as all sorts of provincial malcontents. It was no longer the group of Tervingi that Fritigern and Alavivus had led across the Danube the year before, and Ammianus recognizes this fact by ceasing to speak of Tervingi and beginning to speak generically of *Gothi*, 'Goths'. These *Gothi* roamed more or less at will in the land between the Haemus mountain chain and the Danube during 377 and most of 378. The rationale behind these movements is totally obscure, but it is striking that neither the Roman nor the Gothic side seem to have made any effort to negotiate throughout this period of more than a year. It is possible that Valens is to blame. If the Roman generals on the spot acted indecisively, it may be that they had received no guidance from an imperial court more interested in Persian affairs. The Goths, after all, were barbarians, and northern barbarians had always taken second place to Persia. In those circumstances, lacking direction from above and not wanting to take the wrong decision with so unpredictable an emperor as Valens, Rome's Balkan commanders can hardly be faulted for trying to contain the Gothic threat rather than suppress it.

The Imperial Response

At some point in 377, however, Valens became convinced of the seriousness of the problem. He determined to patch up a truce with the Persians over Armenia, sending his longest-serving general, Victor, to negotiate it.[22] In preparation for his own eventual advance, he sent the generals Profuturus and Traianus to keep the Goths in Thrace under control. Meanwhile, Valens' nephew Gratian likewise realized the gravity of the situation. He despatched two good generals, Frigeridus and the *comes domesticorum* Richomeres, to support the eastern troops, but also to ensure that the trouble was contained in Thrace and Moesia and did not spread westwards into Pannonia and the Latin provinces.[23] Gratian's intervention demonstrates how worrisome the Gothic revolt had become during the course of 377. Western generals did not, as a rule, intervene in eastern affairs, nor junior emperors in those of their seniors, lest it look too much like provocation. As recently as 366, Valentinian had declined to help Valens face down the usurpation of Procopius, a far more direct threat to dynastic control than the Goths could hope to be. Only the prospect of chaos along the whole Danube frontier can have prompted Gratian's intervention.

As it happened, Frigeridus fell ill and returned to the West for a time, leaving Richomeres to lead the western troops to their rendezvous with Valens' generals Profuturus and Traianus. In late summer 377, they brought the Goths to battle near a site called Ad Salices ('the Willows'). The precise location of this site remains unknown, though it probably lay somewhere between the coastal town of Tomi and the opening out of the Danube delta into its many channels, very near the imperial frontier rather than in the immediate vicinity of Marcianople. The battle of Ad Salices that followed was a major one, but a draw, for the Goths were secure within their well-guarded wagon train and could retreat into it as necessary. The Roman forces seem to have been smaller than the Gothic, and Profuturus himself fell in battle, but superior drill and training saved the army from total destruction. Having suffered too many losses to continue the assault, the Roman troops retreated south again, back to Marcianople, where the revolt had first begun in earnest.[24] At roughly the same time, Frigeridus returned to the East, fortified Beroe, and inflicted a major defeat on another Gothic noble, Farnobius, who had been raiding through Thrace. Frigeridus sent the survivors of the slaughter back to Italy, where they were settled as farmers, a useful reminder that barbarian settlement within the empire could work perfectly well when managed with a minimum of care.[25]

Despite Ad Salices, Richomeres and the other generals had inflicted serious damage on Fritigern's Goths. Many of them withdrew into the safety of the Haemus mountains for the winter of 377–378. Richomeres went back to Gaul as autumn fell, planning to collect a larger force for the following year's campaigning season. Valens, for his part, re-enforced his troops in Thrace with a more senior commander, the *magister equitum* Saturninus. He, with Traianus as his lieutenant, block-aded the Goths in the Haemus passes and deprived them of food. He hoped that by reducing them to desperate hunger and then removing the guards from the passes he could lure them into the open country and destroy them in pitched battle. The plan failed. Rather than moving north and standing to battle in the plains between the Haemus and the Danube, the Goths allied themselves with some unspecified Huns and Alans, and made their way south into Thrace. In that country's wide open spaces, with their excellent roads, Fritigern could move freely, lay-ing waste great stretches of land between the Haemus, the Rhodope, and the shores of the Hellespont and of the Bosporus near Constantinople.[26] So badly ravaged were the provinces of Moesia and Scythia that the emperor officially lowered their tax burden in 377.[27] Indeed, by early 378, much of Thrace itself was inaccessible to the outside world: Basil of Caesarea wrote to an exiled fellow-churchman, Eusebius of Samosata, then resident in Thrace, commenting on the unprecedented difficulty of communication and expressing surprise that Eusebius had managed to survive there at all.[28]

Valens Prepares for War

Valens' generals Saturninus and Traianus may have had only limited success, but Gratian's commanders managed to quarantine the revolt.

By early 378, Frigeridus had fortified the Succi pass, the vital conduit between Thrace and the western Balkans.[29] Thereafter, Fritigern's
Goths were effectively confined to Thrace. In that same year, not just
Richomeres but Gratian himself led a large portion of the western army
into the eastern empire to assist his uncle. He had wanted to come
sooner, but some Alamanni in the Rhineland detained him: hearing of
the troubles in Thrace and Gratian's plans to assist in their suppression,
they seized a chance to raid into the western provinces.[30] Only in 378
could Gratian spare his main army for the Gothic war. By then, Valens
had settled eastern affairs to the point where he felt able to march to
Thrace. He arrived in Constantinople in spring 378, staying there for
perhaps twelve days and facing down riots among a discontented populace, one no doubt frightened at the continuing Gothic presence on
their doorstep.[31] Valens' first move was to reorganize his officer corps,
dissatisfied with their conduct up to this point, and not without good
reason. In place of Traianus – whom Valens personally blamed for
failing to stop the Goths at Ad Salices – the retired western general
Sebastianus was made commander-in-chief and was perhaps given a
strike force drawn from the emperor's own seasoned palatine troops.[32]
Certainly, he quickly won a couple of surprise victories over Gothic
raiding parties.[33] But this welcome success brought an unexpected side
effect: fearing lest his various followers be picked off piecemeal, Fritigern ordered them to form together and operate as a single unit. From
their rendezvous point at Kabyle, a well-watered and easily defensible
site in the plain between the Haemus and Rhodope mountain chains,
the whole of the Gothic force began to make south for Adrianople.
There Sebastianus was headquartered, sending back to Constantinople
reports of his recent successes. On 11 June, Valens left Constantinople
for what would prove to be his last journey.

THE BATTLE OF ADRIANOPLE
What actually happened on the battlefield of Adrianople is remarkably ill documented for so decisive a moment in Roman history, and
one so comprehensively discussed in contemporary writings. Unfortunately for the modern historian, contemporary interest was chiefly
concerned to explain why the disaster happened, not how it unfolded.

Ammianus, as so often, gives us our only detailed account of the battle, but his outline of events includes substantial gaps – some of his own making, some the product of a faulty manuscript tradition – so that a tactical description of the battle is impossible. Nevertheless, Ammianus' broad outline seems clear and is corroborated by other sources. In the first week of August, Valens marched his field army – between 30,000 and 40,000 men, in all likelihood – out from its staging post at Melanthias, just west of Constantinople. The emperor made for Adrianople with all haste, supposedly jealous of the successes that Sebastianus had won and wanting a share of his general's glory. Fritigern's Goths bypassed Adrianople and its substantial garrison, making instead for the road-station at Nike. There the Gothic army was observed by the imperial scouts who fanned out in advance of the emperor's main force. The intelligence they brought back was misleading, suggesting that the Gothic forces numbered only 10,000 men, much less than their real number. This news gave Valens, eager for battle and a victory he could call his own, all the excuse he needed to attack at once.[34]

Advancing to Adrianople, he fortified a camp in the suburbs of the city and impatiently awaited the arrival of his nephew's army. Perhaps on the 7th of August, the general Richomeres arrived with the western advance guard, advising Valens to wait the very short time it would take for Gratian's main force to arrive.[35] Delay, however, did not suit Valens, and he called a meeting of his high command to debate the issue. The generals themselves were deeply divided, but which generals argued for which plan is unclear: in the aftermath of the disaster, contemporaries strove to shield their favourites from blame and shift it onto others, a task made easier by the death of almost all those who had witnessed the debate. Thus Ammianus claims that Sebastianus led the group which argued for an immediate assault on the Goths, while the *magister equitum* Victor led those who argued for the delay that would guarantee victory. Eunapius, by contrast, defended Sebastianus, as is clear even from the very confused Eunapian chronology preserved by Zosimus.[36] Regardless, the council decided on the course of swift action. Valens favoured it, and his civilian officials played upon his natural jealousy, suggesting that he ought not to share with Gratian the glory of an inevitable victory.

Roman victory was, after all, expected by everyone, not least the Gothic leader Fritigern. At Adrianople, within striking distance of the imperial army, he showed himself more eager for a peaceful settlement than at any time since the very first crossing of the Danube. Perhaps he feared risking battle in the continuing absence of the Greuthungi under Alatheus and Saphrax, whom he had long since sent for. Perhaps, on the other hand, he worried that the Goths could not defeat a proper imperial field army when their victories had thus far come only against smaller, provincial commands. Be that as it may, on 8 August he sent a Christian priest and some provincials of humble status to offer terms to the emperor: he and his followers, poor exiles driven from their own lands and with no place else to go, wanted only Thrace with its crops and its lands. In exchange for that, he could offer the emperor lasting peace. Thus ran Fritigern's public message. With it came a private message for Valens himself, in which the Goth assured the emperor that he really did want peace, but that for him to enforce himself upon his followers, the emperor would have to keep his army mustered and active as a visible threat to the Goths. Valens distrusted these overtures, and at any rate wanted very much to fight a battle he was convinced he could win.[37]

Thus on the morning of the 9th, leaving his civilian court officials and his treasury safely inside the walls of Adrianople, he marched his troops northeastward out of their encampment into the rolling plain where Fritigern and his army were based. We cannot really be sure how many men either side fielded, but tens of thousands of men went into battle on that August morning. Not long before noon, the Romans spotted the Gothic camp, probably near the modern village of Muratgali. Massing on a low ridge line in front of their wagon circle, the Gothic warriors were well rested and eager for battle. Valens began to dispose his troops in line of battle, cavalry units on each wing, and the mass of his infantry in the centre. Neither side was as prepared for a pitched battle as they might have been: the left wing of the Roman army was still scattered in columns-of-march, while the Greuthungi under Alatheus and Saphrax had not yet arrived. Fritigern therefore played for time, sending envoys to beg for peace while the imperial forces roasted in the blazing sun, and choked on the fires which he had lit to punish them further. Watching as the condition of his troops deteriorated, Valens thought better of his refusal to negotiate – possibly he even decided wait for Gratian – and made ready to send higher-ranking officials to meet representatives of the Goths.[38] This was a mistake, and one cannot imagine Valentinian or Constantius II opening protracted negotiations with the enemy while their soldiers' readiness withered away in the wake of a forced march. Yet as so often happened in ancient battles, fighting began by accident, before either side was ready.

Two units of the elite *scholae palatinae*, the Scutarii under Cassio and the Sagitarii under Bacurius, probably on the right wing and near to the emperor where *scholae* were usually posted, advanced prematurely and engaged the enemy.[39] Their move disrupted the imperial line of battle, which was then disordered still further by the sudden appearance of Alatheus and Saphrax and their followers, in company with a unit of Alans. What followed was a military disaster, described by all our sources in lurid colours. The Roman left wing drove too far beyond the Gothic line and was cut off, surrounded and slaughtered. With the main infantry's left flank thus exposed, the Roman line was compressed in on itself, hampering the ability of the soldiers to fight and causing many to die from wounds inflicted by their own side. Towards late afternoon, the Roman infantry line broke and the rout began. The imperial bodyguard and the *scholae palatinae* must have been almost totally destroyed, for Valens was forced to take cover with the Mattiarii, a unit of the regular field army rather than an imperial *schola*, but seemingly one of the few Roman units to have stood its ground. Some of the generals attempted to rally the auxiliaries who had been held in reserve, but these had already melted away off the battlefield. Seeing that further attempts at rallying the disintegrating army were useless, the generals Victor, Richomeres and Saturninus fled the field. There, the butchery continued until nightfall.[40]

The fate of Valens was uncertain even at the time. Some said that towards evening he was struck by an arrow and fell dead amongst the common soldiers. Others claimed that, mortally wounded, he was carried off the field by a few loyal bodyguards and eunuchs, and hidden in a farmhouse; there, as the emperor lay dying, Goths surrounded the farmhouse and, rather than waste time breaking in, set the house ablaze and burned to death the emperor and his attendants. Only one man escaped through a window and explained that the Gothic firebrands had just deprived themselves of the glory of capturing a Roman emperor on the field of battle. Whichever story – if either of them – was true, Valens' body was never recovered.[41] With him at Adrianople fell the generals Traianus and Sebastianus, the tribune and Valens' relative Aequitius, thirty-five senior officers, and fully two-thirds of the army that had taken the field on the morning of 9 August 378.[42] As Themistius would put it five years later: 'Thrace was overrun, Illyricum was overrun, armies vanished altogether, like shadows'.[43]

THEODOSIUS AND THE GOTHS

CHAPTER SEVEN

T HE PSYCHOLOGICAL IMPACT OF ADRIANOPLE WAS IMMEDIATE. Pagans at once interpreted the defeat as punishment for the neglect of the traditional gods. In distant Lydia, the pagan rhetor Eunapius of Sardis composed what has been termed an instant history, to demonstrate that the empire had headed inexorably towards the disaster of Adrianople from the moment of Constantine's conversion. For Eunapius, it seems, the Roman empire itself had ended at Adrianople: 'Strife, when it has grown, brings forth war and murder, and the children of murder are ruin and the destruction of the human race. Precisely these things were perpetrated during Valens' reign'.[1] From a distance of longer years, and with considerably greater penetration, Ammianus made the same argument, choosing the disaster as the terminal point for his history and loading it with coded venom towards the Christians on whom he, like his hero Julian, blamed the empire's decline. No Christian response was immediately forthcoming, though Nicene Christians seem to have blamed Adrianople on divine punishment for the homoean beliefs of Valens, and Jerome ended his *Chronicle* in 378, just as Ammianus did his history. This dialogue of blame and excuse, the pagan side of which is now largely lost to us thanks to suppression by the Christian winners, went on throughout the fifth century, exacerbated by Alaric's sack of Rome. After all, how could the barbarian scourge have stung so painfully if God or the gods were not murderously displeased?

For the modern scholar, too, the battle of Adrianople is a turning point of major importance, though we seek historical rather than divine explanations. As we saw in the last chapter, the causes of the disaster lay not in any single event but in a series of human errors. The aftermath of the battle, however, represents a new phase in the history of both the Goths and the Roman empire. In this new phase, the historian's framework of analysis changes dramatically. We can sum up the core of the change quite simply: until 378, Gothic history was fundamentally shaped by experience of the Roman empire. The central fact of Gothic existence was the Roman empire looming on the other side of the frontier, and much of the political and social life of the Goths can be explained by reference to their relations with Rome. For the empire, by contrast, the Goths were one of dozens of barbarian neighbours, and by no means the most important. They were a marginal force even in the political life of the empire, and invisible to its social and institutional history. After 378, however, the Goths were a constant and central presence in the political life of the empire. Even though the material damage of Adrianople was repaired more rapidly than anyone at the time could have imagined possible, tens of thousands of Goths now lived permanently inside the Roman frontiers. In a very short time, that fact profoundly altered the way in which the imperial government dealt not just with the Goths, but with barbarian peoples more generally. Before long, imperial institutions from the army to the court changed in response to the challenges of the new situation, and the social world of many regions was profoundly altered. In many ways, the Gothic settlement in the aftermath of Adrianople laid the foundation of the new and changed world of the fifth century.

JULIUS AND THE ASIAN MASSACRE
Contemporaries found making sense of the disaster a slow and painful process, but practical responses could not wait. In the Balkans, the

immediate aftermath of Adrianople was chaos, just as one would have expected. Gratian halted at Sirmium, where he was joined by those generals who had escaped the slaughter. He went no further east. The Goths laid siege to Adrianople itself without success, then pressed on to Constantinople where they were again repulsed, in part thanks to a troop of Arab auxiliaries so bloodthirsty that they terrified even the triumphant Goths. Not until 381, three years after the battle, did most of the Balkan peninsula again become safe for Roman travellers. In the interim, to those outside the region, Thrace produced nothing but rumour. So confused was the situation that, for the latter part of 378 and much of 379, the eastern provinces had basically to operate without reference to any emperor at all. Government ticked over in the hands of those imperial officials who were in place in August 378, and they were left to make their own decisions as best they could. Most of all, they had to decide how to stop the Balkan unrest spreading into the rest of the eastern empire.

This was a real possibility, as is demonstrated by events in Asia Minor. There, and perhaps in other parts of the East, riots broke out amongst native Goths in various cities. The exact outline of the episode, and the extent of it, has always been unclear, because Ammianus and Zosimus, the latter relying on Eunapius, give very different accounts. Ammianus says that in the immediate aftermath of Adrianople, the *magister militum* of the East, Julius, forestalled the eastward spread of the Balkan troubles by systematically calling up all the Gothic soldiers from the ranks of the army and having them massacred outside the eastern cities.[2] Ammianus favoured this approach as the correct way of dealing with barbarians, but when he wrote – in the 380s – he may have been holding up the bracing harshness of Julius as a reproof of the emperor Theodosius' Gothic treaty of 382. Zosimus tells a different story. According to him, when Julius found himself unable to contact the emperor or anyone in Thrace, he instead sought the advice of the Constantinopolitan senate, which gave him the authority to act as he thought best. With that licence, he lured the Goths of Asia Minor into the cities and there had them massacred in the confines of urban streets from which they could not escape. Zosimus, moreover, suggests that these slaughtered Goths were not soldiers, but rather the teenage hostages who had been handed over to the Roman government in 376 to guarantee their parents' good behaviour. Finally, Zosimus dates the massacre not to the immediate aftermath of Adrianople, but rather to 379.[3]

Although the patent contradiction between these accounts is often resolved by accepting Ammianus over Zosimus, additional evidence suggests an alternative.[4] Two sermons of Gregory of Nyssa, the younger brother of Basil of Caesarea, mention depredations by Scythians in Asia Minor in 379.[5] This corroboration of Zosimus points the way forward: Ammianus, for polemical purposes, has telescoped a long process into a single swift move by Julius, while Zosimus preserves the longer time frame and the sense of uncertainty that followed a battle which left no one in real control of the eastern empire. What probably happened is that Julius, knowing that there were Goths in the local army units as well as any number of young Gothic hostages of very nearly military age and prone like all teenage males to violence, decided to prevent any repetition of the Thracian debacle. He began with the forts in the frontier provinces – the *castra* mentioned by Ammianus – but his actions were either meant to, or interpreted as meaning to, prefigure a systematic massacre of Goths in the eastern provinces. As word spread, those Goths who were in a position to riot did so, and were killed in large numbers across Asia Minor and Syria.

THE ACCESSION OF THEODOSIUS

That so many – presumably quite innocent – Goths should have been done away with in this fashion emphasizes as nothing else can the scale of the dangers, and also the scale of the confusion. For us, looking back dispassionately and trying to work out what happened, it is easy to forget how hopeless of repair the whole situation must have seemed. But we can only explain the failure of Gratian and his generals to coordinate a systematic response if we remember the depth of the shock that Adrianople caused. Rather than system or coordination, survivors switched to habitual, automatic responses to deal with the crisis. We have seen this already with the response of Julius and, presumably, other eastern officials as well. Most of them carried on doing what they normally did, the state continuing to function without any clear notion of what it was continuing for. Gratian's immediate reaction was a similarly conditioned response: with the Balkans in chaos and the Goths running riot, he turned not to the immediate problem, but rather to the Alamanni, a foe that was always worth fighting and against whom he had a reasonable chance of success. As we saw, some Alamanni had attacked Gaul the minute they heard that Gratian intended to march east.[6] Given Valens' catastrophic failure, Gratian must have felt it necessary to hurry back to the West lest equivalent disaster strike there.

Into this vacuum stepped Theodosius, a thirty-three-year-old Spanish aristocrat and the son of one of Valentinian I's great generals, also named Theodosius. The younger Theodosius would go on to become augustus and, as with all emperors, our sources are coloured by retrospective judgements. Just as Valens was indelibly marked by the catastrophe of Adrianople, so Theodosius was forever after associated with the defence of Nicene orthodoxy and the suppression of paganism. In the ecclesiastical histories of the fifth century, Theodosius became Theodosius the Great, a name which he still bears in the casual usage of modern historians. The appellation was bestowed more for his pliability in theological matters than for any signal achievements in public policy, but the image of greatness seeped into every other corner of his reign as well. Thus a recent biography of Theodosius is subtitled 'the empire at bay', conjuring the image of a wounded empire, turning with its last strength to savage the attackers besetting it on all sides.[7] However compelling that image might be as theatre, it is hardly in accord with the reality of an emperor who never won a major battle under his own command and who rarely campaigned at all after 381. However easy it is to let later ecclesiastical authors colour our impression of Theodosius' greatness, the difficulties of his early reign are suggested by the darkness that shrouds his accession to the purple.

Theodosius had in the early 370s stood on the verge of a prominent military career: he was *dux Moesiae*, a rather senior post for so young a man, no doubt secured for him by his father's influence. In 374, as *dux*, he had won a victory over the Sarmatians.[8] In 376, however, the elder Theodosius fell victim to the palace intrigues that followed

Valentinian's death. His eponymous son chose prudent retirement to family estates in Spain, lest he too die by the hand of an executioner. Isolated in his Spanish exile, Theodosius was abandoned by most of his former friends, a man irrevocably damaged by his father's disgrace, or so it seemed. It is thus very hard for us to imagine why Gratian should have chosen to call him out of retirement in this moment of crisis and send him to deal with the Balkan emergency. In fact, only one source – the ecclesiastical history of Theoderet of Cyrrhus – records this summons of Theodosius by Gratian, and its accuracy has correctly been impugned. Theoderet wrote his ecclesiastical history in the later fifth century, when the legend of Theodosius' greatness and orthodoxy were firmly established as true. Part of his story of Theodosius' accession is palpably fictionalized.[9] Far more significant is the silence of nearly contemporary sources, particularly the orators Themistius and Pacatus, on the route by which Theodosius climbed to power. Had that path been clean and simple, both panegyrists – and particularly the propagandizing Themistius – would have trumpeted its details in full. Instead, they veil in a deep silence the relationship of Gratian and Theodosius in the immediate aftermath of Adrianople. A more plausible scenario, which makes good sense in light of the period's confusion, has recently been suggested.[10] Already in 378, when the extent of the Balkan violence and Gratian's plan to march east were generally known, Theodosius and his remaining friends at court spotted an ideal opportunity to engineer his return to favour. Making much of his Balkan experience and his now-distant success as *dux Moesiae*, they secured his reappointment to that post either shortly before or immediately after Adrianople. Theodosius probably campaigned in the eastern Balkans during late 378, but achieved nothing decisive before his proclamation as augustus on 19 January 379.[11]

Although that was only four months after Adrianople, it would take another two years before Theodosius gained control of the Balkans. Why the reconquest took so long is a matter of controversy, but it might be explained if Theodosius' proclamation had not initially been intended. In fact, there are some grounds for thinking that his accession was the result of a quiet coup by the surviving Illyrian generals who wanted nothing to do with the regime of Gratian. Earlier successes of Theodosius could provide the necessary excuse, and might be magnified in the propaganda if that would make the point. Theodosius duly became augustus, but Gratian need neither have appreciated the move nor had anything at all to do with it. Rather than brand Theodosius a usurper and thereby worsen further the crisis in the eastern provinces, he decided to acquiesce. He received Theodosius' imperial portrait with full respect and began to issue laws in their joint names. But he had no great cause to welcome his new colleague and never did much to help him. Instead, he consigned the Balkans to Theodosius as an insoluble mess, happy enough if the burden of inevitable failure fell squarely on the new emperor's shoulders. The evident absence of western aid certainly helps account for the slowness with which Theodosius brought the Balkans back under imperial control.[12]

THEODOSIUS' GOTHIC CAMPAIGNS

In the year and a half that followed his imperial accession, Theodosius made his base at Thessalonica. He did not enter Constantinople, the city he would transform from an occasional imperial residence into the capital of the Roman East, until November 380, nearly two years after his appointment as augustus. That in itself tells us a great deal about the continuing Gothic problem: Thessalonica had good access to the Balkan interior, but could if necessary be supplied entirely by sea. The city was therefore almost impervious to disturbances inland, and could serve as an imperial residence even when the interior was completely occupied by the Goths. The eastern army had been shattered by Adrianople. Sixteen whole units were wiped out without a trace and never reconstituted. One of Theodosius' first concerns was therefore to provide himself with troops. Many of the army units known from the *Notitia Dignitatum*, a thorough but chronologically composite listing of the imperial bureaucracy that describes the eastern army as it existed in mid-394, were first raised by Theodosius between 379 and 380. Several imperial laws from the same years address recruiting problems, and the Syrian rhetor Libanius describes the calling up of farmers.[13] Zosimus tells us that some of the new recruits were hired in from across the

Danube, although they soon proved every bit as ineffectual as those raised locally.[14] The new emperor also needed victories. In the decade after Adrianople, we have evidence for nearly half as many victory celebrations as are attested in the seven previous decades combined.[15] That is a formidable statistic. It illustrates how desperately Theodosius needed to be seen to be dealing with the Gothic problem.

Our only real source for reconstructing the campaigns of 379–382 is the summary of Eunapius that survives in Zosimus' *New History*. We have referred to Zosimus on more than one occasion in the course of our narrative, but his defects are particularly apparent here, where the abridgement of Eunapius is severe and nonetheless still includes confusing doublets.[16] So far as we can tell, in 379, Theodosius and his generals concentrated on clearing Thrace itself and eliminating the immediate threat to Constantinople and Adrianople. The general Modares, himself a Goth in imperial service, won some sort of victory in Thrace before the end of the campaigning season, though its significance may not have been too great.[17] By 380, the different Gothic groups had been driven westwards into Illyricum, but whether that constituted an improvement for anyone but the inhabitants of Thrace is debateable.[18] In that same year, Theodosius suffered a severe setback. Some Goths, perhaps led by Fritigern, marched into Macedonia and confronted the emperor at the head of his new recruits. These promptly failed in their first combat, the barbarians amongst them going over to the victorious enemy, the others deserting *en masse* – no surprise, then, that Theodosius soon had to issue laws on desertion.[19] With this signal success, the Goths were able to impose tribute on the cities of Macedonia and Thessaly, which is to say northern Greece and the southwestern Balkans. A failed Gothic attack on Pannonia even brought Gratian back east in the summer of 380, when we find him at Sirmium, making no effort at all to confer with Theodosius. By the end of the year, he had returned to Gaul, and Theodosius felt able to make his way to Constantinople for the first time in his reign.[20] In 381, Gratian's generals Bauto and Arbogast drove the Goths away from the frontiers of the West and back into Thrace.[21] It must by now have been obvious to Theodosius that his western colleague, far from helping solve the Gothic problem, would do no more than bar the western provinces to the Goths while leaving the eastern Balkans to suffer.

THE PEACE OF 382

Theodosius thus bowed to the inevitable. Seeing no point in throwing still more troops into what was clearly a losing battle, he opened peace negotiations that were finally concluded on 3 October 382.[22] The fact that this peace might well have seemed disappointing, especially after four years of confidently predicted triumphs, was anticipated by such mouthpieces of the imperial court as Themistius. Already in 382, Themistius was arguing that it was better to fill Thrace with Gothic farmers than with Gothic dead, and that because of the peace, the Goths themselves gained so much that they could celebrate a victory won over themselves.[23] He hammered the same point at inordinate length a year later in his thirty-fourth oration: this masterpiece of political spin rewrites the history of the previous half-decade in order to absolve Theodosius of any imputations of incompetence in failing to wipe the Goths out altogether.

Despite Themistius' grandiloquence, actual evidence for the treaty is minimal. Synesius claims that the Goths were given lands, Themistius echoes the classic topos of swords being beaten into ploughshares and locates his Gothic ploughmen in Thrace, Pacatus claims that the Goths became farmers.[24] This sort of rhetoric was routine in describing any agreement with barbarians, and permits no conjecture as to the mechanisms or location of the settlement. Perhaps the Goths paid, or were meant to pay, taxes: Themistius is studiedly ambiguous.[25] Perhaps the Goths continued to live by their tribal customs: Synesius tells us as much twenty years later, but embedded in a hysterical diatribe against the imperial employment of barbarians, his assertion proves next to nothing.[26] Theodosius surely welcomed the disappearance of the whole generation of Gothic leaders that had won the battle of Adrianople: after 380, neither Fritigern, nor Alatheus and Saphrax, nor Videric are ever heard from again. But that does not imply a deliberate policy to sideline or eliminate them, a task that was, moreover, beyond imperial abilities. All of which is to say that – unfortunately for the modern historian in search of answers and just as with Constantine's treaty of 332 – we cannot work backwards from later events and assume that what did happen was intended to happen in 382. What little we know for certain can be summed up very simply: in 382, the Goths who had terrorized the Balkans since Adrianople ceased to do so, while Roman contemporaries all agreed that the Gothic threat was over.

In the decade that followed, many Goths were called up into regular units of the eastern field army.[27] Others served as auxiliaries in the campaigns that Theodosius led against the western usurpers Magnus Maximus (r. 383–388) and Eugenius (r. 392–394).[28] Many, though not necessarily all, of these Goths were survivors of the group that had won the towering victory at Adrianople and then led Theodosius on a merry chase round the Balkans for nearly three years. For the most part, however, we have little solid evidence for any of the Goths inside the empire until the immediate aftermath of the Eugenius campaign and Theodosius' premature and entirely unexpected death in January 395. Beginning in that year, the young Gothic leader Alaric raised a rebellion that lasted for fifteen years and culminated in the sack of Rome, with which our story began.

ALARIC AND THE
SACK OF ROME

CHAPTER EIGHT

I
N THE DECADES THAT FOLLOWED THEODOSIUS' TREATY OF 382, there is a great deal of evidence for Goths in and around the empire, but remarkably little for those Goths who actually concluded their peace with Theodosius. Indeed, it is very possible that the larger number of these "treaty-Goths" settled down to a life on the land in the Balkan provinces and were never heard from again. Apart from them, however, we still find Ulfila's Goths, the so-called *Gothi minores*, in the Roman province of Scythia. Elsewhere, a Gothic population seems to have lived in Asia Minor, where a serious rebellion broke out in the year 399 under a commander named Tribigild, who probably made use of Goths who had survived the massacres and police actions of 378–379. Beyond the frontier, many Gothic residents remained, even though the upheavals that had led to the Danube crossing seem to have continued. We do not yet have any evidence for Huns in the immediate vicinity of the Roman frontier – indeed, we first meet a Danubian Hun in 400, when a chieftain named Uldin had some dealings with the government in Constantinople.

Instead of direct Hunnic involvement along the Danube, we see during the 380s and 390s a continuation of the political realignments that had started in 376. Although the details of these changes are almost totally invisible to us until the disintegration of the Hunnic empire in the 450s, several different Gothic groups emerge at that point from the shadow of Hunnic hegemony. This suggests that in the decades between 376 and the mid fifth century, many Gothic leaders – men like the *megistanes* whom we met in the *Passion of St. Saba* – retained the authority they had possessed before 376, while others arose to take the place of those who had departed for the empire. Most Sântana-de-Mureş/Černjachov sites west of the Prut river continue without disruption in the last quarter of the fourth and the first quarter of the fifth century, and it is not until after 410 that we begin to see real changes to the material culture of the region.[1] Thus the literary and the archaeological evidence – limited as they are – both suggest that, despite the convulsions of the 370s, a substantial Gothic population survived beyond the old *ripa Gothica*. Indeed, after the events of 376, we have very limited evidence for further Gothic crossings into the empire: only two are on record in the Greek and Roman sources.

The first of them might cause some surprise to readers of the last two chapters, concerning as it does the old Tervingian *iudex* Athanaric. It would appear that, by 380, Athanaric's attempt at going it alone had failed. Deserted even by those who had earlier preferred him to Alavivus and Fritigern, he finally had to make his peace with the empire. The fact that Valens was dead no doubt made the inherent humiliation of this reversal easier to bear, and Theodosius did his best to make the transition painless. The emperor welcomed Athanaric to Constantinople on 14 January 381 with great honours and gave him a lavish state funeral when he died of natural causes soon afterwards.[2] In the midst of a still ongoing Balkan war, the peaceful reception of a noble Goth like Athanaric must have had significant propaganda value for Theodosius, even if the old man had arrived with virtually no following and had no practical influence on the Goths already inside the empire. In fact, it was Athanaric's very harmlessness that made him ideal for Theodosius' needs, and more dangerous Gothic outsiders were not made welcome in the same way. We discover this in the case of our second documented Danube crossing, in 386, when Theodosius celebrated a triumph over some Greuthungi whose request for admission to the empire he accepted, before having them treacherously slaughtered as they made their way across the frontier.[3] This episode illustrates both how central the maintenance of peace in the Balkans had become to Theodosian policy, and also how fluid the political life of the *barbaricum* remained if, as late as 386, a group of Greuthungi without any known connection to the Gothic settlers of 382, felt that settlement inside the empire was preferable to life beyond its frontiers.

GOTHIC OFFICERS IN THE ROMAN ARMY

The treaty of 382 marked the beginning of a new phase in the relationships between Goths and empire in more than one way: beginning in the 380s, we find a remarkable number of Goths, aristocrats 'who were paramount in reputation and nobility' as Eunapius puts it, pursuing careers as officers in the imperial army.[4] There was, to be sure, nothing particularly noteworthy about Goths serving in the Roman military. Whether as the result of treaty terms or simply as mercenaries recruited *ad hoc*, they had done so for many years. On the other hand, the rank of the Goths we now start to find in imperial service is striking. In the middle years of the fourth century, Frankish and Alamannic princes regularly commanded elite regiments of the imperial army, but Gothic officers were more or less totally unknown. The Danube crossing and the subsequent Balkan wars seem to have changed all that.

The fighting and the very fact of physical settlement in the empire disrupted the social hierarchies that had existed amongst Gothic elites back home in the *barbaricum*. Many Gothic noblemen will have quite suddenly found themselves lacking the resources and power that they had enjoyed before 376, and so they turned to Roman careers as the best alternative available. Among attested Gothic officers, we have already met Modares, one of the generals who helped pacify the Balkans for Theodosius in 381 and 382 and also the recipient of a very complimentary letter from bishop Gregory of Nazianzus.[5] Other such generals include Fravitta and Eriulf. The rivalry between these two Gothic nobles stretched back to before their entering imperial service and was only resolved when Fravitta killed Eriulf at a drunken banquet hosted by

Theodosius himself.[6] Thereafter, Fravitta had a distinguished career in the eastern army, marrying a Roman bride and actually putting down a mutiny led by another Gothic general, Gainas. That mutiny, as we shall see, brought down several eastern governments and left thousands of Goths dead in rioting which Gainas himself did not long survive. All of these men illustrate the sudden influx of skillful and important Gothic leaders into the Roman imperial hierarchy, and their rapid assimilation into roles which their Frankish and Alamannic peers had played for many decades already. But a far more significant figure than any of these generals was Alaric, whose career climaxed with the notorious sack of Rome.

THE IMPORTANCE OF ALARIC

Alaric is one of the most important figures in the whole history of the later Roman empire. His career was entirely unprecedented. Like the many Gothic generals just named, Alaric had no power base outside the empire, no kingdom from which he could manage his relationship with the emperor and into which he could retreat if his position became unsustainable. Yet unlike them, Alaric did not follow the well-established path up the career ladder of the army, becoming part of the imperial elite by the only route open to a barbarian. He became a Roman general, but never held a regular military command. He may have been a Gothic king, but he never found a kingdom. In other circumstances, he might have been a splendid anomaly, like Attila the Hun a generation later, a man whose historical impact was so completely the product of his singular personality as to defy parallel or sequel. Instead, Alaric's career was a watershed in the history of the empire, inadvertently forging an entirely new model for a barbarian leader inside the imperial frontiers: Alaric proved that it was possible to dwell inside the empire and play a commanding role in imperial politics, without being absorbed into the structures of imperial government. Unlike anyone before him, Alaric was able to maintain a body of supporters inside the empire whose only connection to the empire came through him. That power-base permitted him to act in ways that no one inside the imperial hierarchy could.

In the process of pursuing his own personal interests, Alaric also re-created the Goths, and what it meant to be a Goth. Although, as we have just seen, there were any number of other Gothic leaders in the army, and large Gothic populations both inside and on the fringes of the empire, Alaric and his followers soon became 'the Goths' as far as contemporaries were concerned. In fact, Alaric's following came to be identified as the direct successor of those Goths who had crossed the Danube in 376; in some sense, they were thought to be the same Goths.[7] Strictly speaking, this identification is simply incorrect: the Gothic groups who had crossed the Danube no longer existed, and the followers of Alaric who sacked Rome were made up not just of Balkan Goths but those from many other places as well. Yet over time the identification of Alaric's followers as 'the Goths' took on a reality all its own. Fifteen years of his leadership gave Alaric's following a sense of community that survived his own death. First under his brother-in-law Athaulf, then under a series of other leaders, Alaric's Goths remained together inside the empire, going on to settle in Gaul. There, in the province of Aquitaine, they put down roots and created the first autonomous barbarian kingdom inside the frontiers of the Roman empire.

THE USURPATION OF MAGNUS MAXIMUS AND PROBLEMS IN THE BALKANS

Alaric came to prominence in 395, but we know that he was already active a few years earlier, in the aftermath of Theodosius' first campaign against a western usurper. Theodosius, as we saw in the last chapter, became emperor in 379, possibly without the approval of Gratian. He was given control of the Balkans in order to end the Gothic wars, but he received only limited western assistance in this task. Gratian's main concern was to confine the Gothic problem to the eastern Balkans and away from Pannonia, while he devoted himself to the Rhine frontier. Back in the West, however, Gratian soon made himself very unpopular with the regular army, supposedly because he showed excessive favouritism to his Alanic bodyguard. In 383, he faced a mutiny in Gaul, led by a general of Spanish origin named Magnus Maximus. Maximus (r. 383–388) overthrew and killed Gratian, taking control of the western regions of Gaul, Spain and Britain, while leaving the twelve-year-old Valentinian II in precarious control of Italy and Africa.

Preoccupied with settling affairs in the eastern provinces, which were still deeply disturbed by the years of uncertainty that had followed Adrianople, Theodosius could not have spared the resources for a campaign against Maximus, even had he wanted to. But it is hard to imagine his having felt much desire to avenge a colleague with whom he had been on such bad terms. In fact, relations had been deteriorating since the early part of 383, half a year before Gratian's death. At that point, Theodosius had raised his own five-year-old son Arcadius to the rank of augustus, a promotion that Gratian's western court refused to recognize.[8] At least initially, therefore, Theodosius may actually have welcomed the murder of Gratian as a chance to entrench his own dynastic control. Certainly he made no move against Maximus. Things only changed in 387 when Maximus invaded the territory of the young Valentinian II. He and his mother Justina fled to Theodosius. Exiled in Thessalonica, they beseeched Theodosius' aid in restoring a legitimate augustus to the throne from which he had been evicted. Theodosius owed his position to a member of the Valentinianic dynasty and he could hardly refuse this request, however uncongenial. With no great enthusiasm, he mustered an army and marched west in 388. Maximus' revolt was crushed thanks to the superior skills of Theodosius' generals, and Theodosius himself remained in Italy until the summer of 391, graciously accepting the excuses and regrets of the many western aristocrats who had collaborated with Maximus.

While Theodosius was away, there was trouble in the Balkans. Units of the army stationed there had been offered money by Maximus to raise a disturbance at Theodosius' rear.[9] We do not know where fighting started, and it is very unclear whether we should think in terms of a major revolt, a long-lasting rebellion of auxiliary troops, or simply wide-scale banditry. Since the depredations of a fractious auxiliary troop and the bands of brigands that haunted many imperial provinces throughout Roman history could look identical even to contemporaries, our own inability to separate the phenomena should come as no surprise. All the same, the scale of the Balkan problem is revealed by the fact that a high-ranking general named Botheric was stationed in Thessalonica in 390. Botheric's murder in a riot led to one of the most famous episodes in Theodosius' career: when the emperor ordered that thousands of citizens be massacred in the circus of Thessalonica as punishment, he was forced to abase himself and do public penance by bishop Ambrose of Milan, who would not admit Theodosius to communion until he had done so.[10] The rioting in Thessalonica probably had nothing to do with the general trouble in the Balkans – it is said to have followed the imprisonment of a popular charioteer – but Botheric's presence there is a sure indication of trouble, because Thessalonica never had a military establishment save in emergencies.

AN IMPORTANT SOURCE: THE POET CLAUDIAN

We do not know how many – if indeed any – of these rebellious units were drawn from the Gothic settlers of 382. Our sources are unusually opaque. The narrative in Zosimus' *New History* is filled with narrative incident, but little historical detail. The poems of Claudian, meanwhile, bathe genuine incidents in a wash of poetic embellishment. Claudian, whose earliest surviving works date to the early 390s, is often our fullest historical witness to events of that decade, which brings with it a number of problems. Claudian – as we call the man born Claudius Claudianus – was a young Egyptian from Alexandria, a Greek speaker by origin, who made his career in the Latin West as a court poet, rising to the rank of *tribunus et notarius* and earning a statue in the forum of Trajan in Rome.[11] He is widely regarded as the last great Latin poet of antiquity, and he has left us work in several poetic genres, all equally accomplished. Most of his career, from what we can tell, was spent in the service of the general Stilicho, a close confidant of Theodosius, the husband of the emperor's niece, and regent for his younger son Honorius from the time of Theodosius' death in 395. Stilicho was undoubtedly the most powerful man in the western empire, and spent much of his career attempting to assert the same level of control over the East. In Claudian, he had a mouthpiece and a panegyrist of genius, who magnified events great and small and transformed poems on every subject into opportunities to praise his patron. Between his panegyric on the third consulate of Honorius, delivered on 1 January 396 and fulsome in its defence of Stilicho's conduct a year earlier, until his own death soon after 404, Claudian is often our only extant source. What is more, his is the only evidence not contaminated by the hindsight of the sack of Rome in 410. Although poetry is not history, and teasing out narrative reference from the poetic context in which it is embedded is not always easy, we learn a great deal from Claudian. Indeed it is one of his poems that gives us our first introduction to Alaric.

ALARIC'S EARLY CAREER

When Theodosius finally returned to the East in 391, he supposedly came close to being killed by Gothic rebels, among whom, we may surmise, was Alaric. Claudian tells us that Theodosius was confronted by Alaric at the river Hebrus, the modern Maritsa.[12] If this episode actually took place, late summer 391 is the only point in Theodosius' career that can accommodate it. We do not know what position, if any, Alaric held in 391. Although it is still often claimed that Alaric ruled the Goths because he belonged to the royal dynasty of the Balthi, the only source for this is Jordanes – and Jordanes at his most transparently fictitious, inventing a 'Visigothic' dynasty to match the Amal family of the Ostrogothic king Theodoric.[13] Jordanes' testimony on this point can be taken seriously only by those whose theoretical superstructure requires an aristocratic *Traditionskern* to transmit Gothic ethnicity. All the contemporary evidence shows that Alaric was a new man and in 391 he was not yet a significant figure, just one of the many bandits and rebels who made the Balkans a festering wound in the body politic. Rather than getting bogged down in Balkan guerrilla warfare, for which he had shown not the slightest aptitude, Theodosius left matters to the general Promotus. When Promotus was killed in an ambush, Stilicho was sent to repair the situation, the first command in which he is firmly attested.[14] Details are lacking, but it seems that he pinned down the rebels and forced them to negotiate peace with the emperor.[15] There is, at any rate, no sign of continuing Balkan disturbances when

Theodosius was again forced to march west against a usurper, this time in 394.

THE USURPATION OF EUGENIUS

Back in 391, when Theodosius left the West after the suppression of Maximus, he had put Valentinian II in nominal charge of affairs. He could hardly have done otherwise when the pretext for attacking Maximus had been to restore Valentinian to his rightful throne. But Theodosius had no intention of ceding power to the youth, and the choice of a regent was made easier by the death of Valentinian's powerful mother Justina sometime during the campaign to restore her son's throne. In the end, Theodosius sent Valentinian to Gaul in the care of the general Arbogast, a trusted and long-serving officer. Unfortunately, Arbogast proved incapable of handling his new charge, with tragic results for all concerned. It is difficult not to pity Valentinian, raised to the purple as an infant in a moment of panic, thereafter dominated by his half-brother Gratian and his mother Justina and disregarded by every other reigning augustus. In 391, left as western emperor by Theodosius, he imagined that the time had at last come for him to rule on his own behalf. Arbogast soon disabused him of that notion, and the young emperor's frustration mounted. When Valentinian attempted to cashier Arbogast, the general tore up the imperial order before his very eyes – he took orders from Theodosius, not from a teenage puppet. Overcome by despair, Valentinian hanged himself. It was the best revenge he could possibly have taken. Rumours of murder were inevitable – indeed are recorded in our sources – and Theodosius could never turn a blind eye, however pleased he may have been by the extinction of the Valentinianic dynasty.[16] Knowing that he could not be restored to favour, the hitherto loyal Arbogast chose preemptive rebellion. He proclaimed a pagan grammarian and minor bureaucrat named Eugenius (r. 392–394) emperor and cast about for allies, finding them amongst the aristocracy of Rome itself. Rome still housed some of the richest and most influential men in the entire empire, many of whom hated Theodosius for his increasingly aggressive Christianity. One of them, Nicomachus Flavianus, made common cause with Arbogast, presiding with him over the usurpation and lending to it the legitimacy that his prestige automatically conferred.

Theodosius, as he had to, prepared for a second western campaign against a usurper. He left his adolescent son Arcadius behind in Constantinople in the hands of the praetorian prefect Rufinus and marched west again in 394, taking with him his younger son Honorius, now likewise raised to the rank of augustus. Flavianus and Arbogast fortified the Julian Alps between Italy and Illyricum and met Theodosius in battle at the river Frigidus on 5 September 394. The fighting was furious and Arbogast was a much better general than Theodosius. But on the second day of the battle, in what Christian writers understandably viewed as a miracle, a hard wind blew straight into the ranks of the western army, stopping their spears and arrows from reaching the Theodosian units and hampering the ability of the western troops to defend themselves. With the wind at his back, Theodosius was victorious, but the battle was more than usually bloody and Theodosius' barbarian auxiliaries suffered tremendous losses after they were placed in the front ranks to absorb the worst of the damage.[17] Flavianus and Arbogast committed suicide in the face of their total defeat.[18]

STILICHO

Theodosius took up residence in Milan. Like Constantius thirty years before him, he had to give serious thought to how he was going to govern the empire. As events had now twice demonstrated, he could not do it alone, and nor would a mere puppet like Valentinian suffice. He needed a colleague on whom he could rely, but his sons were too young and may already have begun to display the pervasive weakness that would characterize their later reigns. We cannot know what Theodosius would have decided, for he had only three months to live. Still a young man by the standards of the Roman elite, he died of congestive heart failure on 17 January 395. The young augustus Honorius was at his side in Milan, and the regency devolved immediately upon Stilicho. In the East, where Arcadius theoretically reigned, power was in the hands of Stilicho's bitter enemy, the praetorian prefect Rufinus. Stilicho, however, had at his command the field armies of both eastern and western empires, and their partial demobilization triggered the crisis that would soon envelop much of the empire.

Stilicho himself is a sympathetic figure, but one badly compromised by hostile accounts both ancient and modern. He had the misfortune to command the western empire in the face of severe external threats and do so for an emperor incapable of inspiring confidence even as a puppet and figurehead. No one could have countered every challenge that Stilicho faced, and his enemies sought explanations for his periodic failures: latching on to the fact of his Vandal descent on one side, they argued that Stilicho demonstrated the inevitable treachery of the barbarian. Modern scholars have followed suit, imagining that 'Germanic' blood gave Stilicho more in common with barbarian enemies than with the empire he served, a foolish canard whose time should long since have passed. As we can see both in his actions and in the testimony of Claudian, he was only ever a Roman commander, of proven competence on the battlefield, and the most trusted of Theodosius' military subordinates. More than that, he was by marriage a member of the imperial family, the spouse of Theodosius' niece and adopted daughter Serena, whose son Eucherius was acknowledged by Theodosius as his grandson. Even before Theodosius' death, Stilicho had been made the legitimate guardian of Honorius, and by marrying Stilicho's daughter Maria, the young emperor became his son-in-law in 398. In other words, Stilicho's many years of conflict with the eastern court should not be understood in terms of his Vandal blood, or more general barbarian ambitions to dominate Roman interests, but rather as the political intrigue that attends any royal minority and which, in the present instance, broke out the moment Theodosius was dead.

ALARIC'S REVOLT

In 395, Stilicho sent some of the auxiliary units that had served at the Frigidus back to the East. At the head of one of these units was Alaric, who had presumably been brought into the ranks of the imperial army shortly after the Balkan rebellion of 391.[19] In 395, we are told by Zosimus, Alaric grew angry at not having been given a proper command, instead remaining in charge of just those barbarians he had led on the campaign against Eugenius.[20] This anger is quite plausible. Particularly given that barbarian auxiliaries had borne the brunt of the fighting at the Frigidus, Alaric may well have felt he deserved a promotion for having won Theodosius his victory. Regardless, while *en route* through the Balkans, Alaric rose in revolt. At first, he was joined only by the troops he already commanded, but his following soon burgeoned. We should probably envisage Alaric's followers growing in the same way as did those of Fritigern between 376 and 378, an initial core being joined by a varied group of the dissatisfied and dispossessed who saw in the rebellion a chance to better their condition. In the Balkans of the early 390s, the Gothic settlers of 382 and their descendants may have had especially good reasons for dissatisfaction and may therefore have supplied the largest number of new recruits as Alaric's following grew, but we lack evidence to that effect. Certainly nothing supports the common assumption that Alaric gathered behind him all the Goths of the 382 treaty, or even a majority of them.

Besides, his earliest goals were more personal and more limited. He wanted a proper command and, in 395, he marched on Constantinople to demand it. We are told that Rufinus bribed Alaric to withdraw from the city by giving him leave to sack provinces elsewhere in the Balkans, but Claudian, our source for this, was always ready to slander Stilicho's enemies, Rufinus very much among them.[21] More plausibly, as it nearly always did, Constantinople simply looked like too dangerous a target, so that Alaric turned instead to the softer options of Macedonia and Thessaly. Rufinus, for his part, could hardly mount an effective defence, still less go on the offensive, lacking as he did the eastern field army, which remained in Italy under Stilicho's command. Before 395 was out, however, Stilicho had marched across the Alps and into the Balkans to deal with Alaric.

STILICHO AND RUFINUS

From the moment of Theodosius' death, Stilicho always claimed guardianship of both Arcadius and Honorius, on the grounds that this had been the deathbed wish of Theodosius himself. Contemporaries could not have verified that claim any more than we can. Making good on it would have meant displacing the powerful eastern officials who already controlled Arcadius, and they, of course, rejected Stilicho's position entirely. But by marching his army into the Balkans to deal with Alaric, Stilicho could also apply crippling pressure to the regime of Rufinus. Or so one might have thought, save for the puzzling results of the actual expedition: before the end of 395, Stilicho had returned the eastern army to Constantinople under the immediate command of the Gothic general Gainas, and had himself retired from the campaign against Alaric without having brought him to battle.[22]

Claudian would have it that Stilicho, a loyal servant to both emperors, was only acting in response to Arcadius' request for the return of the troops, but that cannot be the whole story and may be entirely false.[23] Instead, we may suspect that, when Claudian insists on Stilicho's firm discipline and skill in leading two armies that had recently fought one another at the bloodbath of the Frigidus, he is covering up the fact that Stilicho had found it impossible to control both eastern and western field armies on a single campaign.[24] Unable to trust the eastern troops in a pitched battle against Alaric, and knowing that the eastern frontier needed its field army, Stilicho sent them back to Constantinople under the command of the general Gainas. When the army was mustered for inspection there in November 395, Rufinus was seized and torn to pieces by the soldiers. The regency in Constantinople was taken over by the eunuch Eutropius, Arcadius' trusted grand chamberlain, who had himself been plotting against Rufinus for some time. Eutropius' interests and those of Stilicho coincided only briefly, and when the eunuch proved no more deferential to Stilicho's claimed regency over the East than Rufinus had been, he became the new target of Claudian's poisonous invective. By then, Stilicho had beaten a tactical retreat to Italy. Alaric did not as yet pose any threat to the western empire, and leaving him at large could only help undermine Eutropius in Constantinople.

ALARIC AND EUTROPIUS

Stilicho spent most of 396 in Gaul, repairing the frontier that had been weakened during the civil war between Eugenius and Theodosius.[25] Alaric, meanwhile, advanced into Greece via the pass at Thermopylae and remained in the peninsula until 397, raiding as far south as the Peloponnese, in an action recorded in Eunapius' *Lives of the Sophists.*[26] In 397, while Eutropius' eastern regime was still enfeebled by competition over the regency and faced the added burden of Hunnic raids across the Armenian frontier, Stilicho again felt ready to intervene in the Alaric affair. In early April, he led a naval expedition to Greece, making landfall in the south and forcing the Gothic leader to retreat up into the mountainous province of Epirus, though failing to bring him to submission.[27] Eutropius took this invasion very badly. He viewed it, with good reason, as a deliberate attempt to undermine him in the same way that Rufinus had been destroyed. Having decided that, of the two potential threats, Alaric was far preferable to Stilicho, Eutropius persuaded the compliant Arcadius to declare Stilicho a public enemy – *hostis publicus.* At the same time, Eutropius entered into negotiations with Alaric, granting him some sort of official position in the eastern military hierarchy.[28] This clever manoeuvre outflanked Stilicho, for now Alaric, not he, was the legally constituted authority in the region and he had no reason to think that the local *curiales* and landowners in the Balkans were more likely to listen to him than to Alaric. Having been left little choice, Stilicho withdrew once again back to Italy.

We do not know for certain what position Alaric actually received. Claudian provides our evidence and he is chiefly concerned to demonstrate the multiple ways in which Eutropius had betrayed the empire. Thus according to Claudian, Alaric was given charge of all Illyricum, commanding the services of imperial factories he had once looted and sitting in lawful judgement over cities his men had so recently plundered.[29] Once we cut through the rampant hyperbole, it seems likely that Alaric was given a military command that allowed him to legally request the services of the civilian government in Greece. The post of *magister militum per Illyricum,* which is generally conjectured by scholars and was certainly vacant in 397, fits the evidence well. Yet what happened to Alaric and his followers after 397 is much less clear: Zosimus' account leaves out an entire decade's worth of material when he switches sources from Eunapius to Olympiodorus. It is possible that between 397 and 401, Alaric's followers were billeted on the cities of the southern Balkans and supplied by civilian administrators in the same way as any other unit of the imperial army would have been. On the other hand, some scholars argue that Alaric's followers returned to the land as farmers, perhaps even the land they had been assigned in the peace of 382. Any conclusion will depend on whether one believes that Alaric led a Gothic army or that he had mobilized the treaty-Goths of 382, not on the evidence which is largely absent. Regardless, we hear nothing of Alaric or his followers for nearly four years between 397 and 401.

The problem of Alaric thus fell into temporary abeyance. This was just as well for Stilicho who now had more pressing concerns. Eutropius suborned the *comes Africae* Gildo, a north African aristocrat who had been given his sweeping imperial command by Theodosius twelve years earlier.[30] Gildo transferred his allegiance from the western to the eastern government and cut off shipments of African grain to the city of Rome. Rome's urban population was prone to rioting at the best of times, and a food shortage would have guaranteed disaster and might easily have led to the collapse of Stilicho' regime. Until Gildo was suppressed, Stilicho would have no time for the East. At Constantinople, in the meantime, the eastern court dissolved into an orgy of political intrigue. Eutropius was unpopular both because he was a eunuch and because of his role in the religious controversy to which eastern cities were always prone. Despite his success in personally leading a campaign against the Huns in Armenia and Asia Minor – and the consequent award of the consulate for 399 – his enemies were on the lookout for any opportunity to bring him down. In the end, a nasty revolt in Asia Minor destroyed not just Eutropius' regime, but that of his successor Aurelian as well, while also poisoning forever Alaric's good relations with the eastern empire.[31]

GAINAS, TRIBIGILD AND THE EASTERN COURT

We have already briefly met the Gothic leaders Gainas and Tribigild, the one a commander in the army that Theodosius had taken to fight Eugenius, the other in charge of troops at Nacoleia in Asia Minor. Tribigild, perhaps having decided to imitate Alaric and win a promotion for himself, raised a rebellion in spring 399 and defeated the first imperial army sent to fight him. Gainas, sent to suppress the rebellion, decided that Tribigild was too powerful to defeat. He recommended that the imperial court enter into negotiations, which he undertook to manage. Tribigild's chief condition for renewed allegiance was the deposition of Eutropius. As the eunuch already had powerful enemies in the palace, the empress Eudoxia chief among them, Arcadius was finally persuaded to abandon a chamberlain whom he sincerely trusted. Eutropius was cast out of office along with his supporters in August 399, enjoying a short exile in Cyprus before being executed on spurious treason charges.[32] An experienced eastern bureaucrat named Aurelian became praetorian prefect and replaced Eutropius as the chief minister of Arcadius.

That, however, did not satisfy Gainas, who now bargained on his own account, rather than as an intermediary with Tribigild. In April 400, Gainas marched his army to Chalcedon, on the Asian side of the Bosporus opposite Constantinople. He demanded what Alaric had received three years before – a senior military command – and also the consulate. Several other senior generals had held the consulate and Gainas clearly felt his own services had earned similar recognition. He also demanded the deposition of Aurelian. Two of the three requests were granted – Aurelian was deposed and Gainas was designated consul for the following year. However, the new praetorian prefect Caesarius was just as hostile to Gainas as Eutropius and Aurelian had been, and the Goths were unpopular with the people of Constantinople as well. In July, Gainas decided that it would be safer to move his troops away from the city and into Thrace. But mobilization provoked riots, and thousands of Goths, mostly civilians, were massacred inside the city by the urban mob, many burned alive in the church where they had taken shelter. Gainas was forced to flee after being defeated in battle by the general Fravitta, and did not return alive from his attempt to get across the Danube. Tribigild too was suppressed, and the longevity and stability of Caesarius' regime put paid to any hope Alaric might have had of renewing cordial relations with the eastern court. Caesarius' government in Constantinople lasted for fully three years, and by the time he was eventually replaced in 404, Alaric had left the eastern empire behind.

ALARIC IN ITALY

Late in 401, Alaric and his followers set out for Italy, arriving there on the 18th of November.[33] How many of them there were is beyond us. Some scholars maintain that Alaric took with him to Italy most of the Gothic settlers of 382, but there is nothing in the sources to suggest that. Even his motives are a blank, although it seems clear that he no longer regarded the eastern empire as a reliable negotiating partner, and the death of Gainas at the end of 400 may have made Alaric's own position worryingly anomalous. Crossing the Julian Alps, Alaric hovered on the frontier of Italy, threatening Stilicho with invasion and hoping to extract concessions that are not, at least at this point, specified in our sources. In the spring of 402, Alaric invaded and Stilicho brought him to battle twice in northern Italy, first at Pollentia in April on Easter Sunday, then at Verona a couple of months later. Alaric had been able to cross the Alps while Stilicho was detained in Raetia, and he won a victory over a small Roman army before going on to besiege Milan, a grand city which was frequently an imperial residence. Stilicho marched to the relief of the city, then drove Alaric to Pollentia. The battle of Pollentia was a modest but real success for Stilicho: he seized many prisoners, including Alaric's wife and children, and took possession of all the treasure that Alaric had amassed in half a decade's plundering. Stilicho granted Alaric a truce, in which he was meant to withdraw from Italy for good; perhaps Stilicho wanted to preserve a chastened Alaric as a potentially useful tool, perhaps he simply regarded Alaric as too powerful to destroy.

But very soon, Stilicho claimed that Alaric had violated the terms of the truce and brought him to battle again, this time at Verona, in July or August of 402.[34] This fight was no more conclusive than Pollentia had been and even Claudian admits that Alaric was able to consider attacking Gaul or Raetia in its immediate aftermath. If some of Alaric's support melted away in the absence of a decisive success, he was nonetheless able to avoid further confrontations and retreated into the Balkans again.[35] From 402 to late 404 or early 405, Alaric occupied the northwestern Balkans, perhaps the province of Pannonia II, shunted by Stilicho into the *de facto* no-man's land between East and West. In this corner of Illyricum, Alaric could not aggravate the state of almost continuous cold war between the eastern and western courts, or at least not until one side or the other decided to deploy him in its own interest. This time it was Stilicho who took the initiative. He decided to grant Alaric the same sort of office that Eutropius had granted him half a decade earlier. Probably in 405, Alaric's followers again returned to Epirus, their leader once again bearing the codicils of office appointing him *magister militum*, but now supplied by the western rather than the eastern empire.[36] Eastern propaganda chose to see this move as Stilicho's preparation for a full-scale invasion of Illyricum, an interpretation modern scholars have been too willing to accept. In fact, Stilicho's move represented nothing new. Granting Alaric his new title was no more than the reassertion of a hegemony that Stilicho had always claimed to possess, and it involved taking no action whatsoever – Alaric was already in Illyricum, and he might just as well be put to some use as an irritant to the eastern court. Even had Stilicho actually planned to take action himself in Illyricum, and there is not the slightest evidence that he did, events in Italy and Gaul rapidly made such plans unfeasible.

CRISIS IN THE WESTERN EMPIRE

Late in 405, a Gothic king named Radagaisus, hitherto completely unknown to history, crossed the Alps from central Europe, marched through the province of Raetia, and invaded Italy. More than a year passed before he was finally subdued. To make matters worse, on the last day of either 405 or 406 a large band of Vandals, Alans and Suevi crossed the Rhine near Mainz and spread devastation in the northern provinces of Gaul.[37] That invasion provoked a string of usurpations in Britain, the third of which, led by a common soldier named Constantine (r. 407–411), spread across the Channel and soon removed Gaul, Britain and Spain from the control of Honorius' government in Italy. For obvious reasons, Stilicho had to deal with the threat to Italy before he could attend to a Gallic usurpation. In August 406, he chased Radagaisus down near Florence and won a crushing victory that left thousands of the Gothic king's followers enslaved – so many that the bottom fell out of the market for able-bodied slaves.[38] With Radagaisus dead, Stilicho could turn to other matters, particularly suppressing the Gallic usurpation of Constantine, for which purpose Alaric might prove very useful. Unfortunately for Stilicho, Alaric had now lost patience.

There is no question that Alaric had recouped whatever losses of manpower he had suffered at Pollentia and Verona, and, after three years as a legitimate commander in Illyricum, he may well have begun to rebuild his financial position as well. But Illyricum and Greece had been plundered repeatedly since the early 390s and it is hard to see how they could have yielded revenues on a large enough scale to replace the spoils that Stilicho captured at Pollentia. Having already been resident in the eastern empire for so long, Alaric seems to have decided its potential as a target was limited. The West offered richer pickings. Thus in 407, he marched on Italy again, taking up position in Noricum – modern Austria – and demanding 4,000 pounds of gold if he was to spare Italy from another full-scale invasion. Stilicho, whose first attempts to deal with the Gallic usurper Constantine had not succeeded, decided to turn Alaric loose on him instead. He therefore convinced Honorius and the Roman senate to part with the sum demanded.[39] Stilicho's plan was sensible and based on a realistic assessment of the dangers inherent in the present situation, but it weakened his own position fatally. The senators who had to pay for this massive subvention understandably resented it, and their sympathisers at court began to play upon the suspicions of the emperor. Like Valentinian II before him, Honorius had ambitions to rule in his own right and, again like Valentinian, he was a dreadful judge of character, totally incapable of recognizing where his own best interests lay. Unlike his late predecessor, however, Honorius possessed a certain low cunning. Rather than confront Stilicho prematurely, he allowed enemies at court to undermine the general's position. Matters were only exacerbated by Stilicho's insistence that Honorius marry his younger daughter Thermantia when the emperor's first wife Maria, Stilicho's elder daughter, died.[40]

The breaking point came through purest chance – Arcadius died in May 408 and both Honorius and Stilicho determined to go to Constantinople to assert western control there. Honorius already mistrusted Stilicho's motives. He now allowed the *magister officiorum* Olympius to persuade him that Stilicho was planning to seize the throne for himself and his own son Eucherius, thereby displacing the Theodosian dynasty. Given that the well-timed death of a puppet emperor had secured the position of that same dynasty only fifteen years before, one can see why Honorius might have believed insinuations along such lines. At any rate, he acquiesced in an organized coup against Stilicho. At Ticinum, modern Pavia, regiments destined for the Gallic war mutinied, lynching several officers. Stilicho was blamed, and Olympius had him declared a public enemy by Honorius. Loyal to the Theodosian dynasty to his last breath, Stilicho refused to attack the emperor who had betrayed him, even given the vast resources at his disposal. Instead, he allowed himself to be removed from the sanctuary of the church in Ravenna in which he had sought refuge and went quietly to his execution on 22 August 408. His supporters were purged in cities around Italy; his young son was hunted down and executed; and the wives and children of his barbarian auxiliaries were massacred by the thousand.[41]

THE FIRST SIEGE OF ROME

The death of Stilicho meant that the full force of Alaric's anger was unleashed on Italy. Olympius refused to honour the promises which Alaric had been given. Thousands of barbarian soldiers, their wives and children dead, deserted and joined him in Noricum.[42] He gave Honorius one last chance, demanding a sum of gold – how much is not specified – and an exchange of hostages, perhaps hoping for the return of such civilian dependents of his new followers as still survived.[43] When this overture was rebuffed, Alaric marched straight down the Italian peninsula to Rome. During the winter of 408/409 he besieged the city – the first of three sieges – and blockaded the river route up the Tiber from Portus, thereby threatening the Romans with starvation. Panic gripped the city, and scapegoats were sought.[44] Stilicho's widow Serena was strangled by order of the senate, posthumous vengeance on the man they blamed for Alaric's continued existence.[45] While the senate dithered, Alaric's following grew as barbarian slaves, some of them the survivors of Radagaisus' Gothic army, fled to join him from all over Italy. Finally, the Romans gave in and begged for a truce. In exchange for Alaric's letting food into the city, the senate promised to send an embassy to Ravenna and convince the emperor to make peace with him. Alaric agreed. For him, Rome was a bargaining counter, not an end in itself, and if he could get more out of allowing the Romans to eat than he could from keeping them starved, then so much the better. The senate's embassy departed early in 409 and achieved what it had set out to do. Olympius conferred high office on the Roman envoys, and Alaric was invited to meet with representatives of the emperor.

Negotiations took place at Rimini in 409, while a Gothic army camped outside the city walls. The imperial legation was led by the praetorian prefect of Italy, Jovius, a former ally of Stilicho and rival of Olympius, and perhaps an old acquaintance of Alaric. Relying on the strength of his position, Alaric set his demands quite high. He demanded money and grain, but also the highest generalship, the *magisterium utriusque militiae*, or command of both services, which Stilicho had held before him. Jovius, it would seem, favoured this arrangement, but either the emperor or Olympius balked at giving another barbarian the codicils of office. They conceded as much grain and money as Alaric might want but no position in the imperial hierarchy.[46] Outraged by the refusal, Alaric turned away from Rimini and began the march down the via Flaminia towards Rome, intending to renew the siege. Olympius' hold on Honorius soon collapsed, and Olympius himself fled to Dalmatia, but this brought Alaric no comfort.[47] Having himself lost face through his failure to manage the negotiations smoothly, Jovius now joined the side of the intransigents, supposedly swearing himself and his cronies to never again attempt peace with Alaric.

THE SECOND SIEGE AND THE USURPATION OF PRISCUS ATTALUS

Alaric thus lost all potential support at the court of Honorius. As a result, when he calmed down at some place on the road between Rimini and Rome, and offered up much less stringent demands (a moderate amount of grain and a couple of unimportant provinces like Noricum in which to dwell), these were twice rejected and he found himself forced to consider stronger measures.[48] Renewing the siege of Rome was an obvious tactic, but it had not got him what he wanted last time and there was no reason to think it would now. Something more drastic was needed. Alaric had been involved in imperial affairs long enough to realize that usurpers concentrated the imperial mind wonderfully. He therefore decided to set up an emperor of his own, one who would both meet his demands and perhaps also force Honorius to take a more reasonable stance in negotiations. In December 409, therefore, he declared the Roman nobleman Priscus Attalus emperor. Attalus was one of the senate's leading lights. He had held office already under Theodosius, and had been prominent in embassies to the imperial court earlier in the reign of Honorius. During Alaric's first siege of Rome, he had been one of the three senatorial ambassadors who went to Ravenna and arranged for the parley at Rimini. Appointed *comes sacrarum largitionum* – head of the emperor's treasury – and then prefect of the city of Rome, he was meant to keep the senate and the Roman population firmly on the side of Ravenna despite the threat posed by Alaric. He was still serving as urban prefect when Alaric offered to make him emperor.

Alaric may have intended this manoeuvre to serve only his own interests, but the new augustus had real imperial pretensions as well. Having seen how little the court at Ravenna valued the safety of Rome and the wishes of the Roman senate, Attalus appears to have turned decisively against Honorius. All our extant sources derive at one or more remove from the now fragmentary account of Olympiodorus, an eastern ambassador to the West in the 420s and the most careful and thorough Roman historian since Ammianus.[49] Though it is often hard to recover Olympiodorus' insights from the sources like Zosimus that used him, it would seem that Attalus presumed to speak for the Romans of Rome, preparing a restoration of imperial majesty with a thoroughly Roman flavour. Attalus bestowed top military commands on Alaric and his brother-in-law Athaulf, but the rest of his nascent regime was plucked from the upper echelons of Roman senatorial society. His self-confidence was ill placed, however, and he seems either not to have realized, or to have willfully ignored, how much his position depended on Alaric. Very soon after his proclamation, Attalus began refusing to take Alaric's advice. He did not act quickly enough to secure Africa and its grain supply and then his first attempt at seizing control of the province failed when his general Constans was defeated and killed by the pro-Honorian *comes Africae* Heraclian. Yet having failed, he still refused to allow Alaric to send a small force of 500 Goths – all Alaric believed it would take – to conquer Africa and with it Rome's grain supply. Instead, Attalus marched on Ravenna and, with Alaric at his side, opened negotiations from Rimini. When Honorius offered some sort of collegiate rule as a compromise – an astonishing concession for a legitimate emperor to make and proof of the weakness of his position – Attalus proved stupidly intransigent, insisting that Honorius should be deposed and go into exile on an island.[50]

We cannot know why Attalus was so adamant. Perhaps he mistrusted the good faith of the Ravenna government, and genuinely believed that Rome's interests could not be safe while Honorius occupied the throne. Perhaps it was misplaced arrogance, the unsheathed contempt of a Roman aristocrat for the upstart dynasty of Theodosius and the present, supine incumbent. Or perhaps, with Alaric at his back, it just seemed foolish not to push for the highest prize of all, sole rule over the western empire. Suddenly, though, his grand plans collapsed. Nearly 4,000 eastern soldiers arrived at Ravenna by ship. These had been requested so long before – while Stilicho was still in power – that no one could possibly have expected their arrival. Ravenna, surrounded by marshes and thus difficult to assault, could now be actively defended as well. Honorius thus had no more need to negotiate at all. Alaric by now clearly regretted his choice of puppet, Attalus having proved neither competent nor pliable. Indeed, for us as for Alaric, it is hard to decide whether Honorius or Attalus was less suited to the task of ruling an empire. Honorius at least possessed the one sole merit of legitimacy, and so early in 410, Alaric deposed Attalus, perhaps as a result of secret negotiations with Ravenna, perhaps as a precondition for opening them.[51]

THE THIRD SIEGE AND THE SACK OF ROME

This produced results. Alaric led his forces to within sixty stades – just under 13 kilometres – of Ravenna, at a location whose name has been lost in the corrupt textual tradition. He hoped to bring two years' worth of fruitless half measures to some permanent conclusion. As we saw in our prologue, the position of his men was deteriorating, and continued delays could only make matters worse. All might have gone well, but for yet another chance complication. While Alaric prepared to negotiate in good faith, he was attacked by the Gothic general Sarus, a man who had been in imperial service since the days of Stilicho. We do not know why Sarus intervened at precisely this moment. One source tells us that he regarded the prospect of Alaric's coming to terms with Honorius as a danger to his own position.[52] It thus does not look as if he was acting on the instructions of Ravenna, though he might have been. As became clear in the years that followed, Sarus bore a grudge against Alaric's brother-in-law Athaulf, and he may have detested Alaric as well. Regardless of Sarus' reasons, Alaric interpreted the attack as evidence of Honorius' bad faith. Dropping all further effort to negotiate, he turned from Ravenna and marched back on Rome for the third and last time.

This time Rome was not going to be a prop to negotiation. Time and time again that had failed and Alaric's patience was at an end. Alaric put the eternal city to the sack and we have already seen what that meant. For three days, Alaric's Goths sacked the city, stripping it of the wealth of centuries. We may be sure that his followers enjoyed themselves. But for Alaric the sack of Rome was an admission of defeat, a catastrophic failure. Everything he had hoped for, had fought for over the course of a decade and a half, went up in flames with the capital of the ancient world. Imperial office, a legitimate place for himself and his followers inside the empire, these were now forever out of reach. He might seize what he wanted, as he had seized Rome, but he would never be given it by right. The sack of Rome solved nothing and when the looting was over Alaric's men still had nowhere to live and fewer future prospects than ever before. Alaric had shown a new way forward, in his career of intermittent honours and recognition, and those who followed the same road in later decades would realize the potential of the tactics he had pioneered as a simultaneous insider and outsider to the empire. But Alaric's own road soon came to an end. The sack of Rome ended on the 27th of August 410. Within a couple of months, he was dead.

THE AFTERMATH
OF ALARIC

EPILOGUE

THE TRAUMA OF THE SACK OF ROME WAS AS MUCH psychological as physical. Those three painful days of August 410 entered into ongoing debate about the effects on the empire of the imperial conversion to Christianity, a debate that had been going on since Adrianople. It had flared up in practice, as we saw, in the besieged Rome of 408, when some suggested that the only way to stave off Alaric was to offer sacrifices to the old gods who had protected the city for so long. Those sacrifices, in all likelihood, were never offered, and then the city was sacked. Thus did pagans find themselves vindicated, though it was a melancholy satisfaction when Rome still smouldered around them. The sack put Christian authors on the defensive and they set out to rebut the pagan charge – now so much more plausible – that Christianity had brought about Rome's decline. A Spanish priest named Orosius produced an apologetical work in seven books which he called a *History Against the Pagans*. Orosius' history aimed to show that Rome's pagan past had been filled with many more disasters than its more recent Christian era. Far more subtle was St. Augustine's *City of God*, more than a thousand pages of closely argued history and theology, meditating on the divine plan for the world, and the role of the Roman empire in it, and the contrast between an earthly and a heavenly city, which latter offered up the prospect of eternal peace.

Needless to say, the simplistic and tendentious response of Orosius proved more popular. He, in his zeal to defend the role of Christianity, downplayed the horror of the sack of Rome. To be sure, the city had been plundered, but Alaric had given orders to protect the holy sites, particularly the basilica of the apostles Peter and Paul, and to avoid bloodshed as much as possible. Christian nuns were spared violation, and when one was found in possession of church treasures that had been hidden from the besiegers, Alaric ordered that she and all the gold and silver that belonged to God should be returned under escort to their church.[1] We need not believe very many such stories – Orosius' history, for all its length, is throughout remarkably short on substance. But his tactic of minimizing the horrors of the sack proved very popular, and was used by many Christian authors of the fifth century. Even church historians like Sozomen, who relied heavily on the pessimistic and pagan Olympiodorus, could rewrite his words to show that the city revived at once from the rigours of the sack.[2] On that point, at least, they were probably right. Much of the city's vast portable wealth may have left in the Gothic wagon train, and many aristocrats may have fled as far afield as North Africa and Palestine, but Rome's urban population bounced back almost at once. Within a year or two, the urban prefect again found it impossible to satisfy the needs of all the population entitled to free grain.[3] Seven years later, the Gallic nobleman Rutilius Namatianus, returning home after having been honoured with the urban prefecture, was able to speak of an *ordo renascendi*, a world in the process of rebirth, even as he sailed past the ruins of Etruria, its fields still barren, its houses still in ruins.[4]

As Roman contemporaries struggled to make sense of what had happened, or went about the more practical business of rearranging shattered lives, Alaric himself was at a loss. All he had hoped for was gone. Sated by three days of sack and surrounded by fabulous heaps of plunder, his followers were no better placed than they had been before. The regions around the city were still devastated. Food would soon run short again. And what good was fabulous plunder if there was nowhere to spend it and no safe haven in which to show it off? Every problem that Alaric had confronted on the night of August the 24th loomed up again just as large on the morning of the 28th. At a loss, he decided to make for the south of Italy, attempting to cross from Rhegium to Sicily. Perhaps he thought the island's still unravaged grain fields could support him and his followers while he cast about for some permanent solution to their problem. Perhaps he intended to make for Africa, the land that supplied Rome with its loaded grain ships – ships to which Alaric had been as much a hostage as the Romans whom he had besieged. We cannot know for sure, but it does not matter – the crossing from Rhegium was thwarted. One story claimed that a sacred statue, possessed of magic powers, prevented the barbarians crossing.[5] Others, more prosaically, attributed the setback to a storm at sea. Either way, the path forward was blocked and Alaric turned back. But seized by fever, he died not far from the city of Consentia, the modern town of Cosenza. It was, perhaps, Rome's revenge for the sieges and the sack: the endemic illness that would kill so many of Rome's would-be conquerors in centuries to come claimed the very first of them as well.

Jordanes tells an elaborate story about Alaric's funeral rites: the course of the river Busentus was diverted, Roman captives were marched onto the river bed where they dug a grave for the dead leader. Then, when Alaric had been placed in it with many treasures from the sack of Rome, the river was let back into its normal channel and the diggers were killed so that they could never reveal the site where Alaric had been laid to rest.[6] It is a beguiling story, and one generally retailed as fact. But it is out of place in its early fifth-century setting and it is unmistakeably influenced by the elaborate funerary customs common among the princely elite of the Hunnic period and later. Perhaps Jordanes invented the story, perhaps it had long since begun to circulate to explain why no one knew where Alaric lay buried. Perhaps it is even true.

Jordanes also reports the black mourning that descended upon Alaric's following after his death. That, at least, one can well imagine: along with Alaric died any connection to the imperial government, still the only power that could truly guarantee the Goths' secure existence. Alaric's successor, Athaulf, realized that very fact and spent his brief reign trying hard to restore a satisfactory relationship with Ravenna. Athaulf, as we have seen, was Alaric's brother-in-law. He was probably a powerful Gothic noble in his own right, and certainly the deadly enemy of the Gothic general Sarus who had scuppered the last set of peace talks between Alaric and Honorius. In 411, Athaulf marched the Goths into Gaul, first joining briefly in the usurpation of a Gallic nobleman and in the process managing to attack and kill Sarus, then bringing down the usurper and returning Gaul to the allegiance of Honorius' government in Ravenna. Yet this signal aid bought no goodwill from Honorius. There were many reasons for that, but chief among them was the intransigence of Honorius' new commander-in-chief, Constantius. A soldier of great skill, he was also a politician of genius, and had emerged victorious from the court intrigues that followed the death of Stilicho: Olympius, who had engineered Stilicho's murder, was beaten to death with clubs at the instigation of Constantius, and every other potential enemy at court was done away with just as decisively. Constantius then took charge of the whole government of the western empire, and did so, like Stilicho, from the post of *magister utriusque militiae* – 'master of both services', the highest military command. He did not, in other words, use a position in the civilian hierarchy, for instance the praetorian prefecture or the mastership of offices, to dominate the government – an early sign of the major divergences between eastern and western empires that would grow more pronounced as the fifth century progressed.

Another cause of this divergence, though, was the fact of the Goths themselves. When Alaric's followers finally found a permanent home and permanent security for themselves, it was inside one of the western provinces, where they were from then on a complicating factor in the politics of the western empire. It was, however, a long time before that permanent settlement arrived, because for many years Constantius would brook absolutely no compromise. Until the Goths were prepared to humble themselves and genuinely subordinate their own plans and wishes to the needs of imperial government, Constantius was not interested in accommodation. By 413, moreover, his hands were free to act. In that year, Constantius suppressed the last of the usurpations that had plagued the western provinces from Gaul to North Africa ever since 406. He therefore determined to come to grips with Athaulf, who had been eking out a desultory existence in southern Gaul for a couple of years. The Gothic king, ignored and rejected by Constantius and Honorius despite his best efforts to make himself indispensable to them, decided to once again try the manoeuvre that had worked briefly for Alaric: he again made Priscus Attalus emperor. Attalus, who had traveled in the Gothic train ever since his deposition in 410, accepted the dubious honour despite the disastrous precedent of his first proclamation during Alaric's second siege of Rome. Perhaps he had genuinely grown to like his position within Gothic society – certainly he was baptised by a homoean Gothic priest named Sigesarius.[7] In 415, he even pronounced the *epithalamium* – the nuptial poem – at an unprecedented wedding.

In the southern Gallic city of Narbonne, Athaulf married Galla Placidia, the sister of Honorius and a hostage of the Goths since the sack of Rome. It is hard to know what prompted this match, and what political effects it was meant to have, but it is clear that Placidia profited by it in the long-term: for the rest of her life, she possessed a loyal troop of Goths which served as her bodyguard and helped make her a political force in her own right. At the time, though, the wedding only exacerbated the tension between Athaulf and Constantius, who blockaded the southern coast of Gaul and starved the Goths out of the province and into Spain. There, Placidia bore a son by her new husband and named him Theodosius – the name of her own imperial father and a clear sign of dynastic ambitions, given that Honorius remained without heir. But the infant died in Barcelona, and with him yet another dream of reconciliation between Honorius and the Goths. Athaulf soon followed his child to the grave, felled by the dagger of an assassin while he inspected his horses in their stables. The Gothic noble who profitted by this murder was himself killed after only seven days, and the new Gothic king Wallia made peace with Constantius in return for food.

He restored Placidia and Priscus Attalus to the imperial government. The widowed Placidia returned to Italy, where she was married to Constantius, whom she hated. Yet surrounded by an enormous fortune and protected by Goths loyal to her and the memory of her first husband, she went on to become the mother of an emperor: Valentinian III, born in 419 to her and Constantius, ruled the disintegrating western empire for thirty years (425–455). Attalus, humiliated, led in triumph, and physically mutilated, was exiled to the island of Lipari where he lived out his days in moderate comfort, no doubt regretting the cruel fate that had seen him lose the imperial purple not once but twice, while the useless Honorius reigned blissfully on. As for Wallia's Goths, once properly fed and housed, they went into action as a Roman army, clearing the Iberian peninsula of barbarians – the same Vandals, Alans and Sueves who had crossed the Rhine in 405/406 and then settled in Spain after traversing the Pyrenees in 409. In 418, Constantius called off this hugely successful campaign and settled Wallia's Goths in Gaul, in the province of Aquitania Secunda and a few of the cities on its fringes. Wallia did not live to see this settlement take place, but under his successor Theoderic (r. 418–451), a distant relative of Alaric by marriage, the Goths became more or less loyal subjects of the Roman emperor in Italy.

The settlement in Gaul begins a new phase in the history of the Goths, and of Gothic relations with the Roman empire. No longer one of many barbarian groups hovering on the fringes of empire, the Aquitanian Goths instead became the first barbarian kingdom inside the empire. In 418, their settlement may not have been viewed as permanent; certainly no one imagined that part of the western empire was being given away to a Gothic king and his followers. But that is precisely what happened over time. As the fifth century progressed, Theoderic I and his successor Theoderic II acted not as imperial officials, but as autonomous rulers within the larger Roman empire. In time, the Gothic settlement became a Gothic kingdom. The precedent set by Alaric also had a long future ahead of it. Alaric's own career was a failure – it is hard for us to judge it as anything else, and it is quite clear from the sources that he regarded it in the same way. But his career had demonstrated the power it was possible to exercise if one possessed a military following with no ties to the structures of imperial government save personal loyalty to an individual leader. As the fifth century wore on, more and more commanders in the western empire – not just barbarian kings, but Roman generals of every sort – turned to the strategy which Alaric had pioneered and used extra-governmental pressure to win political advantage for themselves inside the government. This new dynamic of imperial politics helped bring on the collapse of the western Roman empire in the 460s and 470s, but that is an altogether different story than the one we have been trying to tell in this book.

Our own story comes to a close with Alaric precisely because his career is both an end and a beginning in the history of the Roman empire's dealings with the Goths. Alaric was the child of a Balkan settlement that had been made necessary not just by the Gothic success at Adrianople, but by the imperial rivalries between the houses of Valentinian and Theodosius. In that sense, it follows in the footsteps of Gothic history throughout the fourth century – conditioned by, and in some sense conditional on, the actions of Roman emperors both beyond and within the imperial frontiers. As we have seen, the Goths themselves were created by the pressures of life on the Roman frontier, and the whole of their social and military history, from its beginnings in the third century until the Gothic wars of Valens in the 360s, developed in the shadow of Rome. Adrianople, and still more the lifetime of Alaric, changed all that. No longer products and victims of Roman history, the Goths – and the many other barbarian settlers who followed in their footsteps – now made Rome's history themselves.

GLOSSARY OF ANCIENT SOURCES

❋ ❋ ❋

Ambrose *see Biographical Glossary*

Ammianus Marcellinus from a well-connected family in Syria, perhaps Antioch, he joined the elite military corps of *protectores* as a young man, but retired after the death of the emperor Julian, going on to write a history of Rome which he completed around the year 390. This *Res Gestae*, which ran from A.D. 96 to 378 and is extant from 353, is our single most important source for fourth-century history and our most detailed treatment of the Adrianople campaign.

Arrian c. 86–160, governor of Cappadocia under Hadrian, author of a famous history of Alexander the Great, and also the *Order of Battle against the Alans* (c. 135).

Aurelius Victor governor of Pannonia II (361) and prefect of Rome (389), author of a short epitome of Roman imperial history, the *Caesars*, running from Augustus to Constantius II and completed in about 360, which is particularly important for the history of the later third and parts of the fourth century.

Basil of Caesarea c. 330–379, bishop of Caesarea in Cappadocia and the most important Greek theologian of the later fourth century. His letters provide important information about the Gothic martyr Saba, as well as general statements about the conditions in Thrace in the chaotic years that preceded Adrianople.

Cassiodorus c. 490–c. 585, official at the court of several Ostrogothic kings of Italy, most importantly Theodoric, before abandoning the Gothic cause around 537 and retiring to Constantinople. Author of many surviving works, but also of a now lost Gothic history in twelve books which Jordanes used, though to what extent is controversial.

Claudian born Claudius Claudianus in Alexandria in Egypt, Claudian made his career as a poet in the Latin West; his earliest poems date from the early 390s and after mid-395 he was the chief spokesman for Stilicho. His poems provide much of our information on Alaric and court politics from 395 to 404.

Dexippus third-century Athenian historian who wrote a universal history in twelve books and an account of the third-century Gothic invasions from 238 to c. 275 called the *Scythica*. Though both survive only in fragments, they were used by Zosimus in his *New History*.

Epitome de Caesaribus a later fourth-century account of Roman history which preserves some fragments of information not in Aurelius Victor or Eutropius.

Eunapius of Sardis author of a classicizing history of his own times written in the aftermath of Adrianople which survives only in fragments but which formed a major source for Zosimus' *New History*. Eunapius also wrote a volume of *Lives of the Sophists*, some of which sheds light on Alaric's invasion of Greece.

Eutropius imperial administrator and author of a *Breviary* or abridgement of Roman history from its beginnings until the death of Jovian, which he dedicated to Valens and which preserves some otherwise unknown information on the third and fourth centuries.

Gregory Thaumaturgus c. 213–c. 270, bishop of Neocaesarea in Pontus, his canonical letter is the most vivid and important testimony to the effects of Gothic raids in Asia Minor during the 250s.

Gregory of Nyssa c. 330–395, bishop of Nyssa, younger brother of Basil of Caesarea, and like him an important theologian. Two of his sermons record the depredations of Goths in Asia Minor in the aftermath of the battle of Adrianople.

Herodotus fifth century B.C., author of a large history, completed before 425 B.C., and centred on the wars between Greece and Persia. This work provided a model for much later Greek history and invented the stereotype of the Scythian that was so prevalent in third- and fourth-century accounts of the Goths.

Historia Augusta late fourth-century collection of imperial biographies from Hadrian to Carus and Carinus, based on generally good sources for the second century, but descending into almost total fiction by the end of the third. Nonetheless, the *Historia Augusta* preserves a few details of Gothic history derived from better sources like Dexippus and otherwise lost.

Jerome Christian priest and polemicist, c. 345–420, author of many works, including a *Chronicle* that translated into Latin and continued the chronicle of Eusebius of Caesarea; Jerome's *Chronicle* provides some information about Gothic history not known – or at least not dated – in other sources.

Jordanes sixth-century historian from Constantinople who wrote both a Roman and a Gothic history (the *Romana* and the *Getica*), the latter at some point after 550. Jordanes made some use of Cassiodorus' Gothic history – how much is controversial – but he added a great deal to it and thoroughly endorsed the destruction of the Gothic kingdom of the Ostrogoths by Justinian.

Julian *see Biographical Glossary*

Lactantius c. 240–c. 320, a Latin rhetorician at Nicomedia, among whose many works is a polemic *On the Deaths of the Persecutors* which provides accurate details of imperial history in the third and fourth centuries, including the death of Decius in a Gothic war.

Olympiodorus of Thebes Greek historian, before 380–after 425. Wrote a detailed history of the years 407 to 425 which, though now preserved only in fragments, was a major source for Sozomen, Philostorgius and Zosimus, and thereby central to our understanding of Alaric's actions in Italy just before the sack of Rome.

Orosius Christian priest from Spain who wrote a polemical *History against the Pagans* in seven books which continued down to 417 and argued, against pagans who saw Adrianople and the sack of Rome as divine anger for the imperial conversion to Christianity, that Rome had been much worse before the conversion.

Panegyrici Latini collection of speeches in honour of emperors compiled in late fourth-century Gaul and including eleven panegyrics from the late third to the fourth century, many of which attest otherwise unknown imperial campaigns against barbarians beyond the frontiers.

Paulinus deacon of the church of Milan and author in c. 422 of the *Life* of Bishop Ambrose of Milan, which helps establishes the sequence of events in 397.

Philostorgius c. 368–c. 440, author of a now fragmentary Greek church history written from a homoean point of view, drawing on the (also now fragmentary) history of Olympiodorus and preserving otherwise unknown information on Ulfila.

Socrates fifth-century lawyer and author of the earliest of several Greek church histories extant from the fifth century, continuing the ecclesiastical history of Eusebius. Socrates provides a great deal of unique information on the fourth and earlier fifth century, particularly on the eastern provinces.

Sozomen fifth-century lawyer and church historian whose church history offers a parallel, and rather different, perspective to that of Socrates, with considerably greater interest in secular history, and much more evidence for western affairs, most of it drawn from the now fragmentary history of Olympiodorus.

Synesius philosopher, and later bishop of Ptolemais, resident in Constantinople in the later 390s, where he wrote two treatises, *De regno* and *De providentia*, which are key to understanding the political manoeuvres at the eastern court surrounding the revolts of Alaric, Tribigild and Gainas.

Tacitus senator and historian, c. 56–c. 118, author of histories of the early Roman empire and of the *Germania*, an ethnographic account of Germany and its *gentes* which provided early modern humanists with their most important material for inventing a Germanic, non-Roman history.

Themistius c. 317–c. 388, Greek philosopher, rhetorician and spokesman for Constantius II, Valens and Theodosius I. The author of numerous works, several of his 34 surviving speeches are the best available evidence for imperial attitudes and policy towards the Goths.

Theoderet of Cyrrhus c. 393–466, monk and bishop of Cyrrhus in Syria, his church history drew on that of Socrates and preserves much information otherwise unknown.

Theodosian Code compilation of imperial constitutions from 312–438, put together at the behest of Theodosius II (r. 408–450), beginning in 429. It is our major source for the legislation of the later Roman empire and preserves a vast amount of historical detail on imperial administration and political history.

Zosimus imperial bureaucrat in the later fifth or the early sixth century, author of a *New History* in six books, running from Augustus to 410, but concentrated on the later fourth century, and probably unfinished. The history drew heavily on Dexippus, Eunapius and Olympiodorus, and is our fullest evidence for their contents and for the history they recounted.

BIOGRAPHICAL GLOSSARY

Aequitius tribune and relative of Valens, killed at the battle of Adrianople in 378.

Alanoviamuth father of the sixth-century author Jordanes.

Alaric Gothic chieftain, perhaps king, 395–410, first attested in 391 as a bandit in the Balkans. After service on Theodosius' campaign of 394, he raised a rebellion in 395. After several years in the eastern provinces he led his followers to Italy and repeatedly attempted to negotiate a peace with the government in Ravenna, finally allowing his troops to sack Rome in 410.

Alatheus Gothic *dux* and co-regent with Saphrax for the Greuthungian child-king Videric. Together they led some of the Greuthungi across the Danube in 376, eventually joining forces with the Tervingi of Fritigern and fighting at the battle of Adrianople in 378.

Alavivus Gothic leader of the Tervingi, and with Fritigern one of two chieftains primarily responsible for the Danube crossing of 376. Last heard of in 377 when the Gothic revolt broke out at Marcianople.

Alexander Severus emperor 222–235. Last emperor of the Severan dynasty, his murder in 235 began the political crisis of the third century.

Alica Gothic general who led a Gothic regiment in the army of Licinius during his civil war with Constantine in 324.

Ambrose bishop of Milan 374–397, famous for having imposed public penance on Theodosius after the massacre of Christians in Thessalonica in 390. The prologue of his *On the Holy Spirit* gives important evidence for Gothic royal titles in the period before Adrianople.

Arbogast general of Gratian and later Theodosius, who served with Bauto in the Balkans after Adrianople. In 391 Theodosius left him in Gaul to supervise Valentinian II, but the latter's suicide forced Arbogast to revolt against Theodosius, raising up Eugenius as a usurper in 392 and killing himself shortly after losing the battle of the Frigidus in 394.

Arcadius emperor 383–408, eldest son of Theodosius, named augustus while still a child in 383. Left in Constantinople in 394, he was eastern ruler after his father's death in 395, but was controlled by a series of high-ranking officials opposed to Stilicho, whose final falling-out with Honorius was precipitated by Arcadius' death in 408.

Ardashir founder of the Sassanian Persian royal dynasty, ruling from c. 224 to 241.

Argaith Gothic king in 249, he invaded the eastern provinces along with Guntheric.

Ariaric Gothic king of the Tervingi defeated by Constantine and Constantinus in 332 and forced to hand over his son as a hostage to be raised in Constantinople. He may be the grandfather of Athanaric.

Arinthaeus general of Valens who negotiated peace with the Gothic *iudex* Athanaric in 369.

Arius Egyptian priest whose christology postulated that God the Son was subordinate to God the Father in the holy trinity. This 'Arianism' was condemned at the council of Nicaea in 325, but a variant of it became dominant among Gothic Christians within the empire.

Arminius chieftain of the Cherusci who destroyed three Roman legions in the battle of the Teutoburger forest in A.D. 9.

Arpulas fourth-century Gothic monk and martyr whose relics were deposited at Cyzicus by the Gothic noblewoman Dulcilla.

Athanaric Gothic *iudex* – 'judge' or 'king' – of the Tervingi. Defeated by Valens after three-year Gothic war, 367–369, he sought refuge in the empire in January 381 and died two weeks after being welcomed to Constantinople by Theodosius.

Atharid son of the Gothic king Rothesteus, he commanded the execution of the Christian Goth Saba in 372.

Athaulf Gothic leader, perhaps king, 410–415, brother-in-law and successor of Alaric. He led the Goths out of Italy into Gaul, then Spain, and married the emperor Honorius' sister Galla Placidia before being murdered in Barcelona in 415.

Augustus *princeps* or first citizen, 27 B.C.–A.D. 14, and thus the first Roman emperor.

Aurelian emperor 270–275. Very active general who fought a Gothic war among many others. The city of Rome was fortified by the massive 'Aurelianic' wall during his reign.

Aurelian (2) praetorian prefect of the East in 400, he succeeded Eutropius as the chief power at the court of Arcadius. Like Eutropius, he was brought down by the revolts of Tribigild and Gainas.

Aureolus general of Gallienus who campaigned against the Goths, but rebelled in 268.

Auxonius praetorian prefect of the East under Valens, and principally responsible for organizing the supply of the Gothic wars of 367–369.

Bacurius tribune of an elite *schola palatina* unit, the Sagitarii, he and Cassio began the fighting at the battle of Adrianople in 378.

Basil of Caesarea *see Glossary of Ancient Sources*

Bathouses fourth-century Gothic priest and martyr whose relics were deposited at Cyzicus by the Gothic noblewoman Dulcilla.

Bauto general of Gratian who in 381 prevented the Gothic revolt in Thrace from spreading into the western provinces.

Bonitus Frankish general of high rank in the army of Constantine during the civil wars with Licinius.

Botheric Roman general stationed in Thessalonica in 390 in response to the Balkan revolt. His murder in the city led to a massacre of civilians in the city's circus on the orders of Theodosius I.

Caesarius praetorian prefect in the East from 400–403 after the collapse of the regime of Aurelian (2). His reluctance to negotiate with barbarians convinced Alaric to leave the East and move to Italy.

Candac barbarian chieftain and employer of Paria, who was the grandfather of the sixth-century author Jordanes.

Cannobaudes Gothic king, possibly fictional, supposedly defeated by Aurelian.

Caracalla emperor 211–217. He issued the so-called Antonine Constitution extending Roman citizenship to almost every inhabitant of the empire in 212. His defeat of the Parthian monarchy allowed the Sassanian dynasty under Ardashir to come to power.

Carinus emperor 283–285, older son and co-emperor of Carus. Defeated by Diocletian at the battle of the Margus in 285, he was killed by his own soldiers.

Carus emperor 282–283, successor of Probus. He was killed on campaign against Persia, paving the way for the accession of Diocletian.

Cassio tribune of an elite *schola palatina* unit, the Scutarii, he and Bacurius began the fighting at the battle of Adrianople in 378.

Cassiodorus *see Glossary of Ancient Sources*

Castalius dedicatee of Jordanes' *Getica.*

Claudius emperor 268–270, winner of a dramatic victory over a Gothic army and thus generally known as Claudius 'Gothicus'. The emperor Constantine I began to claim (fictitious) descent from Claudius after 310.

Cniva Gothic king in 250–251 who defeated the emperor Decius at Abrittus.

Colias Gothic commander of a regular unit in the Roman army along with Sueridus, he joined the revolt of Fritigern in 377 after a dispute with the *curia* of Adrianople.

Constans youngest son of Constantine and emperor 337–350. He defeated and killed his elder brother Constantinus in battle in 340 and thereafter ruled the western half of the empire while Constantius II ruled the East. He was killed in the usurpation of Magnentius in 350.

Constans (2) general of the usurper Priscus Attalus. Sent by Attalus to hold Africa in 409, he was defeated and killed by the *comes Africae* Heraclian who was loyal to Honorius.

Constantine I ('the Great') emperor 306–337, acclaimed emperor at York in 306, by 312 the sole ruler of the West and openly Christian. Defeating his rival Licinius in 316 and 324, he became ruler of the whole empire, waging an important Gothic war in 332.

Constantinus (Constantine II) son of Constantine and augustus 337–340. As caesar, he commanded his father's Gothic campaign of 332. He was killed in a war against his youngest brother Constans in 340.

Constantine III usurper in the West 407–411, raised to the purple in Britain in 407 as a response to the Rhine invasions of 405/406 and in control of Britain, Gaul and Spain from 408 until his defeat and death in 411.

Constantius I emperor 293–306 (caesar 293–305; augustus 305–306) and father of Constantine I, he was a general of Diocletian and Maximian made caesar along with Galerius in 293, when the tetrarchy was created.

Constantius II emperor 337–361. Middle son of Constantine, who outlived his brothers Constantinus and Constans, fighting many wars on the middle Danube, while allowing the Tervingi to grow quite powerful.

Constantius III emperor 419–421, father of Valentinian III. The most successful general of Honorius after 408, he orchestrated the Gothic settlement in Aquitania in 418. He became co-emperor with Honorius after marrying Galla Placidia.

Crispus eldest son of Constantine, left to supervise the West after 324, but executed in obscure circumstances in 326.

Crocus Alamannic king and Roman general instrumental in the proclamation of Constantine I at York in 306.

Decebalus Dacian king 85–106, defeated by Trajan in his second Dacian war, after which the province of Dacia was created.

Decius emperor 249–251, killed in battle at Abrittus by the Goths of Cniva.

Diocletian emperor 284–305. With Maximian as co-emperor from 285, he formed the tetrarchy in 293 by appointing Constantius and Galerius as his caesars, thereby ending the long period of political crisis in the third century and stabilizing the empire. The Gothic Tervingi are first mentioned during his reign.

Dulcilla daughter of the fourth-century Gothic queen Gaatha, she deposited relics of many Gothic martyrs at Cyzicus in Asia Minor.

Eriulf Gothic general and rival of Fravitta, who killed him at a banquet hosted by Theodosius.

Ermanaric Gothic king of the Greuthungi in the decade or more prior to 376, he killed himself after several defeats by the Huns. His story is the subject of much legendary embellishment by the sixth-century author Jordanes.

Eucherius son of Stilicho and Serena, murdered after the fall of his father's regime in 408.

Eudoxia wife of Arcadius and enemy of Eutropius.

Eugenius usurper in the West, 392–394. A grammarian chosen by Arbogast to be a figurehead emperor for his rebellion, he was executed after defeat at the battle of the Frigidus in 394.

Eusebius of Nicomedia bishop of Nicomedia in Bithynia until his death c. 342, he was a homoean sympathiser of Arius and consecrated Ulfila.

Eusebius of Samosata fourth-century bishop of Samosata (c. 360–c. 380) exiled in Thrace during the Gothic revolt and the recipient of an important letter from Basil of Caesarea attesting to Gothic ravages in that province.

Eutropius eunuch grand chamberlain of Arcadius and chief official at the eastern court from the death of Rufinus in 395 until the coup of Gainas in 400.

Farnobius Gothic noble defeated in Thrace by Frigeridus in 377, after which his followers were settled as farmers in Italy.

Fravitta Gothic general in Roman service and rival of Eriulf whom he killed in the 380s. He suppressed Gainas' revolt in 400.

Frigeridus general of Gratian, sent to the Balkans with Richomeres in 377 to assist the generals of Valens against the Goths.

Fritigern Gothic leader of the Tervingi, and with Alavivus one of two chieftains primarily responsible for the Danube crossing of 376. At Marcianople in 377, Fritigern took overall military command of Gothic and other rebels in the Balkans, eventually winning the battle of Adrianople in 378.

Gaatha fourth-century Gothic queen, interested in preserving the memory of Christian martyrs of Athanaric's persecution of the 370s.

Gainas Gothic general in Roman service who led the eastern army back to Constantinople in 395, where he organized the murder of Rufinus. Sent to suppress the revolt of Tribigild in 399, he himself rebelled against the government in 400, but was killed trying to flee the empire after being defeated by Fravitta.

Galerius emperor 293–311 (caesar 293–305; augustus 305–311), he was a general of Diocletian and Maximian made caesar along with

Constantius I in 293, when the tetrarchy was created. He disrupted the planned succession of Constantine I and Maxentius in 305, thereby precipitating half a decade of civil war.

Galla Placidia c. 390–450, imperial princess, daughter of Theodosius I, sister of Honorius, mother of Valentinian III. Captured in the siege of Rome, she married Alaric's successor Athaulf, but after his murder was returned to the imperial government and married to Constantius III.

Gallienus emperor 253–268, his reign is generally portrayed as a long catalogue of disasters, among them devastating Gothic raids in the eastern provinces.

Gallus caesar of Constantius II 351–354 and elder brother of Julian, he was executed by Constantius in 354.

Gildo north African aristocrat given a sweeping command as *comes Africae* by Theodosius in order to secure his loyalty during the usurpation of Magnus Maximus. In 398, he switched allegiance from Rome to Constantinople, but was suppressed by Stilicho and executed.

Gouththikas Gothic priest with whom the martyr Saba intended to spend Easter 372.

Gratian emperor 367–383. The son of Valentinian I, who became the ruler of the western empire after his father's death in 375. He acquiesced in the proclamation of Theodosius in 379 rather than exacerbate the crisis in the East after Adrianople, but was overthrown and killed in the usurpation of Magnus Maximus in 383.

Guntheric Gothic king in 249, he invaded the eastern provinces in company of Argaith.

Gunthigis (Baza) barbarian general in imperial service to whom the sixth-century author Jordanes served as secretary.

Hadrian emperor 117–138 under whom the expansion of the Roman empire ceased.

Heraclian *comes Africae* 408–413 who refused to recognize the regime of Priscus Attalus in 409 and cut off the grain supply of Rome.

Honorius emperor 393–423. Youngest son of Theodosius, nominally the western emperor after his father's death in 395, but in reality controlled by Stilicho, whose daughters Maria and Thermantia he married in succession. After falling out with Stilicho in 408 and sanctioning his murder, his government could not control Alaric, while the many usurpations between 407 and 413 were only suppressed by Constantius III.

Ingenuus usurper against Gallienus in 260.

Jordanes *see Glossary of Ancient Sources*

Jovian emperor 363–364. He was elected by the officers of Julian's field army to extract them from Persian territory after Julian's death, but did so by means of unpopular concessions to the Persians, dying after less than a year on the throne.

Jovius praetorian prefect of Italy and rival of Olympius at the court of Honorius after the death of Stilicho, he attempted to negotiate a treaty with Alaric in 409.

Julian emperor 361–363. Nephew of Constantine and by 354 last surviving male relative of Constantius II, who made him caesar in 355. After becoming sole emperor in 361, he attempted to de-Christianize the empire, but failed to do so because he died prematurely on campaign in Persia.

Julius *magister militum* of the East at the time of Adrianople, he stopped the Gothic revolt from spreading into Asia by instigating a massacre of Goths in the eastern provinces.

Junius Soranus *dux Scythiae* in 373 who ordered the collection of the relics of the Gothic martyr Saba and sent them to his native province of Cappadocia.

Justina second wife of Valentinian I and mother of Valentinian II.

Justinian emperor 527–565 who reconquered territories in the Latin West that had once been imperial provinces but which had been barbarian kingdoms for many decades.

Licinius emperor 308–324, rival of Constantine for control of the whole empire after the civil wars of 306–313.

Lupicinus *comes rei militaris* in Thrace in 376 and with Maximus one of two officials primarily responsible for managing the Gothic crossing of the Danube. He organized the banquet at Marcianople which sparked off the Gothic rebellion of 377.

Magnentius usurper 350–353, he overthrew Constans in 350, but was defeated by Constantius II in 353 in a civil war that badly weakened the Rhine frontier.

Magnus Maximus usurper 383–388, he overthrew Gratian and was briefly tolerated by Theodosius, until his invasion of Italy forced Valentinian II to flee to the East and provoked civil war with Theodosius.

Marcus Aurelius emperor 161–180, his wars against the Marcomanni occupied many years of his reign and disrupted conditions on the middle Danube frontier.

Maria elder daughter of Stilicho and Serena, married to Honorius in 398.

Maxentius usurper, 306–312. Son of the augustus Maximian, Maxentius was proclaimed augustus at Rome but never recognized as a legitimate emperor. He died in battle against Constantine in 312.

Maximian emperor 285–305. Co-emperor of Diocletian from 285, and one of the two augusti in the tetrarchy formed in 293 with the appointment of Constantius I and Galerius as caesars, he was the father of Maxentius, who revolted after Maximian's abdication.

Maximus Roman *dux* of either Moesia or Scythia in 376 and with Lupicinus one of two officials primarily responsible for managing the Gothic crossing of the Danube.

Modares Gothic general in imperial service under Theodosius, he won the first success against Fritigern's followers in 379, a year after Adrianople.

Nero emperor 54–68 and the last member of the Julio-Claudian dynasty.

Nicomachus Flavianus Roman aristocrat who joined the rebellion of Arbogast in 392, lending legitimacy to the usurpation of Eugenius, he killed himself after defeat at the battle of the Frigidus.

Olympius *magister officiorum* of Honorius, and opposed to any compromise with Alaric, he instigated the murder of Stilicho and replaced him as the most powerful figure at court.

Paria grandfather of Jordanes and secretary to the barbarian chieftain Candac.

Postumus usurper 260–269. Proclaimed emperor after successfully defeating a barbarian invasion, he ruled a separate 'Gallic empire' that was not suppressed until the reign of Aurelian.

Priscus Attalus Roman senator of Greek origin who led the senatorial embassy requesting that Honorius negotiate with Alaric. Made urban prefect by Honorius, he then became a usurper with Alaric as his sponsor. He was deposed by Alaric in 410, remaining with the Goths until 415 when Wallia handed him over to Honorius, who allowed Attalus to retire to the island of Lipari.

Probus emperor 276–282. His reign is little known, but he fought many frontier wars against various barbarians, including the Goths.

Procopius usurper 365–366, he could claim kinship with the Constantinian dynasty and rebelled against Valens, but was suppressed in 366. The fact that some Tervingian leaders supported Procopius provided the excuse for Valens' Gothic war of 367–369.

Profuturus general of Valens sent to Thrace with Traianus in 377 to fight the Goths, he was killed at the battle of Ad Salices.

Promotus general of Theodosius sent to suppress the Balkan revolt of 391, but killed there in an ambush and replaced by Stilicho.

Radagaisus Gothic king who appeared suddenly in 405 leading an invasion across the Alps through Raetia into Italy until his defeat by Stilicho outside Florence in 406.

Rausimod Sarmatian king defeated by Constantine at Campona in 323.

Richomeres *comes domesticorum* and senior general of Gratian, sent to the Balkans with Frigeridus in 377 to fight against the Goths, and in 378 leader of Gratian's advance guard before Adrianople. Surviving the battle, he later prevented the Gothic revolt from spreading to the West.

Rothesteus Gothic king and father of Atharid, the Gothic noble who commanded the death of Saba in 372.

Rufinus praetorian prefect of the East, left behind in Constantinople by Theodosius to run the East during the imperial campaign against Eugenius, but killed in 395 by the eastern troops returning under the command of Gainas.

Saba Gothic Christian and martyr under the *iudex* Athanaric, killed at the orders of Rothesteus' son Atharid on 12 April 372.

Sansalas Gothic priest in the village of the martyr Saba.

Saphrax Gothic *dux* and co-regent with Alatheus for the Greuthungian child-king Videric. Together they led some of the Greuthungi across the Danube in 376, eventually joining forces with the Tervingi of Fritigern and fighting at the battle of Adrianople in 378.

Sarus Gothic general in Roman service beginning in 407, he caused the final breakdown of negotiations between Alaric and Honorius and was later killed in battle with his long-standing enemy Athaulf in 412.

Saturninus *magister equitum* and senior general of Valens, promoted to lead the Thracian campaign against Fritigern's Goths after the failures of Traianus and Profuturus. After Adrianople, he continued in the service of Theodosius and helped negotiate the emperor's Gothic peace of 382.

Sebastianus retired western general promoted by Valens in spring 378 to take overall command of the Gothic war, he won some victories but was killed in the battle of Adrianople.

Septimius Severus emperor 193–211, North African emperor of Punic origin and the father of Caracalla.

Serena Theodosius' niece and adopted daughter, wife of Stilicho and mother of Eucherius, Maria and Thermantia, she was murdered during Alaric's first siege of Rome with the approval of her cousin Galla Placidia.

Shapur I Sassanian king of Persia 240–272 and the most dangerous enemy of the Roman empire in this period.

Sigesarius Gothic homoean priest in the entourage of Alaric and Athaulf who baptised Priscus Attalus.

Stilicho Roman general and member of the imperial family, husband of Theodosius' niece and adopted daughter Serena, father of Eucherius, Maria and Thermantia. Stilicho was regent for Honorius after Theodosius' death in 395, but his claims to similar regency over Arcadius in the East were rejected by the eastern court. The death of Arcadius in 408 caused a final breach between Stilicho and Honorius, after which Stilicho was killed.

Sueridus Gothic commander of a regular unit in the Roman army along with Colias, he joined the revolt of Fritigern in 377 after a dispute with the *curia* of Adrianople.

Tacitus emperor 275–276, assassinated while campaigning against Gothic invaders in Asia.

Tacitus (historian) *see Glossary of Ancient Sources*

Themistius *see Glossary of Ancient Sources*

Theoderic I Gothic king 418–451. A relative by marriage of Alaric, he led the Goths after their settlement in Aquitania in 418.

Theodoric ("the Great") Ostrogothic king of Italy 489–526. The lost Gothic history of Cassiodorus was dedicated to him.

Theodosius I emperor 379–395. Proclaimed emperor and recognized by Gratian shortly after emerging from retirement, he concluded the Balkan Gothic war in 382, thereafter facing the western usurpations of Magnus Maximus and Eugenius, before his premature death.

Theodosius 'the Elder' father of Theodosius I and the best general of Valentinian I, executed in obscure circumstances after Valentinian's death in 375.

Thermantia younger daughter of Stilicho and Serena, married to Honorius in 408 after the death of his first wife, Thermantia's elder sister Maria.

Traianus general of Valens sent to Thrace with Profuturus in 377 to fight the Goths, he was killed at Adrianople.

Trajan emperor 98–117, he fought two Dacian wars on the Danube frontier and created the Roman province of Dacia.

Tribigild Gothic general in imperial service, he revolted at Nacoleia in Asia Minor in 399.

Uldin Hun chieftain on the Danube in 400 who killed Gainas.

Ulfila bishop of 'the Scythians' appointed in either 336 or 341 and evangelist of the Goths beyond the Danube. Expelled from Gothia after eight years, he and his followers settled in Moesia, inventing an alphabet in which Gothic could be written and translating the Bible into it.

Valens emperor 364–378. Made emperor by his elder brother Valentinian I in 364, he took command of the East, but was soon challenged by the usurpation of Procopius, which then led to the Gothic wars of 367–369. He admitted the Tervingi into the empire in 376 in order to use them as soldiers on the eastern frontier. When the Gothic revolt became serious in 377, he made peace with Persia and returned to Thrace, where he was defeated and killed at Adrianople in 378.

Valentinian I emperor 364–375. Elected by the army after the death of Jovian, he divided the empire with his younger brother Valens, taking the West for his own part and fighting many campaigns on the Rhine and the middle Danube before dying on campaign against the Quadi.

Valentinian II emperor 375–392. Made emperor upon his father Valentinian I's death in 375, he was always dominated by others, first his mother Justina and his elder half-brother Gratian, then Theodosius I. Restored to his throne by Theodosius after being driven from Italy by Magnus Maximus, he was left behind in Gaul as a puppet emperor under the supervision of Arbogast and hanged himself in 392.

Valentinian III emperor 425–455 and the only son of Galla Placidia and Constantius III, he ruled the western empire for thirty years.

Valerian emperor 253–260, father of Gallienus and active mainly in the East, he was captured on campaign against the Persians and held in captivity until his death.

Vespasian emperor 69–79.

Victor general of Valens who arranged peace with the Gothic *iudex* Athanaric in 369, and later negotiated peace terms with Persia in 377.

Videric Gothic king of the Greuthungi and son of Vithimir, he became king as a child under the regency of the *duces* Alatheus and Saphrax.

Vithimir Gothic king of the Greuthungi and father of Videric, he succeeded Ermanaric but died in battle against the Huns.

Wallia Gothic king 415–418 and successor of Athaulf, he returned Galla Placidia and Priscus Attalus to Honorius and fought on behalf of the imperial government in Spain.

Wereka Gothic priest and martyr whose relics were deposited at Cyzicus by the Gothic noblewoman Dulcilla.

Wiguric Gothic king responsible for the death of the various Gothic martyrs whose relics were deposited at Cyzicus by the Gothic noblewoman Dulcilla.

FURTHER READING

✿ ✿ ✿

THE CRITICAL EDITIONS OF GREEK AND LATIN AUTHORS FROM WHICH I cite are listed at the start of the endnotes. Fortunately for the beginning student and general reader, nearly all the primary sources that bear on the Goths are now readily available in English translation, which should allow readers to check the basis of my conclusions if they wish to do so. Among Latin writers, our most important source is Ammianus Marcellinus, available in an excellent but abridged translation by Walter Hamilton in the Penguin Classics and an occasionally misleading but complete version by J. C. Rolfe in the Loeb Classical Library, which also includes the text of the *Origo Constantini*. For the later period, the poems of Claudian are indispensable, and can be read in the two-volume Loeb translation of M. Platnauer, while Rutilius Namatianus is included in the Loeb *Minor Latin Poets*, volume 2. Lactantius' *Deaths of the Persecutors* is translated in the edition of J. L. Creed (Oxford, 1984), and the Latin panegyrics are translated by Barbara Saylor Rodgers and C. E. V. Nixon, *In Praise of Later Roman Emperors* (Berkeley, 1995). Orosius' *Seven Books against the Pagans* is available in a Fathers of the Church translation by R. Deferrari (Washington, DC, 1964). Jordanes deserves to be read in full, if only to demonstrate how far-fetched the narrative that surrounds his migration stories really is, and the translation of C. C. Mierow (Princeton, 1915) is sound if slightly archaic.

Among the Greek sources, Zosimus' *New History* can be read in the translation of R. Ridley (Canberra, 1982). The fragments of Eunapius and Olympiodorus are readily available in R. Blockley, *The Fragmentary Classicising Historians of Late Antiquity*, volume 2 (Liverpool, 1983), with facing Greek text. The emperor Julian's works are translated in a three-volume Loeb edition; Basil of Caesarea's letters are in a four-volume Loeb. Several relevant Themistian orations are translated in Peter Heather and David Moncur, *Philosophy, Politics and Empire in the Fourth Century: Select Orations of Themistius* (Liverpool, 2001). Substantial parts of Libanius' corpus are now available between four Loeb volumes and two volumes in the Liverpool series: A. F. Norman,

Antioch as a Centre of Hellenic Culture as Observed by Libanius (2001) and Scott Bradbury, *Select Letters of Libanius* (2004). Gregory Thaumaturgus, the documents bearing on Ulfila, the *Passio Sabae*, and the other Gothic martyrologies are all translated in an excellent collection by Peter Heather and John Matthews, *The Goths in the Fourth Century* (Liverpool, 1991). The major Greek church historians, unfortunately, are not well served in English translation: Socrates and Sozomen are available in the Nicene and Post-Nicene Fathers (second series, vol. 2), but the translations were made from old and inaccurate editions, as was the version of Philostorgius in Bohn's Library (London, 1855).

Among the secondary literature, Peter Heather's *Goths and Romans, 332–489* (Oxford, 1991) is the best treatment of its subject available in any language, even though my interpretation of motive and causation in Gothic history differs substantially from his. Unfortunately, Heather's more recent works, *The Goths* (Oxford, 1996) and *The Fall of the Roman Empire* (Oxford, 2005), restate the same arguments as the first book and shear them of all their nuance, advocating instead a neo-Romantic vision of mass migrations of free Germanic peoples. Heather's *idée fixe* – that the Huns were responsible for the fall of the Roman empire and the end of the ancient world – is simple, elegant, and wrong. The literature on ethnogenesis is vast, but Herwig Wolfram's *History of the Goths* (1979; English trans., Berkeley, 1988) is the most widely available. Its mixture of outlandish philological speculation, faulty documentation, and oracular pronouncement remains very influential. Less bizarre, if wholly derivative, accounts of ethnogenesis are available in works by Wolfram's Anglophone apostles: see especially Patrick Geary's contribution to *Late Antiquity: A Guide to the Post-Classical World*, edited by Peter Brown, G. W. Bowersock and Oleg Grabar. Far better are the many works of Walter Pohl, the best of which are not available in English; however, see his contributions to the Transformation of the Roman World series (in *Strategies of Distinction*, 1998; *Kingdoms of the Empire*, 1998; *Regna and Gentes*, 2003). Among older literature in English, the work of E. A. Thompson must have pride of place. His *History of Attila and the Huns* (Oxford, 1948), *Early Germans* (Oxford, 1965), *Visigoths in the Time of Ulfila* (Oxford, 1966), and *Goths in Spain* (Oxford, 1969) were all pioneering, even if their mixture of rigorous empiricism and Marxist dogma reads oddly today. J. M. Wallace-Hadrill's 'Gothia and Romania', reprinted in *The Long-Haired Kings* (Oxford, 1962), also broke new ground in its day.

Much of the most important work on the Goths was done in more general studies of the later Roman empire. J. B. Bury's *Later Roman Empire* (London, 1923) can still be read with great profit and A. H. M. Jones' massive *Later Roman Empire, 284–602* (Oxford, 1964) remains the basic work of reference. Several useful articles appear in the new volumes 13 and 14 of the revised *Cambridge Ancient History*. The only good introduction to the third century in English is David S. Potter, *The Roman Empire at Bay, AD 180–395* (London, 2004), though its treatment of the fourth century is less reliable. For the tetrarchy, Stephen Williams' *Diocletian and the Roman Recovery* (London, 1985) is generally sound, but the key text is T. D. Barnes' *Constantine and Eusebius* (Cambridge, MA, 1981). Hugh Elton's *Warfare in Roman Europe* (Oxford, 1996) is useful on the Roman approach to fighting barbarians. For the reign of Constantius, T. D. Barnes' complex and difficult *Athanasius and Constantius* (Cambridge, MA, 1993) provides the only reliable narrative in English. For Valens, we now have Noel Lenski's *Failure of Empire* (Berkeley, 2002); while it is perhaps too kind to Valens, its approach to Gothic history betters Heather on such points as Gothic conversion. Simon MacDowall, *Adrianople AD 378* (New York, 2001) is an excellent, if speculative, reconstruction of the battle aimed at the hobbyist audience. No reliable modern study of Theodosius has been published in English.

One will get considerably more out of the ancient sources after having read a few studies of them. The literature on Ammianus, in English and every other language, is vast. John Matthews, *The Roman Empire of Ammianus* (London, 1989) and T. D. Barnes, *Ammianus and the Representation of Historical Reality* (Ithaca, 1998) are essential. On Claudian, Alan Cameron's *Claudian: Poetry and Propaganda at the Court of Honorius* (Oxford, 1970) is unsurpassed. Zosimus has yet to attract the English study he deserves, but one can consult the introduction and commentary to the five-volume French edition by François Paschoud (1979–1993). The literature on Jordanes is large and partisan, for the reasons discussed at length in chapter three, and modern Germanist fantasy is regularly retailed as fact. Two responsible alternatives are Brian Croke, 'Cassiodorus and the Getica of Jordanes', *Classical Philology* 82 (1987): 117–34; and Walter Goffart, 'Jordanes' Getica and the disputed authenticity of Gothic origins from Scandinavia', *Speculum* 80 (2005): 379–98. For literary reactions to Adrianople, the basic study is Noel Lenski, '*Initium mali romano imperio*: contemporary reactions to the battle of Adrianople', *Transactions of the American Philological Association* 127 (1997): 129–68. Almost nothing in English exists on the Sântana-de-Mureş/Černjachov culture apart from summaries in Heather and Matthews, *Goths in the Fourth Century*, and Heather, *Goths*. Both of these are broadly accurate treatments of the evidence as it was known in the later 1980s, but lack theoretical rigour in relating archaeological and historical evidence.

NOTES

※ ※ ※

The following abbreviations and editions are used in the notes.

AE = *L'Année Epigraphique* (Paris, 1888–); cited by year and inscription number.

Ambrose, *Ep.* = *Epistulae et acta*, ed. O. Faller and M. Zelzer (4 vols., CSEL 82.1–4). Vienna, 1968–1996.

Ambrose, *De spir. sanct.* = *De spiritu sancto*, ed. O. Faller (CSEL 79). Vienna, 1964. pp. 1–222.

Ammianus, *RG* = *Ammiani Marcellini Rerum Gestarum libri qui supersunt*, ed. W. Seyfarth (2 vols.). Leipzig, 1978.

Aurelius Victor = *Liber de Caesaribus*, ed. F. Pichlmayr, rev. R. Gruendel. Leipzig, 1970.

Auxentius = *Epistula de fide, uita et obitu Vlfilae*, ed. R. Gryson (CCSL 87). Turnhout, 1978. pp. 164–65.

Basil, *Ep.* = *Epistulae*, ed. R. J. Deferrari (4 vols.). London, 1926–1939.

Cassius Dio = *Historiarum romanarum quae supersunt*, ed. U. Boissevain (5 vols.). Berlin, 1895–1931.

Chron. Min. = *Chronica minora, saec. IV.V.VI.VII*, ed. Th. Mommsen (3 vols.). (MGH, Auctores Antiquissimi 9, 11, 13). Berlin, 1892–1898.

Claudian: *Eutr.* = *In Eutropium*; *Get.* = *De bello Gothico*; *Gild.* = *De bello Gildonico*; *III cons. Hon.* = *Panegyricus de tertio consulatu Honorii augusti*; *IV cons. Hon.* = *Panegyricus de quarto consulatu Honorii augusti*; *VI cons. Hon.* = *Panegyricus de sexto consulatu Honorii augusti*; *Ruf.* = *In Rufinum*; *Stil.* = *De consulatu Stilichonis*, all in *Claudii Claudiani Carmina*, ed. Th. Birt (MGH, Auctores Antiquissimi 10). Berlin, 1892.

Codex Theodosianus = *Theodosiani libri XVI cum constitutionibus Sirmondianis*, ed. Th. Mommsen (3 vols.). Berlin, 1905.

CCSL = Corpus Christianorum, Series Latina.

CIL = Corpus Inscriptionum Latinarum.

CSEL = Corpus Scriptorum Ecclesiasticorum Latinorum.

Descriptio consulum = R. W. Burgess, *The Chronicle of Hydatius and the Consularia Constantinopolitana*. Oxford, 1993. pp. 214–46.

Dexippus = *Die Fragmente der Griechischen Historiker (FGrH) IIA*, ed. F. Jacoby. Berlin, 1926. pp. 452–80.

Epitome de Caesaribus = *Pseudo-Aurélius Victor: Abrégé des Césars*, ed. M. Festy. Paris, 1999.

Eunapius = R. C. Blockley, *The Fragmentary Classicising Historians of the Later Roman Empire. Eunapius, Olympiodorus, Priscus and Malchus, vol 2: Text, Translation and Historiographical Notes*. Liverpool, 1983. pp. 1–151.

Eunapius, *VS* = *Vitae sophistarum*, ed. J. Giangrande. Rome, 1956.

Eusebius, *Vita Const.* = *Eusebius Werke I.1: Über das Leben des Kaisers Konstantin*, 2nd ed., ed. F. Winkelmann. Berlin, 1975.

Eutropius = *Eutrope: Abrégé d'Histoire Romaine*, ed. J. Hellegouarc'h. Paris, 1999.

FHG = C. Müller, ed., *Fragmenta Historicorum Graecorum* (5 vols.). Paris, 1841–1938.

Gregory Nazianzen, *Ep.* = *Gregor von Nazianz: Briefe*, ed. P. Gallay. Berlin, 1969.

Historia Augusta: *V. Gord.* = *Vita Gordiani*; *V. Aurel.* = *Vita Aureliani*; *V. Prob.* = *Vita Probi*; *V. Car.* = *Vitae Cari, Carini, Numeriani*, all in *Scriptores Historiae Augustae*, ed. E. Hohl, rev. Ch. Samberger and W. Seyfarth (2 vols.). Leipzig, 1971.

ILS = *Inscriptiones Latinae Selectae*, ed. H. Dessau (3 vols.). Berlin, 1892.

Jerome, *Chron.* = *Eusebius Werke 17: Die Chronik des Hieronymus*, ed. R. Helm. Berlin, 1956.

Jordanes, *Getica* = *Iordanis Romana et Getica*, ed. Th. Mommsen (MGH, Auctores Antiquissimi 5.1). Berlin, 1882. pp. 53–138.

Julian, *Caes.* = *Caesares*, *Or.* = *Orationes*, all in *L'empereur Julien: Oeuvres complètes*, ed. J. Bidez and C. Lacombrade (2 vols. in 4). Paris, 1924–1965.

Lactantius, *De mort. pers.* = *De mortibus persecutorum*, ed. J. L. Creed. Oxford, 1984.

Libanius, *Or.* = *Libanii Opera*, vols. I–IV: *Orationes*, ed. R. Foerster. Leipzig, 1903–1908.

MGH = Monumenta Germaniae Historica.

Notitia Dignitatum = *Notitia Dignitatum accedunt Notitia urbis Constantinopolitanae et latercula provinciarum*, ed. O. Seeck. Berlin, 1876.

Olympiodorus = R. C. Blockley, *The Fragmentary Classicising Historians of the Later Roman Empire. Eunapius, Olympiodorus, Priscus and Malchus, vol 2: Text, Translation and Historiographical Notes*. Liverpool, 1983. pp. 152–210.

Optatianus, *Carm.* = *Publilii Optatiani Porfyrii Carmina*, ed. G. Polara. Turin, 1973.

Orig. Const. = *Origo Constantini: Anonymus Vale-sianus, Teil I: Text und Kommentar*, ed. I. König. Trier, 1987.

Orosius, *Hist.* = *Historiarum aduersum paganos libri septem*, ed. K. Zangemeister (CSEL 5). Vienna, 1882.

Pan. Lat. = *XII Panegyrici Latini*, ed. R. Mynors. Oxford, 1964.

Paulinus, *V. Ambrosii* = A. Bastiaensen, *Vita di Cipriani, Vita di Ambrogio, Vita di Agostino.* Milan, 1975. pp. 51–124.

Peter the Patrician = *FHG* 4: 181–91.

PG = *Patrologia Graeca.*

Philostorgius, *HE* = *Philostorgius Kirchengeschichte mit dem Leben des Lucian von Antiochien und den Fragmenten eines arianischen Historiographen*, ed. J. Bidez, rev. F. Winkelmann. Berlin, 1972.

PLS = *Patrologia Latina Supplementum.*

Procopius, *Aed.* = *Procopii Caesariensis Opera IV: De aedificiis libri VI*, ed. J. Haury, rev. G. Wirth. Leipzig, 1964.

RIC = *The Roman Imperial Coinage* (10 vols.). London, 1923–1994.

Rufinus, *HE* = *Eusebius Werke II.2: Die Kirchengeschichte*, ed. E. Schwartz and Th. Mommsen. Berlin, 1907. pp. 951–1040.

Rutilius, *De reditu suo* = *Rutilius Namatianus: Sur son retour*, ed. J. Vessereau and F. Préchac. Paris, 1933.

Socrates, *HE* = *Sokrates Kirchengeschichte*, ed. G. C. Hansen. Berlin, 1995.

Sozomen, *HE* = *Sozomenus Kirchengeschichte*, ed. J. Bidez, rev. G. C. Hansen. Berlin, 1960.

Synesius, *De providentia and De regno* = *Synesii Cyrenensis opuscula*, ed. N. Terzaghi. Rome, 1944.

Tacitus, *Germ.* = *Germania*, in *Cornelii Taciti opera minora*, ed. M. Winterbottom. Oxford, 1975. pp. 35–62.

Tacitus, *Hist.* = *Historiae*, ed. E. Koestermann. Leipzig, 1969.

Themistius, *Or.* = *Orationes*, ed. G. Downey and A. F. Norman (3 vols.). Leipzig, 1965–1974.

Theodoret, *HE* = *Theodoret Kirchengeschichte*, ed. L. Parmentier, rev. G. C. Hansen. Berlin, 1998.

Zosimus, *HN* = *Zosime: Histoire nouvelle*, ed. F. Paschoud (3 vols. in 5). Paris, 1970–1993.

Prologue: Before the Gates of Rome

1. Sources for the foregoing are Zosimus, *HN* 5.34–50; Sozomen, *HE* 9.6–7; Olympiodorus, frag. 7.1 (Blockley) = 4 (Müller); 24 (Blockley) = 24 (Müller); Rutilius Namatianus, *De reditu suo.*

Chapter One: The Goths Before Constantine

1. For instance the Scythians supposedly recruited into the army by Septimius Severus, in Cassius Dio 75.3, taken as Goths by P. Heather, *The Goths* (Oxford, 1996), 39.
2. Dexippus, frag. 20 (Jacoby) = 14 (Müller); 22 (Jacoby) = 16 (Müller).
3. Jordanes, *Getica* 91 and *Historia Augusta, V. Gord.* 31.1: the *Historia Augusta* is much earlier than Jordanes, but it is more likely that its author – much given to invention and word games – conflated two historical names into one than that Jordanes, a much less adventurous writer, expanded a single name into two. Furthermore, the name Argunt is far less plausible than either Argaith or Guntheric.
4. Zosimus, *HN* 1.23.
5. Lactantius, *De mort. pers.* 4.1, but ascribing the victory to the Carpi.
6. Zosimus, *HN* 1.31–35. In this and the following section, I omit references to the later Byzantine traditions preserved in Syncellus, Cedrenus and particularly Zonaras. Although much valuable information is undoubtedly transmitted in these writers from earlier sources, its precise application is not always clear, as is shown by the best treatment of the subject, B. Bleckmann, *Die Reichskrise des III. Jahrhunderts in der spätantiken und byzantinischen Geschichtsschreibung.* (Munich, 1992), 156–219.
7. Zosimus, *HN* 1.35.
8. Canons 5–10 (*PG* 10: 1020–48 at 1037–47). There is a complete translation in P. Heather and J. Matthews, *The Goths in the Fourth Century* (Liverpool, 1991), 1–11. Note that although the Boradoi of Gregory are probably the Boranoi of Zosimus, we should not correct Gregory's reading to that of Zosimus, as the two words may in fact have slightly different significance. Heather and Matthews do, as the two words may in fact have slightly different significance.
9. Dexippus, frag. 25 (Jacoby) = 18 (Müller); Zosimus, *HN* 1.43; 46.
10. Zosimus, *HN* 1.45.
11. *Historia Augusta, V. Aurel.* 22.2.

12. Ammianus, *RG* 31.5.17, in the aftermath of Adrianople, writes nostalgically of Aurelian's distant successes. For the raids under Tacitus and Probus, see Zosimus, *HN* 1.63.1.

13. Tacitus, *Hist.* 1.4.

14. G. Woolf, *Becoming Roman: The Origins of Provincial Civilization in Gaul* (Cambridge, 1998).

15. Zosimus, *HN* 1.29–30; Aurelius Victor 32–33; Eutropius 9.7–8; *Epitome de Caesaribus* 31–32.

16. For Postumus' victory see the recently discovered victory altar from Augsburg: L. Bakker, 'Die Siegesaltar zur Juthungenschlacht von 260 n. Chr. Ein spektakulärer Neufund aus Augusta Vindelicium/Augsburg', *Archäologische Nachrichten* 24 (1993): 274–77.

17. Zosimus, *HN* 1.42–43; 1.45–46; Eutropius 9.11.

18. Zosimus, *HN* 1.63.

19. Zosimus, *HN* 1.71–72; Eutropius 9.17–18; *Epitome de Caesaribus* 37–38; *Historia Augusta, V. Prob.* 21–22; John of Antioch, frag. 158; 160 (*FHG* 4: 600).

20. Aurelius Victor 38.2.

21. Eutropius 9.18; *Historia Augusta, V. Car.* 8.

22. *Pan. Lat.* 10.4.2; Aurelius Victor 39.18–19; Eutropius 9.20.3. *Pan. Lat.* 10, delivered by Mamertinus on 21 April 289, is our main evidence for the early campaigns of Maximian.

23. *Pan. Lat.* 11.17.1: *Tervingi, pars alia Gothorum adiuncta manu Taifalorum.*

CHAPTER TWO: THE ROMAN EMPIRE AND BARBARIAN SOCIETY

1. The earliest attestation of the word is an inscription from the 220s: T. Sarnowski, 'Barbaricum und ein Bellum Bosporanum in einer Inschrift aus Preslav', *Zeitschrift für Papyrologie und Epigraphik* 87 (1991): 137–44.

2. A. Bursche, 'Contacts between the late Roman empire and north-central Europe', *Antiquaries Journal* 76 (1996): 31–50.

3. M. Speidel, 'The Roman army in Arabia', *Aufstieg und Niedergang der römischen Welt* II.8 (1977), 687–730 at 712. This inscription is often thought to refer to a Gothic recruit in Roman service, both because young Guththa's name may itself mean 'Goth' and because he was the son of one Erminarius, a name similar to many recorded later among the Goths. But the main element of the father's name (Erman- or Herman-) is not found exclusively among later Goths, and naming a child 'the Goth' is more likely to reflect the perspective of an outsider than an insider; perhaps Guththa was the child of a Goth in a non-Gothic environment. All of this is speculative, and it is not at all clear that personal names, in very many societies good evidence for familial relationship, are equally useful in establishing connections to a much broader identity such as that of third-century Goths. For that reason, the Goths (*Gouththon te kai Germanon*) of Shapur's monumental inscription are the first certain attestation of Goths in Roman service: see the text at M. Back, *Die Sassanidischen Staatsinschriften* (Leiden, 1978), 290–91. The opaque evidence of Peter the Patrician, frag. 8 (*FHG* 4: 186) may refer to these Goths as well.

4. W. S. Hanson and I. P. Haynes, eds., *Roman Dacia: The Making of a Provincial Society*, Journal of Roman Archaeology Supplement 56 (Portsmouth, RI, 2004).

CHAPTER THREE: THE SEARCH FOR GOTHIC ORIGINS

1. It has now been shown that the real site of the battle was nearly 80 kilometres distance from Detmold at Kalkriese.

2. Jordanes, *Getica* 316.

3. Jordanes, *Getica* 1.

4. Jordanes, *Getica* 2–3.

5. Jordanes, *Getica* 65.

6. Jordanes, *Getica* 25: *velut vagina nationum.*

7. Jordanes, *Getica* 25–28.

8. E.g., Jordanes, *Getica* 68, where the connection is most explicit.

9. The subtlest and most important work to emerge from this school of thought is Walter Pohl, 'Aux origines d'une Europe ethnique. Transformations d'identités entre Antiquité et Moyen Âge', *Annales HSS* 60 (2005): 183–208.

10. Jordanes, *Getica* 29.

11. Jordanes, *Getica* 47.
12. Jordanes, *Getica* 28.
13. Jordanes, *Getica* 43.
14. The *Gotones* mentioned in Tacitus, *Germania* 44.1 and located somewhere in what is now modern Poland would not be regarded as Goths if Jordanes' migration stories did not exist.
15. W. Pohl, 'Telling the difference: signs of ethnic identity', in W. Pohl and H. Reimitz, eds., *Strategies of Distinction: The Construction of Ethnic Communities, 300–800* (Leiden, 1998), 17–69.
16. But the Greek may actually be a loanword from Sumerian: Jonathan Hall, *Hellenicity: Between Ethnicity and Culture* (Chicago, 2002), 112.
17. Dexippus, frag. 6.1 (Jacoby) = 24 (Müller); Zosimus, *HN* 1.37.2, derived from Dexippus.
18. *Codex Theodosianus* 14.10.2.
19. S. Brather, *Ethnische Interpretationen in der frühgeschichtlichen Archäologie: Geschichte, Grundlagen und Alternativen* (Berlin, 2004). For a short English introduction to the ideas developed at length in Brather's large book, see his 'Ethnic identities as constructions of archaeology: the case of the *Alamanni*', in Andrew Gillett, ed., *On Barbarian Identity: Critical Approaches to Ethnicity in the Early Middle Ages* (Turnhout, 2002), 149–76.
20. E.g., V. Bierbrauer, 'Archäologie und Geschichte der Goten vom 1.–7. Jahrhundert', *Frühmittelalterlichen Studien* 28 (1994): 51–172.
21. P. Heather, *The Goths* (Oxford, 1996), 19.
22. I draw the phrase from R. Reece, 'Interpreting Roman hoards', *World Archaeology* 20 (1988): 261–69, who cites it from M. Jarrett, 'Magnus Maximus and the end of Roman Britain', *Transactions of the Honourable Society of Cymmrodorion for 1983* (1983), 22–35 at 22.
23. Rolf Hachmann, *Die Goten und Skandinavien* (Berlin, 1970).
24. Michel Kazanski, *Les Goths* (Paris, 1993).
25. Bernard S. Cohen, *Colonialism and Its Forms of Knowledge: The British in India* (Princeton, 1996).

CHAPTER FOUR: IMPERIAL POLITICS AND THE RISE OF GOTHIC POWER

1. For the Sarmatian campaign see T. D. Barnes, *Constantine and Eusebius* (Cambridge, MA, 1981), 299 n. 15. For the Carpic, ibid., 300 n. 30.
2. Jordanes, *Getica* 110.
3. *Epitome de Caesaribus* 41.3.
4. Constantine (306/307): *Pan. Lat.* 6.10.2; 4.16.4–5; 7.4.2; Lactantius, *De mort. pers.* 29.3; Eusebius, *Vita Const.* 1.25. Licinius: *ILS* 660 (27 June 310).
5. *Pan. Lat.* 6.2.1.
6. *Pan. Lat.* 4.17.1–2; Optatianus, *Carm.* 10.24–28; *Anon. post Dionem* 15.1 (*FHG* 4: 199); *RIC* 7.185 (Trier 240, 241) for Crispus' victory over the Franks, ibid. (Trier 237–239) for the Alamanni.
7. The victories are recorded in Optatianus, *Carm.* 6.18–21 and Zosimus, *HN* 2.21. *Orig. Const.* 21 describes the victory as Gothic, but the numismatic and epigraphic evidence is decisive.
8. *RIC* 7.135 (Lyons 209–222); *AE* (1934), 158.
9. CIL 1: 2335; for the appropriate date, A. Lippold, 'Konstantin und die Barbaren (Konfrontation? Integration? Koexistenz?)', *Studi Italiani di Filologia Classica* 85 (1992): 371–91 at 377.
10. *Anon. post Dionem* 14.1 (*FHG* 4: 199).
11. *ILS* 8942; *ILS* 696, before 315.
12. Alica: *Orig. Const.* 27, with the emendation of Valesius. The testimony of Jordanes, *Getica* 111 is garbled. Franks and Constantine: Zosimus, *HN* 2.15.1. Bonitus: Ammianus, *RG* 15.5.33.
13. Julian, *Caes.* 329B.
14. Aurelius Victor 41; *Epitome de Caesaribus* 41.13; *Chronicon Paschale*, s.a. 328 (Bonn 527); commemorated on coins: *RIC* 7: 331 (Rome 298); *Orig. Const.* 35 for the *ripa Gothica*.
15. Zosimus, *HN* 2.31.3.
16. *Descriptio consulum*, s.a. 332 (Burgess, 236).
17. Eusebius, *Vita Const.* 4.5.1–2; *Orig. Const.* 31; Aurelius Victor 41.13; Eutropius 10.7.
18. Julian, *Or.* 1.9D.
19. Themistius, *Or.* 15.191a.

20. Jordanes, *Getica* 112.
21. Eusebius, *Vita Const.* 4.5.2.
22. Eunapius, frag. 37 (Blockley) = 37 (Müller); Zosimus, *HN* 4.10; Ammianus, *RG* 26.10.3, which puts the number of Procopius' Gothic supporters at 3,000.
23. Tribute: Eusebius, *Vita Const.* 4.5.2; Ammianus, *RG* 17.12. Military service in 332: Eusebius, *Vita Const.* 4.5 is vague on the Goths and entirely explicit about the Sarmatians being forced to serve in the army as a condition of peace (*Vita Const.* 4.6); cf. the late testimony of Jordanes, *Getica* 112 (Goths send 40,000 troops as a result of the treaty). Service on a case-by-case basis thereafter: Libanius, *Or.* 59.89 for 348; Ammianus, *RG* 20.8.1 for 360 and id. 23.2.7 for 363.
24. See in particular G. L. Duncan, *Coin Circulation in the Danubian and Balkan Provinces of the Roman Empire, AD 294–578* (London, 1993) and E. Stoljarik, *Essays on Monetary Circulation in the North-western Black Sea Region in the Late Roman and Byzantine Periods, Late 3rd Century–Early 13th Century AD* (Odessa, 1993).
25. Alexandru Popa, *Romains ou barbares? Architecture en pierre dans le barbaricum à l'époque romaine tardive (sur le matériel archéologique du Nord-Ouest du Pont Euxin)* (Chisinau [Moldova], 2001), 55–61; Andrei Opait, *Local and Imported Ceramics in the Roman Province of Scythia (4th–6th centuries AD): Aspects of Economic Life in the Province of Scythia*, British Archaeological Reports, International Series 1274 (Oxford, 2004).
26. A. Suceveanu and A. Barnea, *La Dobroudja romaine* (Bucharest, 1991), 260.
27. See the articles in Bente Magnus, ed., *Roman Gold and the Development of the Early Germanic Kingdoms: Symposium in Stockholm 14–16 November 1997*, Kungl. Vitterhets Historie och Antikvitets Akademien, Konferenser 51 (Stockholm, 2001); Attila Kiss, 'Die "barbarischen" Könige des 4.–7. Jahrhunderts im Karpatenbecken, als Verbündeten des römischen bzw. byzantinischen Reiches', *Communicationes Archaeologicae Hungariae* (1991): 115–28.
28. Aleksandrovka: Popa, *Romains ou barbares*, 19–21. Bašmačka: ibid., 22–34. Gorodok: ibid., 42–43. Palanca: ibid., 64–65.
29. Alexandru Popa, 'Die Siedlung Sobari, Kr. Soroca (Republik Moldau)', *Germania* 75 (1997): 119–131.
30. Popa, *Romains ou barbares*, 45–49.
31. See generally Attila Kiss, 'Die Schatzfunde I und II von Szilágysomlyó als Quellen der gepidischen Geschichte', *Archaeologia Austriaca* 75 (1991): 249–60; Radu Harhoiu, *The Treasure from Pietroasa in Romania*, British Archaeological Reports, International Series 24 (Oxford, 1977); id., *Die frühe Völkerwanderungszeit in Rumänien* (Bucharest, 1997); Florin Curta, 'Frontier ethnogenesis in late antiquity: the Danube, the Tervingi, and the Slavs', in id., ed., *Borders, Barriers and Ethnogenesis: Frontiers in Late Antiquity and the Early Middle Ages* (Turnhout, 2005), 173–204. For the fortifications of the site, Popa, *Romains ou barbares*, 66–69.
32. Tomb 14 at Hanska-Luterija, with fragments of many bronze vessels, a gold bracelet, and glass items, is a rare exception.
33. M. Kazanski, *Les Goths* (Paris, 1993) is the best short introduction to Sântana-de-Mureş/Černjachov funerary sites, but see many useful articles collected in the following publications: Herwig Wolfram and Falko Daim, eds., *Die Völker an der Mittleren und unteren Donau im fünften und sechsten Jahrhundert* (Vienna, 1980); Patrick Perin, ed., *Gallo-Romains, Wisigoths et Francs en Aquitaine, Septimanie et Espagne (Actes des VIIe Journées internationales d'Archéologie mérovingienne. Toulouse, 1985)* (Paris, 1991); Françoise Vallet and Michel Kazanski, eds., *L'armée romaine et les barbares du IIIe au VIIe siècle*, Mémoires publiées par l'Association Française d'Archéologie Mérovingienne V (Paris, 1993); Françoise Vallet and Michel Kazanski, eds., *La noblesse romaine et les chefs barbares du IIIe au VIIe siècle*, Mémoires publiées par l'Association Française d'Archéologie Mérovingienne IX (Paris, 1995).
34. See especially Guy Halsall, *Settlement and Social Organization: The Merovingian Region of Metz* (Cambridge, 1995); Bonnie Effros, *Merovingian Mortuary Archaeology and the Making of the Early Middle Ages* (Berkeley and Los Angeles, 2003).

CHAPTER FIVE: GOTHS AND ROMANS, 332–376

1. Ammianus, *RG* 26.10.3
2. Ambrose, *De spir. sanct.*, prol. 17 (= CSEL 79: 23).

3. Hippolyte Delehaye, 'Saints de Thrace et de Mésie', *Analecta Bollandiana* 31 (1912): 161–300 at 276: *Kunstanteinus* (*recte* Kunstanteius) *thiudanis*, which are the Gothic spellings for Constantine and (the correct) Constantius.

4. Eusebius, *Vita Const.* 4.6; *Descriptio consulum*, s.a. 334 (Burgess, 236); *Orig. Const.* 31.

5. Eusebius, *Vita Const.* 4.7.

6. Before 340, both Constantius and Constans had taken the title *Sarmaticus*, implying either a joint campaign or two consecutive ones: T. D. Barnes, *Constantine and Eusebius* (Cambridge, MA, 1981), 262, with references.

7. Ammianus, *RG* 15.8.

8. That is the argument of T. D. Barnes, *Ammianus Marcellinus and the Representation of Historical Reality* (Ithaca, 1998).

9. Ammianus, *RG* 16.5.

10. Sarmatian raids in 357: Ammianus, *RG* 16.10. Campaign in 358: Ammianus, *RG* 17.12–13; Aurelius Victor 42. Destruction of the Limigantes (359): Ammianus, *RG* 19.3.

11. CIL 3: 3653 = *ILS* 775.

12. Ammianus, *RG* 22.7.8.

13. Eusebius, *Vita Const.* 4.5 does not demonstrate religious stipulations within the treaty, merely stating that Constantine subdued the barbarians under the sign of the cross, while no specifics can be read into *Vita Const.* 4.14.1 in which all nations are said to be steered by the single helmsman Constantine. The evidence of Eusebius is on this point surely to be preferred to the fifth-century Socrates, *HE* 1.18 and Sozomen, *HE* 2.6.1 where legendary accretions are to be suspected.

14. Socrates, *HE* 4.33–34.

15. Cyril of Jerusalem, *Catech.* 10.19 (*PG* 34: 657–90 at 688C).

16. Province: Auxentius 35–37 (CCSL 87: 164–65) = 56–59 (*PLS* 1: 703–706); Philostorgius, *HE* 2.5. Nicopolis: Jordanes, *Getica* 267.

17. Philostorgius, *HE* 2.5.

18. Sozomen, *HE* 6.37.

19. Sozomen, *HE* 6.37.11.

20. Philostorgius, *HE* 2.5; trans. P. Heather and J. Matthews, *The Goths in the Fourth Century* (Liverpool, 1991), 144.

21. Ammianus, *RG* 31.3.1.

22. Ammianus, *RG* 29.1.11.

23. N. Lenski, *Failure of Empire: Valens and the Roman State in the Fourth Century A.D.* (Berkeley, 2002).

24. Ammianus, *RG* 26.10.3; 27.5.1–2; Eunapius, frag. 37 (Blockley) = 37 (Müller).

25. Zosimus, *HN* 4.10–11.

26. Valentia: *Codex Theodosianus* 8.5.49; 11.1.22; 12.1.113. Gratiana: Procopius, *Aed.* 4.11.20 (Haury, 149). Valentiniana: *Notitia Dignitatum*, Or. 39.27.

27. Coins: *RIC* 9: 219 (Constantinople 40). Inscription: CIL 3.7494 = *ILS* 770. More generally, Themistius, *Or.* 10.136a–b.

28. Ammianus, *RG* 27.5.6.

29. Themistius, *Or.* 10.133a; Ammianus, *RG* 27.5.7.

30. Ammianus, *RG* 27.5.8–9; 31.4.13; Themistius, *Or.* 10.134a.

31. Ammianus, *RG* 27.5.10; Themistius, *Or.* 10.135c–d; Zosimus, *HN* 4.11.

32. Themistius, *Or.* 10.135a.

33. Socrates, *HE* 4.33–34, and following him Sozomen, *HE* 6.37; Orosius, *Hist.* 7.33.19. See in general, N. Lenski, 'The Gothic civil war and the date of the Gothic conversion', *Greek, Roman and Byzantine Studies* 36 (1995): 51–87.

34. Basil, *Ep.* 154, 164, and 165, following the identification of C. Zuckermann, 'Cappadocian fathers and the Goths', *Travaux et Memoires* 11 (1991): 473–86.

35. Text of the *Passio* in Hippolyte Delehaye, 'Saints de Thrace et de Mésie', *Analecta Bollandiana* 31 (1912): 161–300 at 216–21, with the translation of Heather and Matthews, *Goths*, 111–17.

36. Jerome, *Chron.*, s.a. 369 (ed. Helm, 249i).

37. Delehaye, 'Saints', 279. See also the translations at Heather and Matthews, *Goths*, 125–30.

38. Socrates, *HE* 4.33–34; Delehaye, 'Saints', 276, but the manuscript tradition is faulty and the original name commemorated not entirely clear.

CHAPTER SIX: THE BATTLE OF ADRIANOPLE

1. The whole of Ammianus' Hun excursus comes in 31.2.
2. Zosimus, *HN* 4.20.4.
3. See, e.g., Ammianus, *RG* 31.4.2 where rumour is explicitly cited as the source for people's knowledge of events in the *barbaricum*.
4. Ammianus, *RG* 31.3.1–4.
5. Ammianus, *RG* 31.3.5–8.
6. Ammianus, *RG* 31.4.1–2.
7. Ammianus, *RG* 31.4.1.
8. Socrates, *HE* 4.33–34.
9. Basil, *Ep.* 237.
10. Themistius, *Or.* 10.
11. Ammianus, *RG* 31.4.5–7. Hostages are implied at Eunapius, frag. 42 (Blockley) = 42 (Müller).
12. Attested by Zosimus, *HN* 4.20.6; Eunapius, frag. 42 (Blockley) = 42 (Müller).
13. Ammianus, *RG* 31.4.9; Orosius, *Hist.* 7.33.11.
14. Ammianus, *RG* 31.4.11; Zosimus, *HN* 4.20.6.
15. Ammianus, *RG* 31.4.12–13.
16. Ammianus, *RG* 31.5.3.
17. Ammianus, *RG* 31.5.4–8.
18. See especially Ammianus, *RG* 18.2.13; 21.3.4; 29.6.5; 30.1.18–22.
19. Ammianus, *RG* 31.5.9–17.
20. Ammianus, *RG* 31.6.1–3.
21. But see the account of them in Ammianus, *RG* 31.6–11.
22. Ammianus, *RG* 31.7.1.
23. Ammianus, *RG* 31.7.3–5.
24. Ammianus, *RG* 31.7.5–9.
25. Ammianus, *RG* 31.9.1–5. For another example, see 28.5.15, on the Alamanni.
26. Ammianus, *RG* 31.8.1–8; Zosimus, *HN* 4.22; Socrates, *HE* 4.38; Sozomen, *HE* 6.39.2.
27. *Codex Theodosianus* 7.6.3 (9 August 377).
28. Basil, *Ep.* 268.
29. Ammianus, *RG* 3.10.21.
30. Ammianus, *RG* 31.10.1–20.
31. Socrates, *HE* 4.38; Ammianus, *RG* 31.11.1; Zosimus, *HN* 4.21.
32. M. Speidel, 'Sebastian's strike force at Adrianople', *Klio* 78 (1996): 434–37.
33. Ammianus, *RG* 31.11.1–5; Zosimus, *HN* 4.21; Eunapius, frag. 44.4 (Blockley) = 47 (Müller); Theoderet, *HE* 4.33.2 for Valens on Traianus.
34. Ammianus, *RG* 31.12.3.
35. Ammianus, *RG* 31.12.4.
36. Ammianus, *RG* 31.12.4–7; Zosimus, *HN* 4.23–24.
37. Ammianus, *RG* 31.12.8–9.
38. Ammianus, *RG* 31.12.10–15.
39. Ammianus, *RG* 31.12.16.
40. Ammianus, *RG* 31.12.16–31.13.11.
41. Ammianus, *RG* 31.13.12–17; Zosimus, *HN* 4.24.
42. Ammianus, *RG* 31.13.18–19.
43. Themistius, *Or.* 16.206d.

CHAPTER SEVEN: THEODOSIUS AND THE GOTHS

1. Eunapius, frag. 39.9 (Blockley) = 38 (Müller).
2. Ammianus, *RG* 31.16.8.

3. Zosimus, *HN* 4.25–26. The date is established by the fact that Modares, a general of the new emperor Theodosius, had already won some victories in Thrace when the massacre in Asia Minor took place.

4. All earlier scholarly solutions are summarized in S. Elbern, 'Das Gotenmassaker in Kleinasien (378 n. Chr.)', *Hermes* 115 (1987): 99–106.

5. Scythians repulsed from Euchaita in Helenopontus: *PG* 46: 736–48, at 737A (*encomium* of St. Theodore, dated 17 February 380); young man shot by Scythians outside Comana Pontica: *PG* 46: 416–32 at 424C (sermon on baptism, undated), on both of which see C. Zuckerman, 'Cappadocian fathers and the Goths', *Travaux et Mémoires* 11 (1991): 473–86.

6. Ammianus, *RG* 31.10.1–20.

7. S. Williams and G. Friel, *Theodosius: The Empire at Bay* (London, 1994).

8. Ammianus, *RG* 29.6.14–16.

9. Theoderet, *HE* 5.5.

10. N. McLynn, '"*Genere Hispanus*": Theodosius, Spain and Nicene orthodoxy', in K. Bowes and M. Kulikowski, eds., *Hispania in Late Antiquity: Current Approaches* (Leiden, 2005), 77–120.

11. *Pan. Lat.* 2.10–11; Theoderet, *HE* 5.5–6; Sozomen, *HE* 7.2.1; Orosius, *Hist.* 7.34.2–5; *Epitome de Caesaribus* 47–48.

12. The case for western help, though not accepted here, is best made in R. Malcolm Errington, 'Theodosius and the Goths', *Chiron* 26 (1996): 1–27.

13. Units: some or all of *Notitia Dignitatum*, Or. 5.64–66; 6.33, 62, 64, 67; 7.47, 57; 8.27, 32; 9.41, 46 (= 6.64), 47; 28.20; 31.64; 38.18–19, 32–33. Laws: *Codex Theodosianus* 7.13.8–11. Farmers: Libanius, *Or.* 24.16.

14. Zosimus, *HN* 4.30.2; 4.31.2–4.

15. Evidence tabulated at M. McCormick, *Eternal Victory: Triumphal Rulership in Late Antiquity, Byzantium and the Early Medieval West* (Cambridge, 1986), 41–46.

16. P. Heather, *Goths and Romans, 332–489* (Oxford, 1991), 147–56, clarified the structural defect of Zosimus' account for the first time.

17. Zosimus, *HN* 4.25.2–4.

18. Themistius, *Or.* 14.181b.

19. Zosimus, *HN* 4.31.2–4; *Codex Theodosianus* 7.18.3–5.

20. Zosimus, *HN* 4.33.1.

21. Zosimus, *HN* 4.33.1–2.

22. *Descriptio consulum*, s.a. 382 (Burgess, 241).

23. Themistius, *Or.* 16.

24. Synesius, *De regno* 21 (Terzaghi, 50C); Themistius, *Or.* 16.209a–210a; *Pan. Lat.* 2.22.3, but the reference to military service at 2.32.4 need not necessarily refer to the agreement of 382.

25. Themistius, *Or.* 16.211a.

26. Synesius, *De regno* 19 (Terzaghi, 43D).

27. *Notitia Dignitatum*, Or. 5.61; 6.61.

28. Campaign against Maximus: Philostorgius, *HE* 10.8; Zosimus, *HN* 4.45.3; *Pan. Lat.* 2.32.3–4; against Eugenius, Orosius, *Hist.* 7.35.19.

CHAPTER EIGHT: ALARIC AND THE SACK OF ROME

1. R. Harhoiu, *Die frühe Völkerwanderungszeit in Rumänien* (Bucharest, 1997); M. Kazanski and R. Legoux, 'Contribution à l'étude des témoignages archéologiques des Goths en Europe orientale à l'époque des Grandes Migrations: la chronologie de la culture de Černjahov récente', *Archéologie médiévale* 18 (1988): 7–53.

2. *Descriptio consulum*, s.a. 381 (Burgess, 241).

3. Zosimus, *HN* 4.35.1; 4.38–39.

4. Eunapius, frag. 59 (Blockley) = 60 (Müller).

5. Gregory of Nazianzus, *Ep.* 136.

6. Eunapius, frag. 59 (Blockley) = 60 (Müller); Zosimus, *HN* 4.56.2–3.

7. Zosimus, *HN* 5.5.4; Claudian, *Get.* 166–248; 598–647; Synesius, *De regno* 19–21. For Alaric's Goths described as a *gens*: Claudian, *IV cons. Hon.* 474; *Get.* 99, 134, 169, 533, 645–47.

8. *Descriptio consulum*, s.a. 383 (Burgess, 241).

9. Zosimus, *HN* 4.45.3.

10. Sozomen, *HE* 7.25; Theodoret, *HE* 5.18; Rufinus, *HE* 11.18; Ambrose, *Ep.* 51.

11. *ILS* 2949.

12. Claudian, *Get.* 524–25; *VI cons. Hon.* 104–108.

13. Jordanes, *Get.* 146.

14. Zosimus, *HN* 4.50–51; Claudian, *Ruf.* 1.350–51.

15. Claudian, *Stil.* 1.94–115; *Ruf.* 1.314–22, *III cons. Hon.* 147–50.

16. Eunapius, frag. 58.2 (Blockley) = John of Antioch, frag. 187 (*FHG* 4: 608–10).

17. Orosius, *Hist.* 7.35.19; Zosimus, *HN* 4.58.2–3.

18. Zosimus, 4.58.6; Orosius, *Hist.* 7.35.19; Socrates, *HE* 5.25.11–16; Sozomen, *HE* 7.22–24; Rufinus, *HE* 11.33; Philostorgius, *HE* 11.2; *Epitome de Caesaribus* 48.7.

19. Socrates, *HE* 7.10.

20. Zosimus, *HN* 5.5.4.

21. Claudian, *Ruf.* 2.54–99; Eunapius, frag. 64.1 = John of Antioch, frag. 190 (*FHG* 4: 610).

22. Zosimus, *HN* 5.7.3; Eunapius, frag. 64.1 = John of Antioch, frag. 190 (*FHG* 4: 610).

23. Claudian, *Stil.* 2.95–96.

24. Claudian, *Ruf.* 2.105–23 and 235–39, with *Gild.* 294–96 and *Stil.* 1.151–69.

25. Claudian, *IV cons. Hon.* 435–49; *Stil.* 1.188–245.

26. Zosimus, *HN* 5.5.6–8.; Claudian, *Ruf.* 2.186–96; Eunapius, *VS* 476, 482.

27. Claudian, *IV cons.* 479–83; Zosimus, *HN* 5.7.2. Date: Paulinus, *V. Ambrosii* 45, 48, for the relevance of which see E. Burrell, 'A re-examination of why Stilicho abandoned his pursuit of Alaric in 397', *Historia* 53 (2004): 251–56.

28. Eunapius, frag. 64.1 = John of Antioch, frag. 190 (*FHG* 4: 610); Zosimus, *HN* 5.7.1 – both misdated, but both clearly referring to 397 because of their reference to *Hellas*.

29. Claudian, *Eutr.* 2.211–18; *Get.* 533–40.

30. Claudian, *Stil.* 1.269–81.

31. Main sources for the revolt: Synesius, *De providentia* 2.1–3; Socrates, *HE* 6.6.1–34; Sozomen, *HE* 8.4; Theoderet, *HE* 5.30–33; Zosimus, *HN* 5.18–19; Philostorgius, *HE* 11.8. My narrative follows A. Cameron and J. Long, *Barbarians and Politics at the Court of Arcadius* (Berkeley, 1993).

32. Date: *Codex Theodosianus* 9.40.17 (17 August 399).

33. *Fasti Vindobonenses Priores* 532 (*Chron. Min.* 1: 299).

34. Claudian, *VI cons. Hons.* 201–15; 281–86.

35. Claudian, *VI cons. Hon.* 229–33.

36. Sozomen, *HE* 8.25.3; 9.4.2–4.

37. The arguments of A. R. Birley, *The Roman Government of Britain* (Oxford, 2005), 455–60, very nearly persuade me to abandon my attempt, in 'Barbarians in Gaul, usurpers in Britain', *Britannia* 31 (2000): 325–45, to redate the Rhine crossing from the traditional 31 December 406 to 405.

38. Orosius, *Hist.* 7.37.13–16.

39. Olympiodorus, frag. 7.2 (Blockley) = 5 (Müller).

40. Olympiodorus, frag. 3 (Blockley) = 2 (Müller).

41. Olympiodorus, frag. 5.1 (Blockley) = 2 (Müller); Sozomen, *HE* 9.4; Philostorgius, *HE* 12.3.

42. Zosimus, *HN* 5.35.5–6.

43. Zosimus, *HN* 5.36.1–3.

44. Sozomen, *HE* 9.6–7.

45. Olympiodorus, frag. 7.3 (Blockley) = 6 (Müller); Zosimus, *HN* 5.38.

46. Sozomen, *HE* 9.7.

47. Zosimus, *HN* 5.46.1.

48. Zosimus, *HN* 5.45–51; Sozomen, *HE* 9.7.

49. On Olympiodorus, one should consult A. Gillett, 'The date and circumstances of Olympiodorus of Thebes', *Traditio* 48 (1993): 1–29.

50. Olympiodorus, frag. 14 (Blockley) = 13 (Müller); Sozomen, *HE* 9.8.

51. Sozomen, *HE* 9.8 has the former, Zosimus, *HN* 6.12.2 the latter. Both were drawing on Olympiodorus, but it is unclear which version better transmits the original.

52. Sozomen, *HE* 9.9.2–3; Philostorgius, *HE* 12.3.

Epilogue: The Aftermath of Alaric

1. Orosius, *Hist.* 7.39.4–14.
2. Sozomen, *HE* 9.9.5.
3. Olympiodorus, frag. 25 (Blockley) = 25 (Müller).
4. Rutilius Namatianus, *De reditu suo* 1.140.
5. Olympiodorus, frag. 16 (Blockley) = 15 (Müller).
6. Jordanes, *Get.* 158.
7. Sozomen, *HE* 9.9.1.

INDEX

Ablabius, *54*

Abrittus, *18, 28*

Adrianople: battle of, *139–143*; *curia* of, *135–136*; siege of, *146*

Ad Salices, battle of, *137*

Aequitius, *143*

Africa, grain supply of, *6, 168, 175–176*

Alamanni, *59, 81, 105*; origins of, *39–40, 67, 71*

Alanoviamuth, *49*

Alans, *124–128, 171, 183*

Alaric: *1–11, 157–177, 183–184*; and Attalus, *9, 174–176*; and Eutropius, *166–168*; and Rufinus, *165*; death of, *180*; early career of, *161–162*; first revolt of, *164–166*; demands of, *1–2, 165, 172–174*; followers, *1–2, 4–5, 6, 157, 165*

Alatheus, *126–127, 131–132, 152*; at Adrianople, *141–142*

Alavivus, *128–130, 132–133*

Aleksandrovka, *92*

Alexander Severus, *28*

alphabet, Gothic, *110*

Amal dynasty, *50, 53, 161*

Ambrose of Milan, *160*

Ammianus Marcellinus, *103–105*; *Res Gestae* of, *104–105*; on Adrianople, *140–141, 144, 146–147*; on Huns, *124–125*

Antioch, *117, 129*

Antonine Constitution, *25, 34*

Antoninus Pius, *23*

Apamea, *19*

Aquitaine, *158, 183*

Arabs, *146*

Arbogast, *151, 162–163*

Arcadius, *163, 165, 172*

archaeology. *See* material evidence

Ardashir, *27*

Argaith, *18, 55, 210*

Arianism. *See* Christianity, homoean

Ariaric, *84–85*

Ariminum. *See* Rimini

Arinthaeus, *117*

Arius, *107–108*

Armenia, *129, 137, 167, 168*

Arminius, *47*

army, Roman: as basis of imperial power, *26*; barbarians in, *35–37, 82, 156*; Goths in, *79, 82, 103, 106, 156–157*; losses of, at Adrianople, *150*

Arpulas, *121*

Arrian, *125*

Ascholius, *118*

Asia Minor: Goths killed in, *146–147, 154*; Gothic revolt in, *168–169*

Athanaric, *101*; ancestry of, *85*; death of, *155*; defeated by Huns, *126–128, 131–132*; persecutes Christians, *117–118, 120–122*; Roman wars of, *116–118*

Atharidus, *120*

Athaulf, *10, 158, 175, 177, 180–182*

Athens, *19*

Attalus, Priscus, *9, 174–176, 182–183*

Attica, *19*

Attila, *157*

Augustae, *31*

Augustine, *178–179*

Augustus, *22, 40*

Aurelian (emperor), *8, 20–21, 29–30*

Aurelian (praetorian prefect), *169*

Aureolus, *20, 29*

Aurelius Victor, *30*

Auxentius, *107*

Auxonius, *115*

Bacurius, *142*

barbarians: and imperial policy, *37–39*; concept of, *15, 21–22, 37, 56–60*. *See also under* army, Roman